Ma Vie en Rose

My Sweet Life

Ma Vie en Rose

My Sweet Life

ROSE LEVY BERANBAUM

83 press

For Woody,

who inspires me to
live in the present while
encouraging me
to write the stories of my
past. He has continued to
be my "Partner in Crème"
for over two decades.

Our favorite poem
by Henry Van Dyke,
"For Katrina's Sundial,"
located in her garden of
Yaddo, an artist's colony:

Hours fly,
Flowers die:
New days,
New ways,
Pass by!
Love stays.

COVER PORTRAIT BY ©TAI BLANCHE
PHOTO CREDITS BY TAI BLANCHE, HUGH DILLON,
AND MATTHEW SEPTIMUS

83 Press
2323 2nd Avenue North
Birmingham, Alabama 35203
83press.com

ISBN 978-1-971708-03-4
Printed in China

Time
is
oo slow for those who wait
o swift for those who fear
oolong for those who grieve
oo short for those who rejoice
for those who Love Time is
Eternity
Yaddo
1901
LONG.
73° 46.40 W.
HOURS
WATCH SLOWER
SEPT
OCT
NOV
DEC
W
S
SSE
SE
ESE

Contents

Foreword

My first impression of Rose Levy Beranbaum was that she was a scientist and perfectionist. Her cakes were beautifully presented, and the recipes were carefully written and produced perfect results. After making her acquaintance, I was in awe of the precision that she insisted on. Her kitchen was a laboratory, filled with professional scales, suspended from chemistry lab stands, and timers.

I was fortunate enough to assist Rose for the cooking classes that she gave. Besides learning the techniques, these classes were a lot of fun. I enjoyed tasting freshly churned ice cream while breathing in the aroma of brioche baking in the same room. I enjoyed watching her straining the apricot purée to a silken texture that formed the base for an exquisite soufflé that we watched rise in the oven. It was magic for all the senses. As Rose worked without pausing, she engaged the students with stories about how these recipes came about, the places and chefs that inspired them, and what it took to perfect them. She also shared some travel adventures.

Having grown closer to Rose, I got to test many recipes for her, both sweet and savory. I marveled over her definitive recipes for cheesecake, focaccia, and roast duck, to name just a few. When we would get together for a simple cappuccino or Indian lunch and discuss the recipes, I realized that there was a lot more going on with these recipes and Rose's work. There were fascinating stories that I couldn't get enough of—some that were expected and some that made me blush. All were delivered with absolute honesty and great humor. I loved how Rose was able to share a lot of her personality in her books, especially *The Cake Bible*. Sadly, live cooking demonstrations are rare today. Cookbooks are limited in size. And so much of cooking is taught and learned on television and social media. The personal rapport with a teacher or author is now limited. This book is the perfect antidote to that void.

More than taste memories, dining at the finest restaurants, or studying abroad, Rose's passion and creativity are informed by her journey to the woman that she came to be. Stories are of love, sacrifice, crushing disappointment, and, ultimately, great triumph. They're all featured in this memoir, including several that are still new to me and some that continue to make me blush! Get ready for an interesting ride and fasten your seatbelt!

—David Scott Shamah, *chef and caterer*

2004
IACP
COOKBOOK
AWARD
New York University

Prologue

The announcer declared: "James Beard Awards proudly presents the James Beard Cookbook Hall of Fame Award to Rose Levy Beranbaum." I walked up to the podium, bowed my head, and received the medallion award, suspended on a satin ribbon, on June 14, 2025. This was a full circle from my winning the first James Beard Awards Cookbook of the Year for *The Cake Bible* in 1989 to having *The Cake Bible, 35th Anniversary Edition* published as my last cookbook within the prior year.

Rose and Dr. Jessica B. Harris at the 2025 James Beard Awards

A Short Overview

I failed out of college and got married at 19 (and divorced at 23).

Eventually, I got so bored being a secretary I decided to go back to college. Seven years later, after working full-time and attending night school, and armed with a BS and MA in food science and culinary arts (graduating first in my class cum laude), I landed my first job in food at the test kitchen of *Ladies' Home Journal*. It was better hands-on training than I had gotten at New York University, where it had been theoretical.

I was in the "food world" from its very inception, starting with renowned journalists Clementine Paddleford and Mimi Sheraton in the all-powerful days of *The New York Times*. It was the early days of Julia Child on PBS (Public Broadcasting Service) television. Cecily Brownstone, food editor for the Associated Press, was my mentor and persuaded me to go back to school to get my culinary degrees.

This is the story of my career's evolution from inauspicious beginnings to being a major player in the golden age of food. I am a baker, but I think of myself even more as a writer and storyteller. It probably started when I was a little girl, with my grandmother telling me the story of Scheherazade, the woman who saved her own life by intriguing her murderous husband with 1,001 unfinished stories to keep herself alive. Here is the story of how I evolved from disliking to eat to writing 14 cookbooks and changing the way baking books are written.

I studied with James Beard and, years later, went to France to do a stage at The Lenôtre Culinary School. I was one of the founders of the New York Association of Cooking Teachers and an early member of the International Association of Culinary Professionals when it was still called the Association of Cooking Schools. I have stories to tell of the Southern-born Craig Claiborne (who, oddly enough, was the spitting image, down to the space in his front teeth, of my Jewish dad); Bert Greene, who named my book *The Cake Bible*; Julia Child; Simone Beck; Marion Cunningham (author of *The Fannie Farmer Cookbook* revision); George Lang (a restaurateur who invited me to be the first non-native Hungarian ever to work at Gundel in Budapest); and countless others.

I got my basic training at *Ladies' Home Journal*, started my writing career in the early days of *The Cook's Magazine*, and went on to write for just about every major food publication in America. I chose the first "Grande Dame" of the newly formed Les Dames d'Escoffier, but I wasn't allowed to join until several years later because I was told by then-president Carol Brock that, "first, you have to *be* somebody!" But the biggest impact on my life, of anything I ever did, was writing *The Cake Bible*. I have a soft voice that can easily be overlooked, but after writing this book, my late husband warned me: "Watch what you say now because people are going to listen!"

And, indeed, they did. The book opened doors of possibility, and since then, nothing has ever been the same.

I was wholeheartedly welcomed into the evolving golden age of food. Icons like Charlie Trotter, Norman Van Aken, Emeril Lagasse, Martha Stewart, and Jacques Pépin embraced my expertise in baking. Michael Batterberry said it best: "I was chef to the chefs!"

After eight decades of living, covering it all would be overwhelming, so I've selected the highlights that have shaped the landscape of my existence.

I don't claim to be humble because my success was more a surprise to my family and, most of all, to me! I started out thinking I would never want or have a career or achieve very much, so it's hard to be humble when I reflect on how much I overcame, both from my own lack of aspiration and the world's resistance and interference. Anyway, it's not about humility; it's about a vision that propels us without looking sideways or backwards—only moving toward that inner vision and fighting to be true to it. Now, you know the secrets of my soul.

In her book *Permission*, Elyssa Altman said it best about writing a memoir: "Light and truth move creatives to a place of compassion, humility, self-knowledge, and transcendence."

In 1988, *The Cake Bible* made history after its launch by selling 18,500 copies in one day in an era when cookbooks were used as a write-off for the publisher. *The Cake Bible* was the first cookbook to list weights, to give details about how the ingredients worked, and to offer the revolutionary technique of reverse creaming which was easier, faster, and better. There was little interest in the scientific approach to baking, but the incredible results of the cookbook readers' cakes traveled like wildfire by word of mouth. *The Cake Bible* was the first book to win the James Beard Awards Cookbook of the Year. Even my hero Julia Child called after I was a guest on ABC's TV show *Good Morning America* to say: "Congratulations, dearie!"

In subsequent years, the book was seen not only in a submarine in the depths of the ocean off the coast of Alaska but also in a bookstore at the mountain peak heights of Kathmandu. *The Cake Bible, 35th Anniversary Edition* now sits behind the counter at our favorite restaurant, Thai Palace, near my home.

TIME CAPSULES

Throughout the memoir, I have included dozens of "time capsules" highlighting significant events and changes woven into the evolution of my own culinary journey.

Here is an overall example: Julia Child ignited the evolution for the golden age of the food world. Organizations like James Beard and IACP (International Association of Culinary Professionals) connected the food world to the public. Cookbooks, magazines, and television shows enhanced the quality of cooking in the home. Social media, with instant connections to the entire world, expanded the food world.

Woody's Hirschfeld Design for Our Blog, www.realbakingwithrose.com

1

The Shoulders on Which I Stand

My Maternal History

My life story begins with my great-grandmother Resha Rose Polachek Hurwitz, who was born in Russia in the town of Minsk in the mid-1800s. She was named Rose for her auburn hair, which, in the tradition of religious Jews, she cut after her marriage and wore as a wig called a *sheitel*.

Great-Grandmother Rose

Great-Grandfather Shmuel

Great-Grandmother Rose

Rose's father, Rabbi Polachek, founded the most renowned school of rabbinical studies in Eastern Europe, and Rose married her late sister Nechama's husband (as was the tradition), Shmuel Meir Hurwitz, the youngest student ever to have graduated from the school, who became my great-grandfather. My great-great-grandfather's tomb had the highest honor of being moved to Jerusalem. I wonder what he would think if he knew he were to have a great-great-granddaughter who wrote baking bibles.

Great-Grandfather Shmuel

The family left Russia in 1890 when my great-grandfather had a premonition of the Russian Revolution and World War I and headed for America. His two sons from his first marriage walked to Palestine, which took several years. The two oldest of Rose's eight children, Sol and Becky, emigrated first. They taught themselves Latin and English. Sol became the youngest acting head of pediatrics at Mt. Sinai, and Becky became a dentist, both in New York City. The rest of the family, including my grandmother Sarah who was 16, crossed the Atlantic by ship. She never would have told me about the Arab sheikh who fell in love with her on the ship, but her gossipy younger sister Bertha did. The sheikh went to her father, the rabbi, and asked for her hand in marriage, saying he would make her the number one of his nine wives. That must have gone over like a lead balloon, and apparently, my grandmother never forgave her father for refusing. I found this odd because my grandmother seemed to be so stern and conservative. When she was 75, she and one of her younger sisters went by ship to Israel to see their only surviving half-brother Simon. They hadn't seen each other for 60 years, but they found each other in the crowd of thousands of people meeting the ship, because there was an Orthodox old man dancing, praying, and crying. The crowd pulled back, and he was in the center. Sarah recognized him immediately. She visited for about a month, and he died a few days after she departed.

When the family arrived in New York City, they changed their name from Hurwitz to Horwitt. My grandmother Sarah worked as a sample maker in the garment industry. In Russia, she had been a lace maker. My father's mother, Etta Landesman, also worked in the garment industry as a finisher. I got my love of crafts from both of my grandmothers. But I got my love of storytelling from my grandmother Sarah.

In retrospect, many of my stories contain humor. My mother once said: "Everything is a joke to you." When I told this to my eloquent editor of *The Cake Bible*, Cassie Jones, her treasured response was: "People who can be wildly funny and also deadly serious when necessary are the best kind of people!"

My Paternal History

My father's family arrived in America four generations before my mother's family. His maternal great-grandparents, Sara and Maximillion Fox, emigrated from Hungary around 1868. My dad's paternal grandfather, Adolf Landesman, fought in Emperor Franz Joseph's army and brought Henckels and Zwilling knives to sell in America. (He taught my father how to sharpen knives on a stone, and my father passed on this skill to me.)

Adolf Landesman's granddaughter, my grandmother Etta Landesman, was born in the Pennsylvania Dutch Country in 1885. She once told me that, when she was 16, New York City ended at 14th Street, and after that, it was all woods! Her husband, Herman, was a boxing manager, and his brothers were part of the Jewish gangs of New York, defending Orthodox Jews whose religion forbids fighting back from attacks by other gangs.

Herman left my grandmother, and she started working as a finisher in the garment industry. At the time, my dad and his sister, Ruth, were teenagers, and my dad had to quit high school to support the family. Much later in life, he got his high school equivalency diploma and then went on to graduate from college.

My dad's paternal family was very accomplished. His cousin, Lieutenant Commander Norman Levy, was a nuclear physicist and also a pilot. Norman was killed in 1966 in a fire on an aircraft carrier off the coast of North Vietnam. Their grandmother Rosa was a landlord of many buildings in New York's Lower East Side. Though the Levy family was very wealthy, they did not offer any financial help to their daughter-in-law Etta. Despite my grandmother's very hard life, she lived to be almost 100.

My favorite cousin on my father's side has long been Elizabeth Granatelli. She is half Sicilian royalty, and on a visit to Palermo, the hotel we stayed at turned out to be around the corner from Via Principe di Granatelli! Another favorite is Peter Reich and his wonderful family. Peter was head of environmental studies at University of Minnesota, and for years, he and his wife, Anne, went to Australia to consult on the water table problem.

Inspiring People in My Life's Story

The three people who inspired me and had the most influence on my career were Julia Child as a cookbook writer, M.F.K. Fisher as a food writer, and Marie Curie as a scientist. But there have been many other amazing people in my life. The first person who comes to mind is my great-aunt, Polly, and the second is her younger brother, Nat.

I was around 12 years old, and I was standing on 95th Street off Central Park West in New York City where we lived and where my mother had her dental office. I always remember these words my mother said to me: "Aunt Polly has the most extraordinary friends." I also remember agreeing but silently thinking that no one would ever say that about me. I turned out to be proven wrong. There were many extraordinary people who have graced my life, and there are those who, thankfully, are still present in it. During this same conversation, my mother told me that Aunt Polly thought it was wonderful how I think about other people more than myself. And I remember thinking: "How did I fool such a smart woman!" Years later, I realized she was right. It's not because I'm so virtuous—it's because I'm so curious!

Pauline "Polly" Horwitt Kozma was a truly extraordinary person. Her best friends as a young woman were Babette Deutsch, the poet, and Vera Buch Weisbord, author of *A Radical Life*, in which she featured Polly and our family in great detail. Polly was not pretty at all, but she had long golden blond hair past her hips, until she cut it into a pageboy, and cornflower blue eyes that shined with piercing intelligence.

When I was a very young child, she gave me *Christmas: A Story*, a treasure of a little book, now 75 years old, written by her mentor Eleanor Roosevelt and published by Knopf in 1940. What was most extraordinary about this gift was that Polly was the daughter of a rabbi, and yet, in the years shortly past World War II, she had chosen to give a book with the message of Christ's love to her Orthodox Jewish sister's granddaughter. But Polly was a woman of the world. In fact, she went on to win the Eleanor Roosevelt Award as a member of the American Association for the United Nations. Polly also taught French and Spanish at Julia Richman High School for many years, and when she retired, the school created the Pauline Kozma Day.

Great-Uncle Nat Self-Portrait

How fortunate I was to have had my Aunt Polly as an example of such stellar intellectual and spiritual values. Sadly, she died when I was only 17. And when she knew she didn't have much longer to live, she made a list of suitable wives, who were her friends, for her beloved husband, Laszlo "Leslie" Kozma. Uncle Leslie asked me if there was anything I wanted that had belonged to Polly, and my choice was her wedding and engagement rings (which, coincidentally, had a rose-cut diamond). I told him that I hoped someday to have as happy a marriage as they had. And I do! The ring is now over 100 years old.

Nathan George Horwitt was the most visibly famous member of the family. He was a writer, inventor, farmer, photographer, and designer of graphics, advertisements, interiors, chairs, and books. He invented an adjustable picture frame of which his company Braquette (1933–1980) sold several millions, and he was also creator of the Movado Museum Watch, the first watch with no numbers. He was a visionary, raconteur, and seducer of every female in sight, including his nieces and great-nieces.

He founded the New England Mycological Society and taught me about wild mushrooms. He also taught me about designing and inventing and how to stand up to him. My greatest moment and leap from intimidation was the day he called me asking if I was his "Niece Flower." Without missing a beat, I asked if he was my "Uncle Nut." The absolute silence that followed was my long-won victory. And the year before he died at 92, he thanked me for making the family proud, so I guess I was forgiven for being a smart-ass New York great-niece.

But of all the inspiring people in my life, it is my mother, Lillian Wager Levy, who was my greatest inspiration. She taught me strength, determination, and compassion. Crippled by polio at the age of 3, she got a full scholarship to Cornell University and went on to become the only woman in the entire University of Pittsburgh School of Dental Medicine. She practiced dentistry and orthodonture all her professional life.

Her last note, painfully written from her bed in a nursing home and pinned to the room's bulletin board, stated: "I went to Cornell. I was a dentist." Her motivation was reaching out to the nursing staff to tell them that she was more than just a senile, dying old woman. It so touched my heart. I didn't want a profession like hers. I wanted only to be a full-time mother and to be nothing like mine. And guess what? Here is my story!

2

The Early Years of Enchantment

My parents were married in May 1943 in the midst of WWII. My dad knew he was about to be drafted into the armed forces, so he volunteered as a paratrooper. He didn't like jumping out of planes, and years later, he always thought that people who paid to skydive were crazy. But he did learn one valuable skill—how to land on his feet, cushioning his knees by bending them. He passed this skill on to me and his grandson Alex. Decades later, I watched my little nephew teaching another little boy on a slide in the playground what he had learned from his grandfather. My dad taught us all many lessons, and we all inherited his courage.

Mom

Dad Going Off to War

My Birth Announcement

I was born the following year on April 2, 1944 at St. Joseph's Hospital in Far Rockaway, Long Island, New York, kitty-corner to the Victorian-style house where we lived with my maternal grandparents. I often teased my father that I wished I could have waited just two more days to be born, as then my birth date would have been a perfect 4-4-44 and easy for others to remember. Then, my father would remind me that he had already overstayed his leave from the air force by so many days that he risked sleeping on the prison floor and peeling potatoes for a week.

My dad, paratrooper Robert Maxwell Levy, departed for boot camp the day after I was born. He was never lacking in courage. He even joyfully lifted his mother-in-law up in the air despite her dislike for him (no one was ever good enough for her daughter syndrome). I was 2 months old, when my 30-year-old father's aircraft carrier approached the shores of Normandy. It arrived the day after the D-Day invasion. But the war continued, and he stayed in France for several months. He told me that, every time he jumped out of a plane, his only fear was that he would never see me again, which resulted in a nervous breakdown.

It took a while until my dad was no longer a stranger to me. He lived to be almost 98, which gave us many years to reconnect. He never talked to us about his experience as a paratrooper, except to say that, on his way to Normandy while on the aircraft carrier, no one told the troops that D-Day had already taken place. A friend's father told us that he

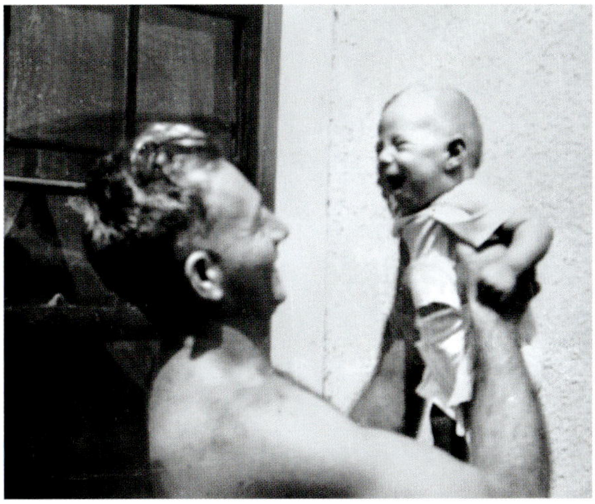

Dad Returns

had encountered anti-Semitism in the military and was tortured by having to stand guard in the rain despite having a high fever from the German measles. The friend reported his saying that: "in the air force, German POWs were no worse than his 'compatriots.'" As an injured paratrooper, my dad ended up in St. Clou, a French hospital in Burgundy.

My mother, after not hearing from my dad for months, feared the worst. When he returned, my dad explained that he knew he was alright, so he thought, somehow, she would know. On the way back from France, he went through Paris and bought my mother a small bottle of Femme perfume which she kept for years, even after it had turned and started to smell dusky. It was a promise of years to come. Growing up, I would surreptitiously smell it and reel back into another era. My father never wanted to return to Europe.

Born in Far Rockaway, in the sunshine by the ocean, the beach was my "play sand," and the ocean was my friend. The first five years of my life were paradise until we moved to New York City. Years later, one of my editors told me that I write in the sunshine.

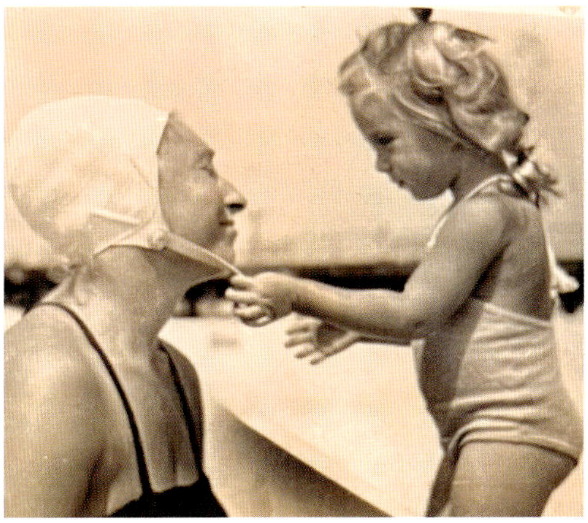

Mom & Rose on Long Island Beach

Rose on Long Island Beach

Rose at the Gate

My father installed a gate on the porch of our home to keep me in, but I metaphorically used it to keep others out. When I saw someone approaching, I would sneakily lock the gate and then laugh hilariously when the person couldn't get in. My dad was so amused he managed to capture it on film.

Grandpa Max

My first experience of profound loss was unforgettable. I was 5½ years old, and my grandfather was my favorite person on earth. When my mother put me in the car to go back to New York, she was in a rush, and I begged her to let me hug Grandpa Max one last time. She roared off despite his running after us saying: "Let the child stay." The image was engraved in my memory. I turned to her and said: "What if I never see him again?" She turned to me asking: "Why would you say that?" He died that night. It's not that I had a presentiment of his death—it was that I had a presentiment of the impermanence of things I loved, and it resulted in my trusting my own intuition.

3

Why I Hated Food
and Was Suspicious of Religion, Plus the Life Lessons from Grandma

Frankie was my first friend. He lived directly across the street in a large house with his big Italian family. One day, I went into their kitchen and saw their grandmother putting what seemed like dozens of corn cobs into a huge pot of boiling water. She asked me if I would like to stay for dinner. I yelled to my grandmother, who was in front of our house, to come over, and when she crossed the street, she whispered in my ear that we couldn't eat their food because we were kosher. At that moment, I decided that, if I couldn't eat my best friend's food, I didn't want to eat any more than was absolutely necessary, and I didn't like religion because it separated me from my best friend.

Grandma Sarah and Rose

When I was about 4, although Frankie and I always played together, one day, Judy, another little girl from around the corner, came over to play with us. Oddly, and for the first time, Frankie peed in front of us. I had never seen a penis before, and I thought it was a string bean! Judy had a mean streak, and to my shock, horror, and near disbelief, she turned to Frankie, when he was done peeing, and pointed to a rock and said: "Why don't you pick up this rock and hit Rosie!" And like a dumb automaton, he did just that. I ran away a few feet toward the street and then froze waiting for it to hit. It did—my right cheek.

Now, here's the really interesting part: As I cried loudly for my grandmother who was across the boulevard, she came running over, and Judy ran away. When I told my grandmother what had happened, she ignored Frankie and went right around the corner to the row house where Judy lived and was sitting on the steps with her older sister. My grandmother lost no time in smacking Judy in the face. Judy's sister protested that Judy hadn't been the one to throw the stone, and my grandmother responded with something like: "But the idea *came* from her." Needless to say, this event ended my friendship with Frankie.

I stood there feeling protected and validated and taking in a major life lesson about human nature, character, male and female relationships, and responsibility, or perhaps I should say culpability. I wonder if Frankie or Judy are still alive and what kind of grown-ups they have or haven't evolved into. I have a pretty good guess.

After my beloved grandpa Max died, my grandmother moved in with us and shared a room with me as I was growing up until I went away to college. Every night, after saying the Shema (the evening prayer), I would ask my grandmother more questions about the old country (pronounced as one word so that I actually thought it was the name of the country). She would admonish me: "You know, you're not allowed to talk after Shema." But I would beg her for just one more story, and that is how I was privy to many tales of life under czarist Russia. I loved the one about the beautiful and clever red-haired cousin, who burned books before the czar's Cossacks arrived because Jews were not allowed to have books. She seduced them with her quick wits.

I often say I was the youngest food critic who was actually paid to eat! Grandma would offer me a quarter to entice me to taste something. She did all the cooking because my mother worked all day as a dentist. Every morning, Grandma would make me an eggnog. After she left the room, I would rush to the sixth-floor kitchen window and pour it down the side of the building. One day, when I was taking a walk, I happened to look up to our window and noticed a white racing streak running all the way down to the street. I disliked most food and considered eating to be a chore I did to please my anxious mother and grandmother, who, it seemed, would go to any lengths to entice my reluctant appetite. One day, my grandmother made an apple pie. I didn't see her use any recipe, so I assumed that she knew it by heart, even though she had never made one before. It was so good that I announced, "*This* I'll eat." To my surprise, she said: "And *this* I won't be making again; it's not worth the effort."

One of the few things I liked was spaghetti, which my grandmother served with ketchup and butter. This was inspired by her prior Italian neighbors' tomato sauce that she thought was ketchup. In those days, Mueller's spaghetti was very starchy, so I worked out a way to wash off the starch by boiling it for 10 minutes, rinsing it, and then boiling it with new water for another 10 minutes. Years later, when I graduated to more sophisticated sauces, I would fry the drained spaghetti in some of the sauce.

No one used the term "supertaster" in those days; it was more like "finicky eater." I didn't know I was a supertaster until many years later, after college, when I took a test which involved placing a gummed paper reinforcement on my tongue, staining the center hole with purple food coloring, and counting the circumvallate papillae (taste buds). I had so many taste buds I couldn't count them all, but suddenly, I realized that quantity is not quality and that over a decade of my smoking might have destroyed some of them. I had tried to give up smoking many times, but what finally helped was when it occurred to me that I was damaging the most important part of my body for my career in the food industry. Fortunately, I still had many unimpaired taste buds!

Another strange delicacy that I loved was Grandma's burnt string beans. Our typical pre-dinner dialogue would go something like this:

> **Grandma (with a hopeful expression shining on her face):** "Rosie, I made string beans tonight!"
> **Me (mildly threatening tone):** "Did you burn them?"
> **Grandma (plaintively):** "It's so hard to wash the *fendl* (Yiddish for pan) when they're burned."
> **Me (unimpressed and openly threatening):** "You know, I won't eat them if they're not burned."

How this all got started was, of course, by Grandma's having accidentally burned the string beans one night. It reminds me of Charles Lamb's "A Dissertation Upon Roast Pig," which is a humorous story of how roasted (read burnt) pork was accidentally discovered in ancient China.

It wasn't until many years later that I discovered Chinese "dry-fried string beans," a recipe in which the string beans are intentionally browned or lightly burned.

But I will always miss my grandmother's version. You see, the string beans burn to just the right degree only when the cooking water is allowed to evaporate (inadvertently) and the beans start to burn just to the point when you suddenly smell them. I was always reassured that they would be perfect when I heard my grandmother cry out: "Oy! The string beans are burnt again!" God was in his heaven, and all was right with the world. By the way, in all these years, I never once burned anything, but that is because I love to cook and bake.

Burnt String Beans on the Grill

My dear friend Elizabeth Karmel, who has written several excellent grilling cookbooks, made string beans on the grill for me that put all thoughts of other past ones almost entirely out of my mind.

Her method is simply to toss the washed and trimmed string beans with salt and a little olive oil and then to toss them on a hot grill rack and continue tossing them with tongs until the beans are deliciously browned, partially blackened, and beginning to shrivel.

My method, based on hers, is to parboil the string beans in salted water for three minutes, drain them, and toss them in the olive oil and salt, though sometimes I use melted bacon fat. Being a baker more than a griller, I like to toss the beans in a grill pan with holes (preferably a disposable foil one) before placing them on the grill to ensure that I won't lose a single one of the skinnier beans to the flames below the grill rack. Either way, season the beans with lots of freshly ground black pepper.

Even as an older child in the 1950s, I still enjoyed going shopping with my grandmother and remember how she selected string beans one at a time rather than by the handful to make sure each one was in perfect shape. When we came home from the market, she would always say: "Someday, there will be a machine to tell us which phone calls we missed." (My Jules Verne grandma.)

Whenever I came into the kitchen to see what my grandmother was cooking, she would say: "Go way and don't bother me." Once, I asked her how often the kitchen floor needed to be washed, and her response was that I had a child's mind. What could I say to that? I was a child.

Rock Candy Solved

Grandma didn't enjoy cooking. She cooked to feed the family, and if, by chance, it sometimes tasted good, she had no objection. The goal, however, was no-nonsense nourishment without frills. So, it always struck me as odd, if not outright contradictory to her character, that from time to time she would make rock candy—a confection consisting of sugar dissolved in water to which a string is added, causing the sugar to transmute into large, transparent crystals that cling to the string and resemble quartz rock.

One day, as I watched her lowering what appeared to be a string into the sugar solution in a small aluminum saucepan, I idly asked her what she was doing. "Adding dental floss," she replied succinctly to put an end to the discussion. This grabbed my attention. "Why dental floss?" I queried. "Vell," she began in her endearing Yiddish accent that I grew up believing all grandmothers had, "I neeted schtring to make it vurk ahnt dere's zo much dental fluss arunt . . ." I roared with laughter. There she was, the mother of a dentist, making the sort of candy which is designed to dissolve very slowly in the mouth—a sure-fire tooth-rotter—and using dental floss, the very purpose of which is to help prevent tooth decay. The irony, however, eluded her, and I laughed alone.

Years later, I decided, for the first time, to make rock candy for the holidays. My cookbook library contains well over 1,000 books, but specific rock candy instructions appeared in only one—a book which had never let me down (before)—*Joy of Cooking*. The instructions called for punching holes in a pan and running parallel rows of string through them on which to crystallize the sugar. This seemed like a rather formal arrangement, but it was pleasing to visualize neat rods of rock candy that I felt certain would ensue if I followed the instructions to the letter (except that as a nod to family tradition, I intended to use dental floss as the string). The instructions called for making a sugar solution and boiling it to the firm to hard-ball stage (247°F to 252°F). No problem—I produced thermometers and was confident of their accuracy. I poured the syrup into the pan, and it was well below the level of the string.

What to do? Knowing better about sugar crystallization but not wanting to waste the sugar, I made a second syrup using double the amount of sugar and poured it over the first. It covered the string but almost immediately started to crystallize into one solid translucent block. I dumped it all out and made a third syrup using three times the amount of sugar. It covered the strings but still crystallized solid.

In desperation, I called my friend Shirley Corriher, who was a research biochemist in Atlanta, Georgia. She explained to me that one of the secrets to making rock candy is that, after pouring the syrup, the container cannot be disturbed or moved at all, and it can take up to a week to crystallize. I tried a smaller batch this time, using a wooden skewer instead of the floss. I didn't even breathe on it and within hours had the same mess of dull crystals, not a single one of which stuck to the skewer. By now, I had used almost 10 pounds of sugar, and the sense of waste was beginning to make me panic.

At this point, my husband stepped in, claiming to have made successful rock candy once years ago. He suggested that the hard-ball stage temperature was too high and that there was therefore too much sugar in proportion to water. This made sense to me, so I followed his vague directions to make a super-saturated solution by stirring sugar into water until no more could be dissolved and the sugar settled out. Again, I stuck a wooden skewer into the solution and put it aside for one week. At the end of this time, the top was like an ice-skating rink, and a few crystals had formed on the bottom, but none were on the stick. At this point, I decided to give up, at least for a while, and work on caramel syrups. But I couldn't get myself to throw out my final rock candy experiment.

Rose Always Questioning

The following week, my husband and I ate dinner at Oceana, one of my favorite New York seafood restaurants. The executive chef Rick Moonen came over to say hello and inquire as to what I was working on. "Caramel," I said, "and I'm having a problem with it crystallizing." He teasingly responded: "But I bet you can't get rock candy to crystallize." I was stunned. "How did you know?" I asked incredulously. He answered: "Because whenever I've tried to make it, all I'd end up with was an ice-skating rink on top and one crystal on the string." I couldn't believe my ears—the very same image I had evolved. Somehow, during the course of the ensuing conversation, it occurred to my husband that he had not thought to tell me the necessity for introducing undissolved sugar crystals into the syrup to prompt the crystallization process. Apparently, the string or skewer needs first to be dampened with water and then dipped into sugar before lowering it into the syrup.

The next day, I checked the two-week-old rock candy experiment and observed that crystals were indeed forming on the skewer, even without the addition of the undissolved sugar, but the process was so very gradual it would surely be preferable to use the added sugar technique. All these years, I had assumed that rock candy was very easy to make because, if it hadn't been, I knew Grandma would not have taken the trouble. But, I guess, as with many things, it's easy if you know what you're doing.

I finally realized it must have been one of the things she learned as the owner of a candy store (another unexplored irony). I recounted this story to my father, who was then reminded of a drink called rock and rye from his childhood. It was administered by *his* grandmother for colds and contained rye whiskey with rock candy.

4

School Years

Grade School

When I was 11, I attended the School of American Ballet and was a toy soldier in the second production of George Balanchine's *The Nutcracker* at New York City Center. It was the first and only time in my memory that my mother and her mother-in-law collaborated to find me the costume that would fit, which enabled me to be in the production. It was a major highlight in my young life.

Soldier in *The Nutcracker*

I was in the sixth grade when I experienced the most humiliating moment of my young life. We were given IQ tests. As usual, I wasn't paying attention and was bored by the test, so I got a very low grade. The worst part was that the teacher gave all the test results to one of the students to bring to the principal's office. I went up to the teacher to protest, saying that my classmate might look at them. The teacher said that would never happen, but of course, it did, and the whole class thought that I was a complete moron. But this experience served to confirm my sense of having a prophetic soul.

Two of my friends were twins named Audrey and Carol Schifrin. One of them read a paper to the class about Maple Manor in Dingmans Ferry, Pennsylvania, where they spent summer vacations with their "Nana." It sounded so wonderful I begged my mother to plan our next one-month summer vacation there with them, and to my amazement, she agreed. It was the summer before starting junior high school, and I was 11. We went horseback riding and swimming and enjoyed the drama of a major hurricane. But the most memorable part was meeting Doug, another guest, who was from France and said he was a mystic. Doug told me he went into the woods at night and had seances to visit his dead sister, and he offered to take me to see my long-departed grandfather, who I was still missing. I was all for it, but my mother (understandably) vetoed it without hesitation.

Doug also offered to read the cards and tell the fortune of four of us little girls who were vacationing at Maple Manor. He started fortune-telling with the twins and didn't say anything memorable. Then, Doug went on to the other little girl saying that she was a sluggish student. She took heated offense, while I was thinking that he could say that about me and I would have had to agree! But when he got to me, Doug said: "You have a great destiny ahead of you." I begged and begged him to tell me what that was, but he refused, saying that, if I knew, I might try to "upset the apple cart." This puzzled me. If something is my destiny, how could my knowing it change it? But when I continued pleading with him, Doug said: "Tell me what is the best thing that could happen to you, and I'll see if you are mature enough to know your great destiny." My answer, without hesitation (and keep in mind that not only were my best friends identical twins so were my first cousins who were my age): "To give birth to twins." Without a pause, Doug said: "You are not grown up enough to know your great destiny."

This was one of the best things that ever happened to me because Doug had only said that to *me*, so it made it credible. Throughout my life, whenever something surprisingly good happened, I would immediately wonder if that was what Doug had in mind. I never expected it, but when good things happened, I fully embraced them. And now, I am no longer wondering because I know, and I am grateful.

High School of Music & Art

I climbed the long stairs to what was called "The Castle in the Sky" for my four years at the High School of Music & Art in New York. One semester, I had a music teacher, Professor Frederick Breydert, who had a very strong German accent. We mocked him when he pronounced schizophrenia as "shitzophrenia" and when he was late to class, explaining to us that he had been listening to Brahms and it always put him to sleep. But one day after school, I saw a group of students who surrounded him in rapt attention. It turned out that he had written an orchestral piece that he had only been able to hear in his mind because he couldn't afford to hire an orchestra to play it. That year, the senior orchestra surprised him by playing his composition. Years later, there was a movie called *Mr. Holland's Opus*, which reminded me of Professor Breydert.

Great-Aunt Polly sometimes served as a substitute teacher for my French class, and I lived in terror that she would call on me despite all the Gigi-esque lessons she had given me. Polly's husband, elegantly old-fashioned Uncle Leslie, was an importer of wine and spirits.

Although I adored them both, they lived in such a rarefied and gracious manner that a visit to their exquisite apartment in the Riverdale neighborhood of the Bronx always held many unknown terrors for me. I was brought up in a much more casual, child-oriented environment. I didn't know that I shouldn't put my feet on the chair rungs or put my hands on the walls or pick up a chicken drumstick with my fingers. And I'd certainly not experienced food that had wine or liquor in it.

Around the time I entered high school and could travel on my own to the Bronx, Polly took it upon herself to civilize and educate me in the finer ways. The afternoon would usually begin with a detested French lesson and then proceed to some other cultural discussion. Dinner would be the final lesson, and one day, when Polly asked me if there was anything I couldn't tolerate to eat, I immediately presented her with a lengthy verbal list. She asked with great surprise if I could possibly be allergic to all those things, and when I explained that it was simply a question of extreme distaste, her horrifying response was, "That's no excuse." Then, she proceeded to serve one of them (canned asparagus—horror of horrors). If only I could return to those dinners now, with my passion for speaking French and my more mature palate. (I still wouldn't want canned asparagus, even if it was imported from France.)

There were many brilliantly talented music and art students at M & A (now called the Fiorello H. LaGuardia High School of Music & Art and Performing Arts). It was a world apart from the snobbery of Birch Wathen junior high school. I had the rare honor of being accepted both for music and, a year later, for art but was not all that gifted in either one. They told me that, since I didn't have an art background, I would have to redo my junior year to catch up, so I stayed with music. This was not easy for me either, because almost all the other music students had parents who were professional musicians and had studied theory which I then failed.

I couldn't believe it when the teacher asked us to listen to a musical piece and then write all four parts of the harmony. My mother hired a tutor because one couldn't graduate without passing all the subjects. The other subject I failed was chemistry. The first day of class, the teacher asked us to commit all the valences from the periodic chart to memory. When I got home and looked at the chart, I couldn't believe that was really the assignment, thinking why bother to memorize something that easily could be looked up. Uncle B, the chemist, came to my rescue for this one. Who would have believed that 17 years later I would graduate with honors, first in my class at NYU! I did, however, excel in sports. In addition to being captain of the volleyball team, I also became captain of the bowling team.

June LeBell, who later became an announcer on WQXR, New York's classical music radio station, for almost her entire career, was in my official class. She invited me to appear on her radio show "Kitchen Classics" in 1990.

When June wrote her first and only book, *Kitchen Classics*, she told me that Julia Child was writing the foreword and asked me to write the dessert part. I agreed and then Julia suggested that, since I knew June much better, I should write the whole thing. It turned out to be one of the best things I've ever written, so I'm sharing it again here.

I advised June to promote the book herself because publishers did very little, but she said: "No need; it's the radio station of *The New York Times*, so they'll feature it." And they did 100% nothing! It's a wonderful book featuring recipes from many musical celebrities. Sadly, June died May 1, 2017.

The Foreword to *Kitchen Classics*

I was born with music in my ears, in my heart, and in my soul. I am sure this is because my mother, who as a young girl studied with Nadia Reisenberg, played womb concerts (the ultimate chamber music) on the piano when she was pregnant with me. She was convinced that, even though I had not yet been born, I would still hear something, if only vibrations, and would grow up familiar with and open to music—one of life's greatest joys. Her theory apparently worked, because as soon as I could walk, I approached the piano and picked out tunes by ear.

If I had been offered the choice of any talent in the world (if I couldn't have been Mozart), it would have been to have a glorious voice and be an opera singer. But since I did not have even a passable singing voice, my instrument became the violin.

One summer, when I was at music camp near Tanglewood, studying with the second violinist of the Boston Symphony Orchestra, my Great-Uncle Nat, who had engineered this opportunity, came to visit me and posed the dreaded question: "Exactly what kind of talent do you possess, concert or drawing room?" The only possible answer was the disappointing truth: neither. As it turned out, despite the fact that I graduated from Carnegie Hall (the High School of Music and Art held all its graduations there), I was an extremely mediocre violin player who preferred listening to performing, but then, the music world does need some appreciative listeners. Our family had its share of them. Legend has it that my Great-Aunt Beck was so moved by a concert at Lewisohn Stadium she got up in the middle and started to dance, explaining afterwards that she couldn't help herself. My mother's theory was that, since she had grown up in Russia, she had the passionate Russian soul. We also had two bona fide performers: Aunt Beck's husband, appropriately named Fiddler, and Uncle Tibor (Kozma), who conducted at the Met under Rudolf Bing and then went on to become head of the music department at the University of Indiana. It is thanks to him that my first "grown-up" birthday party, when I was twelve, was at a Met production of the Fledermaus. *The kids were all very bored (including me—the* Fledermaus *has never been one of my favorites), but their parents were quite impressed. And it was never really a surprise to run into one of the great-aunts during intermission at the opera.*

This generation had my cousin Andrew Schenck (pronounced Skenk), also a gifted conductor, and perhaps, the next generation will have my little nephew Alexander, who, when he first started to sing, had that surprised look, bordering on awe, which clearly said: can these bell-like sounds be coming from me?

Ravi Shankar (the renowned Indian sitarist) once said that for him music is the bridge between the personal and the infinite. It is my feeling that all acts of creativity, approached with the same reverence of total devotion, offer that possibility. Somehow, though, music soars above all others. My soul has been transported by a bite of still warm from the oven Chocolate Domingo Cake, but no food has given me the total corporal and spiritual orgasm music is capable of inspiring.

My mother, whose profession was dentistry, held dear a theory that senses located in the region of the head are the most exquisite and also the ones most intimately connected. As a "food person," I see more and more how true this is. Taste, smell, vision, and hearing have a profound effect on each other's perception. As a very young child, I would not let my mother play the song "Ramona" because it reminded me of chocolate pudding (which I detested). I suppose I must have experienced it as equally thick and sodden with sentimentality.

The connection between food and music is found even in the words used to describe them. In the food industry, the most common word used to analyze flavor is note. Texture is another word food and music have in common. One of my favorite musical memories is of the time I met Isaac Stern at a party celebrating the birth of Jenifer Lang's book Tastings. *I had provided the Chocolate Oblivion Cake that was featured in the book. When George Lang introduced me to Isaac Stern, he rose up, took my hand, and bowed deeply from the waist saying: "Your cake was like velvet." My response: "That is the very word I used to describe your playing the first time I heard you play the Tchaikovsky violin concerto when I was sixteen!" (If any breath had been left, I would have added that it was at Tanglewood.)*

When June LeBell and I were classmates at Music and Art, what seems like only a few years ago, it seemed inevitable that her future would be in music. My fate was far less certain. When we met again, it was when I came to WQXR to advertise my cooking school on the radio. I brought with me my then favorite cake: Grand Marnier et Chocolat. I must admit, I felt that I was entering into a musical temple with something, though quite delicious, perhaps not quite worthy. But June did not seem at all surprised or condescending regarding my transition from violin to cake. In fact, to my relief, it seemed that as far as she was concerned, I was still in the "arts." Several years later, when she started "Kitchen Classics," featuring recipes accompanied by "appropriate" music, I became a frequent guest on the show, which gave us a chance to renew our friendship—often on the air. In fact, we had so much fun catching up and reminiscing, we often forgot that we were on the air! The best part was that we share a similar sense of humor, which is most likely to happen between people whose frame of reference is so similar. Often, we felt like we would make a great vaudeville team. I would read my favorite buttermilk cake recipe, to which June would play a recording of what she referred to (with a gleam in her eye) as "Madama Buttermilk!" We laughed almost the whole show through and got lots of delightful "feedback" from the audience. When June told me about her plans for this book, it seemed like the perfect joyful extension of her show.

The book turned out to be so multi-dimensional and entertaining; it's difficult to do full justice to its depth and breadth.

On a personal note, it's great fun for me to find old childhood friends, now famous musicians, between these covers: the guy who teased me at music camp (Paul Dunkel), the high-school friend who accompanied me home after ice-skating in Central Park, walking his bike alongside (Stephen Kates), the tall, dark, and brilliant harpsichordist who dated my cousin and whose father was my English teacher (Kenneth Cooper).

The humor, intelligence, generosity, and charm June possesses make this book unique. She serves up each "personality" in the most personal of all possible ways: in his or her own voice. These delightful anecdotes, peppered throughout the book, have as their counterpoint favorite recipes contributed by each performer. We know their music, but now, we know another side of them, and they become friends.

And as the proverbial icing on the cake, this book is graced with the incomparable caricatures of our beloved Hirschfeld.

It is a great honor to participate in the 150th celebration of the Philharmonic by being a part of this special book. For me, it is a deeply sentimental and personal book, and I think, in its own way, it will be for everyone who reads it and, most of all, for anyone who cooks from it."

English was my favorite class, and being intrigued by the teacher, Mr. Cooper, I was dying to know what he thought of me and of my writing. When parent/teacher day rolled around, I begged my mother to attend. This required her to cancel several dental patients' appointments. That night at dinner, I eagerly asked her what the teachers said. I only remember that one female teacher said I was perceptive, which I liked, but I was more interested in hearing what Mr. Cooper had to say. My mother responded: "I walked out on him." I was shocked in disbelief! At first, she wouldn't tell me why, saying I wouldn't want to know, but when I insisted, she revealed the reason: "He said you ought to do well with the boys."

My very serious, no-nonsense, flirtless mother was deeply offended and insulted by this put-down of my intellect. Knowing what a womanizer he was, I suspect he actually meant it as a compliment, and I, as an insecure teenage girl, couldn't have been more delighted. This was music to my ears! Coincidentally, Mr. Cooper's daughter, Connie, was in my class. At the time, she hated him. Also, two years ahead of us, my cousin Lois dated his son, Kenneth, who became the famed harpsichordist and musicologist.

Next, it was my father's turn to visit school, so we went together one evening to listen to a performance by the senior orchestra. Much to my annoyance, he asked me why I wasn't in it.

My answer was that I wasn't good enough. "Why aren't you good enough?" he asked. My answer: "Because that's not what I want to do." His next question: "What *do* you want to do?" My response silenced him: "I just want to live." And live I did.

BETTY CROCKER COOKBOOK

1950 *Betty Crocker's Picture Cook Book* was published and is the number one selling cookbook of all time with an estimated 75 million copies sold.

So, I was not a talented musician, but I was the winner of the Betty Crocker Homemaker of Tomorrow Award in my high school. This was not because I knew how to cook. It was because I was a good writer, and the test was based on multiple choice and an essay.

Sadly, my dad suffered all his life from postwar depression and was regularly leaving home to stay at his shop. It became my job (assigned by my mother) to call him and beg him to come home. I had to get permission to leave official class and get to the phone, and finally, the teacher asked for a reason. I burst into tears and then she insisted that I tell the principal, who then put it on my permanent record saying that it was necessary in case my father was needed to be contacted. It was humiliating. I once asked him if he wanted me to have a husband who treated me as badly as he treated my mother.

Rose at the Trevi Fountain

New York Rose at the Trevi Fountain

In my junior year, when I was 16, my mother sent me on the Experiment in International Living. I lived with a lovely Italian family in Trento, in the Dolomites, and also traveled around Italy with the other participants. I made sure to toss some coins in the Trevi Fountain to ensure my return. Woody and I returned when I turned 80, but the scene had changed. It was so crowded I had to employ the New York gesture with my hand to move people aside to get a photo at the fountain.

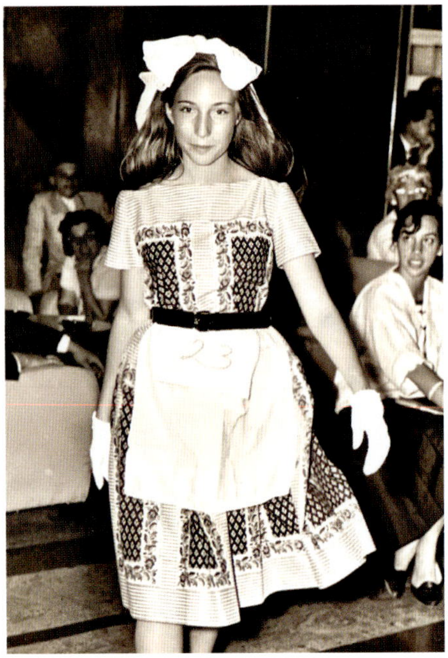

RoseAlice in Wonderland

Rose at High School Graduation

On the ship back home, I won the best costume contest simply by tucking a towel into my belt and making a bow for my hair out of a scarf.

College Years and My Introduction to Baking

University of Vermont: My grade advisor in high school recommended that I apply to a college home economics program instead of liberal arts because I would have a better chance of being accepted. My plan had been to transfer out of the home economics program to be an English major which I accomplished. But one food class that I took before the transfer paved the way to my future career. The teacher explained why coffee never tasted the way it smelled, saying that when using a percolator, the volatile oils in coffee that make it smell so wonderful are going into the air and leaving the coffee! I was intrigued, and it became a lifetime ambition to keep those oils in the coffee.

Over the years, after something like 10 coffeepots (and bean roasters and grinders) later, including a very noisy vacuum pot, I arrived at my goal—first, the Chemex with its filter system and, now, the Nespresso, where the coffee is in a pod and stays the freshest. Color me coffee! Years later, when I had an interview for a job as secretary of the tumor service at NYU Medical Center with the head surgeon, he asked why I was divorced, and my answer was: "One coffeepot too many!" In fact, during the final year of our marriage, my first husband said that he was going to get me the newly created Chemex pot but decided not to feed my neurosis. This is the neurosis that led the way to writing a book of extreme precision—*The Cake Bible*.

My Vermont boyfriend David Gibbs, who became my first husband, introduced me to the virtue of cast-iron frying pans, saying that it was unequaled for frying bacon and many other purposes. I was longing to have one, and one day, when we were shopping, I hefted an 11-inch model. I think it was about $7, which was more money than either of us could afford. We had so little money, we counted it in A&W root beers.

We walked through the store, and reluctant to leave the pan behind, I hadn't yet returned it to its hook. We left the store without buying anything and walked into the parking lot when, to my astonishment, I discovered that the heavy frying pan was still hanging from my right hand. I suppose I had gotten used to the weight, and it had become a part of my arm. "Oh, my goodness!" I said. "We'll have to return it." David, in shocked disbelief, said something along the lines of: "We'll be in more trouble if we try to bring it back—just keep it!" I was horrified and delighted all at the same time. I still feel a little guilty. And I still have and treasure the pan.

My first baking experiences were a total failure. When I made an oatmeal cookie from the recipe on the back of the oatmeal box, it was just that—a cookie. During baking, all the batter merged to form one giant sheet.

Conversely, my first cake, from a mix no less, came out of the pan in three pieces. (The instructions had said to grease the pan but hadn't mentioned flouring it.) Puzzled and disappointed and with my little brother at my elbow asking what I was going to do, I glued the cake pieces together with frosting from a can.

Two things happened when I returned home for college vacations. The first was when I decided to make my father's favorite pie—the cherry pie I had learned to make in one of the food classes. Unknown to me, my grandmother used the oven to store pots and pans, and she kept her kosher soap in the broiler beneath it. My mother and I emptied the oven, and together, we tried to figure out how to light the oven. Fearing an explosion, my mother made a long paper wick, lit the oven, and took me into the living room, putting her hands over her ears for protection. I did the same. Of course, by the time the flame reached the gas, the explosion she had feared, but had actually created, took place. **RECIPE: Cherry Pie** (**page 238**)

JAMES BEARD SCHOOL

1955 James Beard's Cooking School classes begin in New York City. He taught at his own schools in New York City and Seaside, Oregon, and also traveled to lecture at other venues for the next 30 years. Thirteen years later, I was given a holiday present to attend several of his classes.

Next, I didn't realize that the thick cherry juice needed more than just slits in the top crust to release the juices as they bubbled out, so when I opened the oven toward the end of baking, I saw that the slits had sealed together and the juices had burst through and had flooded onto the oven floor. My grandmother came running in crying out "the soap, the soap" because it had all melted in the broiler beneath. Next vacation, I tried putting cut paper straws into the slits to keep them open. But once again, my grandmother tried to rescue her melting soap saying: "Don't you ever learn?" To which I said: "Don't *you* ever learn that an oven is for baking?"

JOY OF COOKING

1931 *Joy of Cooking* was published. Many revisions later, my signature Lemon Poppy Seed Pound Cake was included.

Returning to college, I tried making a lemon meringue pie, and the filling wouldn't thicken even when, in desperation and scientific curiosity, I added three-quarters of a box of cornstarch. Because I was living in a rural area at the time, I suspected that the only possible culprit might be the water, so I had it tested. Sure enough, it was at the highest level of mineral content. The nascent food science professional in me was born, and years later, I created my idea of the perfect chocolate chip cookie. **RECIPE: My Dream Chocolate Chip Cookies** **(page 240)**

When I transferred to the liberal arts program, I told my boyfriend, David, that I wanted to be a writer like him. His discouraging response was that I had nothing to write about. But I discovered the writer in me when I took a class in creative writing, and the teacher read out loud to the class the following part of an essay I had written: "Last moments lose their value in the strained effort to sustain them."

After leaving college, in my free time, I borrowed *Joy of Cooking* from my mother's friend Rosalind Street so that I could learn to make bread. She also gave me my first whisk. I knew nothing about bread-making, but after diligently following the clear, friendly instructions, I produced a perfect loaf. I was thrilled and proud. I was also hooked. But I knew so very little about cooking. If someone had suggested that I would someday write a cookbook of my own, I would have thought they were nuts.

5

First Marriage

David Gibbs

When I turned 19, I married David Gibbs, and we lived in Washington Crossing, Pennsylvania. He started studying for his master's degree at Temple University, and I went along with him to watch Julia Child's first PBS show *The French Chef* on one of the TVs in the girl's dorm. We couldn't afford a TV of our own. And every opportunity, I cooked something special for dinner, but David complained that he had trouble concentrating on grading papers when he was smelling my cooking. One night, I made Julia's no-fail cheese soufflé with a coulis de tomate from the show. When I brought it to the table, David said it was very good but asked where the rest of dinner was. That was it!

Since I worked full-time, including a long commute, that was all the time I had to prepare dinner. I'm sure he would have been happier with meat and potatoes, though a few years later, his taste majorly expanded. Then, there was the baked beans. I wanted to please him by making something New England-ish and found a recipe from *Gourmet* magazine, which called for a wide variety of spices. I spent hours on the weekend driving around trying to find all of the ingredients and did. But after the beans spent 48 hours in the oven and were still rock hard, David said that it was costing too much electricity and that I should give up. I didn't know that beans will never soften if salt in any form is put into the water and that the salt pork in the recipe was the added salt.

JULIA CHILD

1961 Julia Child's *Mastering the Art of French Cooking* was published, and two years later, the first cooking show was on PBS. I was inspired to watch the show by my cousin Lois Schenk who had met Julia in person.

That Christmas, David gave me two presents: The first was a book on New England cooking. He seated me on his knee and opened the book to the baked beans saying this will be a simpler way to make them. He read the recipe out loud, and it started with "first go out and dig a hole." This gave us a good laugh. So much for simplicity.

The second gift was another book and just what I was hoping for—my own copy of *Joy of Cooking*. I was off and running. First came the Velvet Spice Cake because I loved the idea of a velvety texture. It was every bit as velvety as promised, but I didn't like the taste of the spices. This was the first cake I had ever baked from scratch, so I didn't understand that the spices could have been omitted without sacrificing the desirable texture.

The next recipe title to intrigue me was Angel Pie, which proved to be both delicious and a miracle of textures, but it had an unappetizingly chartreuse-colored filling, because I had failed to turn to the cross-reference concerning egg cookery, where I would have been warned about cooking an egg yolk mixture in an aluminum pan. (This experience was to influence my decision, many years later, when writing *The Cake Bible*, not only to offer theories and pointers for success but to have helpful tips in sidebars next to the recipe, where they are more difficult to avoid.)

Both these experiences served to keep me from ever losing sight of how magical and mysterious baking seems to a beginner and how frightened one is to deviate from a recipe without understanding the principles. I also learned from that experience to pay attention to the entire title of a recipe, the headnote, and any sidebar note.

Chicken Breasts Cockaigne, another *Joy of Cooking* classic, precipitated an argument in the supermarket when my young and struggling husband suggested I buy the less-expensive chicken thighs. Still not daring to deviate from the guidelines of a recipe, I raised my voice in protest and indignation and all but yelled: "I want breasts!" Cringing in embarrassment as other shoppers turned to stare at me in amusement, I stood my ground, however, and the recipe was superb and delicate as intended. In fact, everything I ever tried from *Joy of Cooking* was essentially a success, except for the venison stew, and even that was a learning experience. Someone who hunted had given us a leg of venison, and as it was cooking, I found myself futilely hoping that it wouldn't taste the way it smelled. It wasn't the fault of the recipe though; it was the age and subsequent gaminess of the meat. So, as far as I was concerned, *Joy of Cooking* was THE book, even after I began to expand my cookbook collection to over 1,000. That said, I had two other failures.

Our first Thanksgiving together, David and I bought a small turkey, and to my disappointment, it didn't seem to contain the giblets. After roasting it and carving it, I found that the bag of giblets had been tucked into the neck cavity—the usual place.

Then, there was the pumpkin pie. I was sure that my New England husband would love it, but to me, it tasted like a barnyard. He made a face and asked me what I put in it. My answer was pumpkin. He asked: "What about eggs and spices and sugar?" I thought that a can of pumpkin was a complete pumpkin pie filling. It seems like a century ago that I knew so little, but actually, it's more than a half-century ago.

The first summer in Washington Crossing, David had a two-month vacation from teaching. Our neighbor, George Bush, editor at *Better Homes & Gardens* magazine, gave him a dream assignment to review restaurants in southern Vermont. These were places David could not afford to visit when he was growing up there. But since he wasn't going to be paid by the school until the fall, we didn't have the money for the trip, so we asked my mother to loan it to us. David was counting on my knowledge of food, though it was only slightly more than his.

The first restaurant we went to was Mama Grosso. Her son sat with us as we enjoyed an excellent dinner despite my great faux pas when I complimented him on what I thought was the soup, and it was actually an onion condiment. He looked horrified, probably imagining what an uneducated review we were going to write. When David and I returned to our motel room, we rolled on the bed, laughing with hilarity. Fifty-nine years later, I got an honor from the same magazine, praising me as one of the 2024 Stylemakers. Life had come a full circle.

New York City

I was sad to leave Buck's County, Pennsylvania, to return to my hometown of New York City, but David longed to live in the big city. For my 21st birthday, my present was the money to buy the ingredients for paella. We had just tasted it for the first time at the World's Fair in Queens, and I was longing to have it again. Craig Claiborne had a recipe in *The New York Times* which turned out to be excellent. When I met him years later at Restaurant Daniel where I had a press party for one of my books, I got to tell him the story.

The first job I found was thanks to my mother. The wife of her former boyfriend ran the NYU Courant Institute of Mathematical Sciences, and though I wasn't a mathematical typist, she was willing to give me a try to learn on the job. The mathematicians were an interesting group, but I also met Bobby—a colleague who changed my life. She introduced David and me to her partner, a jazz drummer, who later became very famous. This drummer offered David a pill of LSD, and I asked to share it, thinking the whole pill would be harmful to him. However, even the half pill gave him a "bad trip," though I actually enjoyed mine. It was the beginning of the dissolution of our marriage.

Bobby reported to me that the famous drummer "had eyes for me," which required a definition. She suggested that I go to live with him for a few weeks.

David thought it would be a good experience for me to see how other people lived. It was the 1960s, an era of "free love," so I packed my down pillow and moved a few blocks downtown to the drummer's loft in SoHo and a whole new world of jazz musicians and junkies. I slept with his heroin stash hidden under my pillow while he sat with a friend taking heroin and nodding off. Once, he even let me accompany him to Astor Place where he sold it. It horrifies me now to think how close I came to ending up in the Women's House of Detention in Greenwich Village. One thing for sure: I wasn't going to end up like the partners of some of his colleagues, supporting their jazz geniuses by prostitution.

One day, I asked the famous drummer if I could try cocaine. He offered a smidgen of the white powder, and when I asked how to take it, he said: "You gots to snort it, baby." I asked with incredulity: "In my *nose*?" I had never even let my mother put nose drops in my nose as a child. That was the deal-breaker and may have saved me from addiction. After I left him, the drummer asked me to come back, but I declined.

When David called to tell me that it was time to come home, he announced that, although he said he would always love me, he didn't say he would stay married to me after I left him for the famous drummer. I was so devastated, and after a few weeks, I started having severe intestinal cramps. I went to my gynecologist/endocrinologist, Dr. Ernest Kulka, who was an Austrian physician who had been analyzed by Freud himself—no doubt why he had the metal speculum on a heating pad! When he asked me about the last time I had a bowel movement, I reported that it had been several weeks. To my shock, this refined and elegant doctor's response was: "Ach zoh, you are full of shit!" He went on to say that not since WWII had he seen anything like this.

David and I continued to live together for several weeks. When he finally moved out, we both cried. It wasn't long before David met his life partner, who turned out to be a distant relative of mine through marriage. It took me seven years to find my second husband and decades for David and me to become long-distance friends.

6

On My Own, Entering the Food World

I was 23 when I started Jungian therapy and fell in love with my married therapist, which is normal and called "transference." What was less normal was that he also fell in love with me, which was called "counter-transference," and acted on it. We became lovers for a short time until I met an amazing older man who was also married and responsible for my going back to school, getting two degrees, and finding my true profession.

Living in New York again spearheaded my career. Everyone came through the city, and I went to every event when I was invited. New York became the epicenter of the burgeoning interest in food. Dean & DeLuca, the gourmet market, was three blocks from my house, and Balducci's was not much further.

Shopping at Balducci's

The one thing that my grandmother made that I adored were gribonyes. She cut up chicken skin and fried it until crisp. But she never let me have more than one or two pieces, saying that they were undigestible and were intended for my father who had "an iron stomach." So, the first thing I did, when living on my own, was to try making gribonyes. The problem was that I didn't realize it was chicken skin—I thought it was chicken fat. I watched as the chicken fat melted into smaller and smaller pieces and realized my mistake.

The next time I planned to make them, I was standing in line in the meat section of the wonderful Greenwich Village grocery store Balducci's and overheard the older gentleman in front of me asking the butcher for a duck that was both skinned and boned. Timidly (and I pretended jokingly), I asked him if I could have the skin and bones. "Sure," he responded, "but what are you going to do with them?" I informed him: "Fry the skin crisp and make stock from the bones. Are you sure you don't want them?" He said: "They're all yours." Then, he disappeared into the crowded store. Despite my delight with my treasures, curiosity soon got the better of me, so, as soon as the butcher wrapped the duck skin and bones and filled my order, I set out in pursuit of the old gentleman to find out exactly what he was planning to do with the skinned and boned duck. Unfortunately, he must have been moving very quickly as he was nowhere to be found.

My career covered a wide expanse of different professions, but all the things I tried until I fell upon my ultimate profession was an amalgam of all of them. No one at the beginning would have guessed that food would be my true calling.

My First Job in the Food World and Studying with James Beard

In 1967, I was fortunate to find a secretarial job in the public relations department of Reynolds Metals Company that changed my life. They didn't have a test kitchen, and the two home economists were not interested in food, so the boss, Eleanore Lynch, gave me recipes from the book she was writing to test at home. As a Christmas present, she gave me and one of the other women, Helen Hatton, several classes with James Beard. One of the classes featured paella and strawberry savarin. By sheer coincidence, the week before, I had made these exact dishes for Helen. She lost no time in telling Mr. Beard, and he made the mistake of asking whose was better—his or mine. Helen was always very outspoken, and her answer was "hers!" He wasn't too upset, because I was in charge of sending boxes of aluminum foil to editors, and I kept him well supplied. (Helen went on to start a PR company called "Speak Easy"—no surprise!)

Another class featured making a cake roll. When I tried it at home, it was a total disappointment because my oven was not level and needed to be propped with a stick to keep the door closed. Consequently, one end of the cake was very thin, and the other end was very thick, which made rolling it a recipe in disaster.

The recipe I remember best was for duxelles, which involved an hour of finely chopping mushrooms (this was before the food processor did it in seconds). Duxelles is a great addition to many dishes such as grains and beef Wellington, and James Beard used it in between layers of crêpes. I also valued the technique of folding egg whites into a mixture with my hand, even though my gold pinky ring slipped off never to be found.

One day, back at the office, the teletype machine started clattering away in the next room. Eleanore asked me to check it, saying that she was working on something important for Clementine Paddleford, who was the most important and demanding food journalist in the country. I checked and called to her from the machine room, telling her that she didn't have to worry about Clementine. Understandably, Eleanore was shocked that I would dare to say such a thing until I explained that we just got the teletype message that Clementine had died.

The most wonderful thing Eleanore did for me was to introduce me to Cecily Brownstone, food editor of the Associated Press. I lived in the West Village only a few blocks from Cecily, so Eleanore sent me to see her with some pastry tarts shaped using foil instead of tart pans. Cecily became my mentor, telling me to go back to college and that she would launch my career when I graduated. Seven years later, Cecily gave me some articles to write for her. One I wrote was on challah, which some clueless editor in the Midwest headlined as "Bake Challah for Passover." Cecily didn't think it was funny, especially when I said, to be sure, no one would write a headline as "Yum Yom Kippur." And when I thanked her, Cecily said: "I merely threw you a bone." That was the truth!

After leaving Reynolds, for a brief period of time, I started a manuscript typing service. I was blessed with very fast reflexes and clocked in at 180 words per minute on an IBM Selectric. My mom warned me that people would not pay when leaving. Only one tried, and I said in no uncertain terms: "I did the work now, so I want to be paid now." I came close to having had the esteemed writer Baron Roy Andries de Groot as a client but missed the moment. I was shopping across the street at a store called Opera Deli and noticed a very tall man with the largest German shepherd I'd ever seen. I said to the man, "That's a very large dog." He looked down at me from his towering height, smiled, and said: "Big man, big dog." After he left, the store clerk told me who he was and that he was blind. The clerk explained that most of the man's life he had vision, so he didn't appear to be blind. Then, he told me the man had been looking for a typist, but I had no idea where he lived, though I found out later it was just a few houses down the street.

When I was in my late 20s, I felt that I did not have enough energy, so I returned to Dr. Kulka, who was a professor to all the NYU gynecologists. He started off by telling me I had large teeth and bucolic eyes (translating that to be cow-like) which, like Mussolini, indicated a hypothyroid condition. He measured me like a tailor measuring for a suit and pronounced that, in addition to my other inadequacies, my arms were long. Then came the pelvic exam when he asked me how my hair growth had been. Finally, I thought I could impress him with something positive, so I shared that I used to have hair down to my knees. "Ach zoh!" he cried out. "Zoh, vat hahpent?" I explained that it was in a long braid and that I always wore it to one side. "Yah yah?" he encouraged me to continue. So, I added that my head started tilting to one side. He sighed and said with great disappointment (no medical history paper to be written), "Ach zoh, ze hair on your head!"

He prescribed thyroid pills which I took for a few years until I started working as a medical secretary for a doctor who asked me if I had ever had a protein-bound iodine test to determine whether I had hypothyroidism and added that Dr. Kulka was known to prescribe thyroid medication to every woman patient. So, I stopped the thyroid pills and, after a few weeks without them, took the test. I was on the upper limits of normal!

A few years later, when working as secretary of the tumor service at NYU Medical, again, I was always tired. I went to Dr. Many Blum, the top specialist who worked at Bellevue Hospital once a week (where I didn't have to pay). He asked me what I did during the day, and I said I worked there. And what did I do every night? Go to school was my answer. "Every night?" he asked. "And you wonder why you are tired?!" I had just assumed that if I weren't going to school, I would be doing something else equally tiring. But this lifestyle of working day and night became my permanent lifestyle for years to come.

My Long Hair Down to My Knees

The Family Friend Who Changed My Life

Forty years older than me, a brilliant general practitioner offered me amazing emotional support. He started a mental health association and had graduated second in his class from the University of Virginia School of Medicine. (Yes, he was an "old man," but I am now more than 20 years older than he was at the time!) He told me that he wished he had my intellect and told me to go back to school and graduate first in my class (both of which I did after seven years of night school). Had he not been physiologically impotent, we would have been lovers.

We adored each other and wrote many letters, all of which I've saved. I would take the subway home from work every day at lunch hour, which was a half hour each way, just to see if there was a letter in the mailbox from him, and there always was. We tried to separate several times, with him saying that I needed to have a whole life, but all I wanted was him. I told him one day that I wanted men to be interested in my mind and not my body. He asked if I didn't want to have sex appeal, and I got the point! After several years, we both realized that we had to end the relationship. What changed my life the most was that, in 1967, he got a job for me as a medical secretary for his colleague, an internist specializing in diabetes.

My Tenure as a Medical Secretary

I didn't have any medical training, but the general practitioner said I would learn on the job. The internist's office was on the main floor of an Upper East Side brownstone that had once belonged to Eleanor Roosevelt. He and I had lunch in the waiting room every day and exchanged many stories and thoughts, including his having a relative who was a Rhodes Scholar, to which I informed him that there were two Rhodes Scholars in my family. In addition to one-upping him, I loved making him laugh. When he said that, as a student at Williams College during WWII, gas was scarce, so he used hair tonic in its place, I asked him if he called his car Wild Root Charlie! And when I told him that his calculator wasn't working, he said that it's always the person not the machine. I suggested that he try adding a few numbers, and it turned out to be the old machine that was at fault. He laughed when I started using a Chinese abacus.

At first, the internist allowed me to make lunch over a Bunsen burner in his tiny lab. But then, he said it had to stop because his office was starting to smell like a short-order joint! Also, his wife wasn't pleased that he was gaining weight and had no appetite for dinner. They invited me to babysit for their younger children (they had seven children in all before they adopted an eighth from Korea) in their home in Tenafly, New Jersey, and they also invited me to their farm which he called the Beyond Hope Farm because it was outside the little town of Hope, New Jersey (where, coincidentally, I now have been living for over 30 years). His oldest daughter worked for a fashion magazine. Little did I know that, many years later, we would be working together on a food magazine and that I would be making her daughter's wedding cake.

The internist and I weren't in love; we were in admiration. He taught me how to do EKGs (electrocardiograms), and one day, a blue blood patient reached over to pinch my behind. I told him that the doctor could see every move he made on the EKG readout, and the man actually believed me! The internist was furious and told me that the patient had promised his wife to change his ways and be faithful, but the guy invited me to the famous Sardi's restaurant in the Theater District, and I couldn't resist. The food was bad, and I never saw him again.

The internist's associate at the office, who was a surgeon, had a history of seducing his medical secretaries, and the internist told him that, if he tried that with me, he would be fired as a partner. This resulted in his talking to me as little as possible. One day, however, after the surgeon had given a colonoscopy, I went into the exam room to ask him a question, and he actually started a polite conversation, until he suddenly looked down and saw that the colonoscopy machine he was cleaning was sending out a fine spray of shit covering his pants. His response was: "That's what I get for standing here talking to *you*!" I ran to my desk trying to hide my laughter, but he probably heard it, just as he heard me cry one day after he had insulted me.

THE COOK'S MAGAZINE

1980 Chris Kimball started *The Cook's Magazine* to offer a scientific, no-nonsense approach to cooking, distinct from lifestyle magazines. The magazine focused on rigorous recipe testing for home cooks.

1993 It became *Cook's Illustrated*.

About 20 years went by, and one of the internist's eight children became the founding editor of *The Cook's Magazine*. My first two magazine articles, "Understanding Génoise" (1981) and “Understanding the Layer Cake” (1982), were the start of my career as a food writer. I continued to write for the magazine through 1989. Soon after, I received a photo in the mail from the internist; it was a picture of him making a cake for his wife’s birthday from my recipe in his daughter’s magazine!

After the departure of the surgeon, the internist needed a new associate to share his office, so that was how I met the replacement for the surgeon, who was a general practitioner, and how I discovered that he was addicted to the narcotic codeine. There were several signs that triggered my suspicions, but, to me, at that point, it was unimaginable that a doctor would become an addict. For one thing, the internist had explained to me that, in order always to have an adequate supply of painkiller for his patients, a doctor would sometimes prescribe medicine to a patient, and the doctor would keep it.

However, when the general practitioner asked me to go to the pharmacy to pick up a prescription like that, it turned out it was for a patient who had died the week before, and that struck me as odd. When I was at the pharmacy, I also purchased some toothpaste for myself, and it was in the same bag as the medicine, though I paid for it separately. When I returned to the office, the very agitated general practitioner asked for the prescription, and I nervously handed him the whole bag. The first thing he pulled out was my toothpaste, and he cried out: “Where is my medication?” He was visibly perspiring, which I had noticed was the case even when he came dressed only in a two-piece suit on a cold day. One day, when we were sitting in the waiting room eating lunch, I saw the general practitioner lift his food with a fork to his mouth and pause for a fraction of a second, and my mind immediately jumped to the vision of my former boyfriend, the famous jazz musician who had been on heroin, being slightly offbeat when he was high. Finally, I hesitatingly voiced my suspicions to the internist, prefacing it with: “I’m sure it’s not true.”

To my shock, the internist informed me that he and his colleagues had been trying to accuse the addicted general practitioner for years and couldn’t find a definitive way to do it, thanking me for giving them the irrefutable ammunition. I assumed that the general practitioner was sent to a rehab facility, but the internist never told me.

During the two years I served as a medical secretary, I also went to night school at the Fashion Institute of Technology (FIT) and loved it, despite both my grandmothers having said not to go into the garment industry. One day, my mother’s best friend, Celia Hindin, who was a phlebotomist at NYU Medical Center, told me that there was a wonderful job opening there. She said that Iris, the secretary of the tumor service, was getting married and leaving and her job was open. She explained that, instead of my spending my days in a dark hole, I would be walking from Bellevue to the VA Hospital to NYU Medical Center every day, and they would pay my tuition to go back to school at NYU. The internist encouraged me to move on, saying that I was too refined for Seventh Avenue (the garment industry).

7

How I Got My BS & MA in Seven Years of Night School:

Working as a Full-Time Medical Secretary at New York University

In 1968, I was accepted at NYU and transferred all my credits from FIT. NYU gave me nine free credits per semester. Eventually, I would joke about how I went from draping fabric to draping fondant!

My grade advisor, Roseanne Black, assured me that she would be there to guide me through the required courses, even though some were during the day when I was working, and that anyone who can grow her hair down to her knees would have the perseverance to get through it. What finally helped me decide to spend years going to night school was one day, as I was walking through Washington Square Park, I realized that those years would pass, and it would either be with or without a degree. But then, Roseanne's husband got a job in China. I'll always be grateful that she confided in me that she was leaving, even though she had not yet informed the head of the department. She said that she didn't want me to hear about it after the fact and worry, and she assured me that I was on a good course. It was a great kindness, and she turned out to be right but not without some major bumps in the road.

My mother, concerned about my future career possibilities, offered to send me to a special study at NYU, which, at the time, was an expensive $800. The concept was that, over a period of several days, I would take various tests administered by a psychologist, at the end of which my grades and responses would be compared to those of people who were happy in their profession.

The results of the special study were that I should be either a writer or a landscape architect. I got in the 99% in every area, except design where I got 15%. The design test was based on comparing two abstract drawings—one symmetrical and the other asymmetrical. Finding the abstracts unappealing, I chose the least offensive, which were the symmetrical ones. The test I liked best was the psychological one.

When I was asked if I could be anyone living or dead, I chose Psyche (from the myth of Cupid and Psyche) because she was given wings, a halo, and immortality. (See page 114 for how my wish came true!)

KITCHENAID CELEBRATED ITS 50TH ANNIVERSARY

1969 KitchenAid released the Model K-45 stand mixer, a cornerstone in the brand's history that solidified the iconic design still popular today. While not a specially colored limited edition, the anniversary model is considered the precursor to the modern Artisan mixers designs.

One of my responsibilities working at NYU tumor service was to help organize and set up the walk-in mammography clinic. One day, I was almost scammed walking back to my office when two girls pretended to have found an envelope filled with money and offered to share it with me. After one of them told me that her mother had breast cancer, they must have been totally shocked when I said with full sincerity that she deserved to have all of the money. Then, in all naivety, I saw a policeman nearby and suggested we tell him about it but then added that he would probably keep it himself. I saw the look of panic on the girls' faces, and a lightbulb went off. I hurried away, saying I was late for work. My innocence protected me.

Saving My Grandmother

The surgeon who was head of the breast clinic at New York University Medical Center was the top breast cancer surgeon. He was very handsome, and his sister was an actress. He was always trying to fix her up with his colleague Dr. Elliott Beranbaum, who was not interested in a celebrity and, soon after, married me (before I became one). The cancer surgeon was always ogling my breasts, so I found it quite hypocritical, when I went to him as a patient, that he suggested first that I stop eating chocolate. And before my mouth could drop open, he followed that with another suggestion that I stop drinking coffee, which made me gasp because I cannot live without coffee. I asked him what that would accomplish, and he told me that my breasts will shrink and I will feel more comfortable. Oh, how I wanted to respond with: "If you stopped eating chocolate and drinking coffee, would your cock shrink?!" Instead, I informed him that I was not uncomfortable.

I saved my grandmother (the one who brought me up and who had kidnapped me from the hospital shortly after I was born because she thought they were not treating my minor infection correctly) when she was 92 from having an unnecessary mastectomy. My grandmother, who was completely senile and living in a nursing home in Great Neck, New York, was diagnosed with breast cancer, and they were planning a mastectomy. The rule was that she was not allowed to bring in her own doctor, or she would lose her standing in the nursing home. But when they heard her doctor was the great breast cancer surgeon, they made an exception. He was willing to go because he lived in Great Neck, so it wasn't out of the way. He told them that a woman of 92 needed only a lumpectomy.

He told me that he had never been in a nursing home before and thanked me for the experience. He also told me that, now that I have cancer on my maternal side, it greatly increased the chances of my getting it. This time, I rose to the occasion and said: "That's not true!" He was totally shocked that a lowly medical secretary would dare to contradict him, but he was curious enough to ask me why. I explained: "Most people don't have 92-year-old grandmothers, but if they did, most of them would have breast cancer." He graciously agreed. I am forever grateful that, thanks to him, my grandmother wasn't tortured by the nursing home staff's desire to practice surgery on her.

Typing the Grant Proposals

In 1968, the person who was supposed to train me as a medical secretary left shortly after my arrival to join her new husband where he was stationed in Texas because he had experienced a change of heart, and she was compelled to join him and reassure him that the marriage was not a mistake. I was so overwhelmed by all I needed to learn on my own that I told the doctor, one of the two chairmen of the tumor service, that I couldn't handle it and had to quit. I was surprised by his reaction, refusing to accept my resignation and saying that all work is complicated and difficult unless one is a cab driver or butcher! I guess he didn't know about my working in the clerical end of a brake lining factory. So, it was back to the drawing board.

I once stayed up three nights in a row without sleeping to finish typing the reapplications for the grant for the National Institutes of Health. If it hadn't been submitted by the deadline, the department would have lost its grant, and the co-chairman was convinced that it was beyond any human being to be able to do all that typing on time. But as a speedy manuscript typist and with that "persistence," I pulled it off.

A few months later, the co-chairman said that the department needed more grant money. I had the temerity to suggest that they give me a new title, such as organizational specialist instead of medical secretary. He roared back: "They would laugh us out of Washington.

You are only a secretary. You are only a secretary." When I took dictation from him, he was so slow I usually fell asleep between sentences, and once, when I didn't wake up in time, he caught me!

A few years later, the co-chairman came into the office after hours where I was dictating a recipe to my boyfriend, Dr. Elliott Beranbaum, who was a radiologist, which the co-chairman really had wanted to be but had realized he'd make more money as a surgeon. Then, years later, when married to Elliott, I ran into the co-chairman at my dentist's office, and he gave me a huge hug, saying that seeing me was the best thing that's happened in months. When I told Elliott, a man of few words, he commented: "Years!" Apparently, while on retirement, the co-chairman would visit Elliott while he was reading X-rays which annoyed him immensely.

I was asked to attend a lecture given by a cancer surgeon to the American Cancer Society (ACS) to ensure the continuation of their grant to the department. I was duly shocked when he burst out enthusiastically: "We at NYU *love* cancer!" I found it such an unfortunate expression I used it for a paper on cancer for one of my classes and got an A.

So, while working at NYU Medical every day and studying every night, I gradually learned the job and managed to reduce the hours spent to such a degree that I was also able to have a manuscript typing service again, using the office copy machine to make copies and charge for them. One day, the cancer surgeon, who finally noticed that I was doing very little actual hospital work, came to my office and put the question to me: "Exactly how many hours a week do you spend on your job?" I cast my eyes heavenward trying to calculate accurately to give him an honest answer. He must have thought I was trying to come up with a lie, but he realized it wasn't the case when I responded: "About three hours!" He asked: "Three hours a day?"

"No, a week!" I answered honestly. I thought, maybe, he would fire me on the spot, and for a moment, he was too flummoxed to answer, but then he said: "Well, try to make more of your job. Help Miss Schomer type reports." She didn't ask me to do them because she knew I hated it. She once let me take the day off to make curtains for her and covered for my absence at work.

My Student Teaching Experience

Five years passed, and I was close to getting my BS degree to teach about food in high school, but there was a problem. Student teaching required being in the school all day every weekday for the entire semester. I approached my boss with the problem, and he asked why I couldn't do the student teaching part-time over two semesters. I told him that I had already asked, and they said it couldn't be done. A life lesson: my boss said, "Call again and ask someone else." I did just that, and the person I spoke to this time said: "It's never been done before, but why shouldn't you be the first?"

So, I went back to my boss with this great news to which he said: "We'll have to put you down as part-time at work." He told me that, if the grantors found out that I was only working part-time and getting a full-time salary, their department would lose their grants. I told him that it wouldn't work because I had to be full-time in order to get the tuition remission. He relented and took the enormous risk.

I did my student teaching that year and then there was only one course left to get my BS degree, but instead of taking it, I started taking classes on the master's level. NYU only offered six tuition-free credits per semester on the graduate level, but since I was technically still an undergraduate, I was able to take nine. After completing them, I took the final three-credit course to get my undergraduate degree which left NYU scratching its head because they had never given a MA until a year after the BS, and they had no idea how I had done it in just one semester! Another life lesson.

I had to wait the year and then I graduated cum laude and number one in my class. I should have gotten a degree in fighting and beating the system. It's still one of my favorite things to accomplish. Today, BS and MA degrees from NYU would cost over a quarter of a million dollars. And I got more than my money's worth in life lessons.

In one of my classes in teaching, the esteemed cookbook author Jean Anderson gave a lecture to inspire us students. She shared how wonderful it is to write a cookbook that will earn royalties for years to come. I thought to myself that this would never happen to me. The irony is that it did happen with many of my books, but it doesn't usually happen to most authors. For the class, we were also required to do cooking demos, and I was thrilled when the teacher told me that I was a born teacher.

In another class, we were required to choose any "exercise" that was new to us and to keep a progress chart to show the learning curve. I chose standing on my head, and after several days, I actually accomplished what I thought was impossible. In still another class on international cuisine, we were each given a very small budget to feed a class of 30. I made pesto and had $1 leftover which I used to make a beautiful parsley bouquet. The only problem was that I hadn't realized the necessity to cut the bottom of the stems for the water below them to penetrate, so they quickly wilted.

In a class on home design, I was asked to do a presentation on window design. I started by saying that the first thing to consider about windows is how much to let in and how much to keep out. I was delighted when everyone applauded the unexpected metaphor. Also in that class, we were given the same test from the study I had taken, comparing two different abstract designs. I told the teacher I could get 100%, choosing the opposite of what I like, because it was based on symmetry and disliking abstracts. I always chose symmetry which is the least offensive to my taste. The teacher promptly disagreed and assured me that the test was a lot more complex than that. I went ahead choosing the ones I liked least, and guess who got 100%?

How I Became Fluent in French

Michèl Mouley was a trained chef I met through an introduction from a French friend who thought we'd really hit it off—and we did. Michèl was originally from Limousin and had just arrived in New York City with only a green card, a fish fileting knife, and no English whatsoever. Since he cooked all day in restaurants, Michèl did not consider cooking recreation. He did, however, make me a pot-au-feu which, the next day, he turned into a beef stew, so glorious with a mirepoix of vegetables as the sauce that the word stew seemed utterly inappropriate.

When I was taking a food class at NYU, I planned to make a poached salmon. Michèl asked me how I was going to decorate it, and I said simply with a gelatin rosé glaze. He was shocked and said: "*Tu vas servir le saumon tu nue?*" (You're going to serve the salmon completely nude?) Then, he offered to decorate it for me. I poached the salmon, and when he arrived, he planted himself in front of the stove to lift the salmon out of the broth, pronouncing it to be "*bien cuit*." I was so proud. He clarified the broth with egg white to absorb impurities and decorated the glazed fish with a lemon cut partially in half with a ribbon of its lemon zest spiraling over it from one side of the fish to the other. Then, he made roses cut from tomatoes with leaves from scallions. It was so magnifique I couldn't bear to cut it when the teacher, Mr. Tarantino, who was totally blown away, asked me to serve it.

The first time we made love, Michèl cried out: "*Jouie, jouie!*" I thought the word to mean *Juif* (Jew) and feared he was a Nazi sadist, so the last thing I could do was jouie, which meant come.

I had studied French for seven years at school, but it didn't include conversation, so my French was limited. Michèl, on the other hand, spoke no English and did fine working in restaurants where most of the kitchen staff spoke Spanish. I told him that I got a degree in teaching, but he said he was "*trop orgueilleux d'apprendre d'une femme*" (too proud to learn from a woman). So, after one and half years of spending every night and weekend with Michèl, my French improved to the degree that French people meeting us asked where I was from in France! And Michèl still didn't speak a word of English.

One weekend, we went to the Hunts Point Produce Market and ate some spicy Italian sausage. In the middle of that night, Michèl woke up in pain on his left side. I told him that it's not likely to be appendicitis since that is usually on the right side, but as his pain got worse, I thought we should go to the ER. I called one of my doctor friends who worked at the VA, but he said he couldn't get him in since it's just for American Veterans. So, I took him to the

Bellevue Outpatient Department, where I worked. Michèl wanted to know where we were, and I gave him the initials in French for OPD which was transliterated as "*au pédé*." Michèl cried out in protest: "*Ah, non!*" Then, I realized that the words in French translated "to the faggots!"

No amount of persuasion worked to get him into that hospital which would have been the best choice. So, I took him to the nearest hospital which was St. Luke's. The attendings stood around him asking me to translate. They asked when was the last time he had a bowel movement which I translated as "*kaka*." They were highly amused that it was the same word in English. They said it was indeed an appendix attack, and he had to be operated on immediately. He refused, saying he would prefer to go back to France for the surgery. I explained that it was likely to burst in the airplane, so he agreed reluctantly and sent me uptown to get his address book. Of course, I had to open it and found the name of a girl he had been flirting with at a recent party. I considered tearing out the page but decided against it.

When I returned to the hospital, they were wheeling the ashen Michèl into the OR. "What's wrong?" I asked. "*Je vais mourir*," he answered (I'm going to die). "Why do you think that, Michèl?" I asked. "Because they asked if I wanted to see a priest," he answered. I reassured him that, with us being at a Catholic hospital, it was a routine request before going into surgery.

Michèl was told after surgery that he was not supposed to climb stairs, and his apartment had more flights than mine. But when I invited him to stay with me for a couple of weeks of recovery, he accused me of wanting to imprison him. In a way, I did.

I wanted to marry Michèl, but he came up with a wide variety of reasons why he couldn't. One was that he had to marry a Catholic. When I asked why, since he claimed to be an atheist, his response was that it hadn't done him any harm (au contraire). Then, Michèl said that I would be called "*la Limousine*"—a woman from Limousin. Next, he said that in France, when a woman is married to a chef, she can't attend family gatherings if he is working. Then, climatically, curling his hands into fists he said, "You are an intellectual, and I am a manual." Finally, I won the battle and lost the war by saying that he couldn't allow himself to love because, to love, one needs trust. In French, this is the reflexive verb "*se faire confiance*" which means to *make* trust not to "*avoir confiance*" which would be to *have* trust. His response: "*Tu parles trop bien, Rose*." (You speak too well, Rose.)

At the time, I still had long hair down to my knees. Michèl said that I should cut it because I would be more of a woman. Who could resist such a suggestion? I cut my hair but lost him anyway. He called me one day, asking how much I would charge to hem his pants. My answer was "nothing," and he realized that meant I wanted nothing more to do with him. I was ready to let go. After all, anyone who gives the reason why so many chefs are fat is because they are handling food all day and it goes directly into the bloodstream was indeed not of my intellectual level. He wasn't joking.

What finally did it was when Michèl and I were in Bear Mountain, and I pointed out that now we know which direction is west because the sun is setting. Michèl, who grew up in the Corrèze Mountains, said: "*Ah, non, le soleil se couche à l'est*." (The sun sets in the east.) In the end, it was worth all the pain because the silver lining was being able to study at L'École Lenôtre in France, and my ability to translate Maurice Bernachon's *La Passion du Chocolat*.

A Climbing Rose

This is a story of the fanciest dinner party in which I ever participated as both dessert maker and guest. It goes back many years to the time before I went back to college to finish my degrees when I worked part-time as assistant to Anna Muffoletto of Cordon Bleu NYC. One of the students, Suzanne Pierrot, was a very attractive society woman, who seemed to be taking the classes as a lark. She was married to a much older and very wealthy man, and they lived in a three-story town house on the Upper East Side.

Suzanne, noticing that there were some very talented cooks in the class, came up with the idea to recruit all of us to make a dinner party for her at her house. Anna politely declined, but we all blindly jumped right in. We each presented an idea for the course that we wanted to prepare. Mine was a cake.

As the evening loomed closer, Suzanne announced that one of her invited friends was Louis Nizer, a noted Jewish American trial lawyer. When I shared this information with my mother, she said: "Our cousin Leon works as his legal secretary!" Leon was a gifted pianist who never made it professionally but used his incredibly skilled fingers for the typing keyboard instead. (I still remember the last piece he ever played for me—Chopin's *Nocturne* in E-Flat—saying it was the most romantic piece ever written.) "Oh, great!" I said with delight. "I can't wait to tell Suzanne about this." My much wiser mother advised: "I wouldn't if I were you."

The evening of the event, all us "workers" arrived early to cook and set up our courses. I was in the upstairs kitchen, having brought the cake already baked and arranging it on the plate, when Suzanne came over to take a look at it and pronounced the verdict: "No one is going to like your cake." I was shocked and puzzled, realizing that she was being competitive and trying to put me down.

In my station as assistant teacher, I was the only one allowed to bring a guest, so I invited my boyfriend, Dr. Herb Edlis, who had a great sense of humor and was very entertaining but always arrived late. During the first course, Suzanne started a game to break the ice called "If you could be any . . ." She started with me, no doubt out to humiliate me further.

The first question was if you could be any bird, and my answer was a hawk. "Why?" she exclaimed. "I thought you'd want to be something gentle (read insignificant) like a dove." I explained that I would love to be able to soar and have incredible vision.

The next question was if you could be any fish. My answer was a shark. "What?!" she cried out. "I would've thought you'd want to be a dolphin. Why a shark?" Calmly, innocently, and sweetly, I explained: "If I am going to be in an ocean with sharks, I'd rather be one of them than to be preyed upon by them. Also, they can regrow their teeth." But then, I took it one stroke too far and said: "I just can't decide whether I'd rather be a male or a female shark because male sharks have two penises."

The food actually dropped out of the mouth of one of the fancy women sitting across the table. And, at that very moment, in walked Dr. Edlis. He took his seat, and Suzanne made the unfortunate mistake of putting the questions to him. I don't remember his answers to the first ones, but when she asked him what flower he would be, without losing a beat, he came up with "a climbing rose." Silence ensued, and that put a fast end to the game for the evening.

When I went up to the kitchen to gather my things, Suzanne was at the sink washing up. When I tried to help her, I accidentally splashed a little water on her Parisian designer dress. Forgetting her elegant manners, she snarled at me. That moment unveiled the full picture of who she was, and I knew it would be the last time I would ever see her. But I was wrong: A few years later, I was doing a baking demo at Macy's, and along walked Suzanne. Our eyes never met.

I Wanted To Be M.F.K. Fisher

After seven years of night school, my final class was one about writing, and it was taught by the dean of the School of Education, Dr. Henrietta Fleck (from Nebraska). She went around the class asking each of us what our dream job would be. It was all women, and without an exception, the response was ennobling goals such as "head of nutrition at Cornell Medical," until at the end she came to me. Could I have provided a better object lesson? My response was: "There's no point in my saying because there's no way I'm ever going to do what I dream of." Dr. Fleck rose up (metaphorically speaking), delighted to make me an example of her superiority, and said: "Why, Rose! Everything needs to be done by someone. Why not you?!"

I sighed and relented with, "OK, I want to be M.F.K. Fisher and travel around the world eating and writing about it." There was a hush and then a few gasps of astonishment.

FOOD WRITER M.F.K. FISHER

M.F.K. Fisher's books began with *Serve It Forth* (1937) and include key works like *Consider the Oyster* (1941), *How to Cook a Wolf* (1942), *The Gastronomical Me* (1943), and her translation of *The Physiology of Taste* (1949), with her writing spanning decades and covering food, travel, and life experiences, often compiled in anthologies like *The Art of Eating* (1954). During college, I had read several of her books and would later encounter her.

I wondered if it was because it was such a self-serving, indulgent goal or because it was so ridiculously ambitious.

A few years later, I wrote my first article for *The New York Times*: "Eating Cake in Tokyo." I sent it to Dr. Fleck, who had since lost her husband (dean of NYU School of Law; they married in their 70s!) and moved back to Nebraska. I thanked her for her encouragement. Her response back was merely to tell me that NYU had just built a Henrietta Fleck room and that I should go and see it and report back to her what it was like. I did nothing of the kind, but I did continue to travel around the world and write about food.

This reminds me of years later when my husband Elliott said one of the nicest things ever said about me. We were at one of his radiological conferences, and at dinner, the chairman of the department went around the table asking each person what he or she did. They were all doctors, and all knew exactly what Elliott did since he ran the Outpatient Radiology Department. So, when it was his turn to talk, he decided it would be about me instead, saying that I travel all over the world discovering recipes and then I bring them home and make them my own.

My three M.F.K. "encounters," two of which couldn't even qualify as encounters, were all unfortunate. It didn't change my appreciation and admiration for her work, but, sad to say, she seemed to take a dislike to me, sight unseen.

The first encounter was when I wrote a paper in college comparing "How to Unseduce a Man" from *How to Cook a Wolf* (which I thought was one of the most brilliantly hilarious things ever written about food) with recipes in *Joy of Cooking*. I got an A.

Years later, this inspired me to send a letter to M.F.K. along with the paper. When I didn't get a response, I told my best friend, Bert Greene, how disappointed I was. "Oh, Rose," Bert said. "You *must* try again. I'll write to her and tell her what a special friend you are, and I'm sure she'll respond. She always does." Reluctantly and not wanting to be pushy, I tried again and still no response.

A few years later, I attended a party for Craig Claiborne given by Jim Dodge, and there was M.F.K. in a wheelchair. Standing next to her was one of my dearest friends, Rosemary Mannel (who did all the illustrations for Julia Child's cookbooks). I went up to her to introduce myself, and Rosemary interrupted me, saying that I was one of her best friends. M.F.K. just looked up at me staring and saying nothing. So, I gave up. I never could figure out what went wrong, but maybe, it was chemistry. I've found that women, with whom I've taken an immediate dislike (and it's rare), often had some negative quality that reflected one in me, and when I get over it, they turn out to be kindred spirits! The happy ending is that, many years later, I met M.F.K.'s daughter, Kennedy Golden, and we became close friends.

My First Fine Dining Experience—Lutèce

When I was in my 20s, Lutèce was considered to be New York City's best restaurant, and it was my dream to have the experience of dining there. One day at work at NYU Medical, the head of the obesity clinic came over to my office. I don't remember his last name, but his first name was Eugene, and I was surprised to see that he was significantly overweight! Somehow, the conversation turned to food, and I shared my dream of going to Lutèce for dinner. He said that he also had a dream, and it was going to a fine restaurant and having the woman pay the bill. My mouth dropped open, but before I could let him know that I wasn't going to be that woman, he said: "Of course, I'll pay—I'll just give you the money ahead of time." So, I understood him to mean that he wanted it to make him look like he was so desirable even a much younger woman would pay for him at an extravagant restaurant. I agreed without hesitation!

COOKBOOK AUTHOR MARCELLA HAZAN

1993 Marcella Hazan published *The Classic Italian Cookbook*, her first of six widely praised cookbooks. Her Osso Buco is our winter holiday tradition.

The night arrived, and we were seated at the restaurant. In those days, it was customary at elegant dining establishments to have two menus—one for the gentleman, which showed the prices, and one for the lady, without prices. I saw at the top of the menu "*Perles de la Volga*." Understanding French, I knew that it meant caviar—from Russia no less. I had only enjoyed this amazing variety of caviar once in my life, and it was when a friend of the family brought it back from a trip. So, seeing no price on the menu, I knew I could get away with it, so I did the daring and inconsiderate thing and said: "Oh, look! What a pretty name—pearls from the Volga River." Eugene took a look at his menu, and seeing the price, he blanched.

André Soltner, Rose, and Giuliano Bugialli

Along came the maître d' to take our order, and I piped up with: "I'll have the Perles de la Volga as my appetizer." I saw, out of the corner of my eye, that Eugene was still rigid and white with panic. But the maître d' saved the day for poor Eugene, and I was forced to hide my anger.

He said: "Oh, Madame! It's caviar! You don't come to a restaurant like Lutèce and order something from a jar; you order something that chef Soltner prepares." So, why the hell did they have it on the menu, I ungraciously wondered to myself. But instead, I responded with false innocence: "Ohhhh—it's caviar? I had no idea!"

Dinner at Lutèce was all I had hoped for, and when dessert rolled around and it was a poached pear that was so delicious, I asked the maître d' how it was made. The response was: "Oh, it comes in a jar!" Uh huh . . .

COOKBOOK AUTHOR MAIDA HEATTER
1974 Maida Heatter published her first of nine classic cookbooks, *Maida Heatter's Book of Great Desserts*.

Eugene never gave me the money to pay the bill (he got out his credit card), and I never saw him again. I had many amazing meals at Lutèce over the years and had the good fortune of getting to know chef/owner André Soltner and considered him to be one of the finest people I've ever known. When I started my cooking school Cordon Rose, he offered to give my brochures to all his clients. And in 2001, just post 9/11, I made the dessert component of a dinner prepared by him and Ariane Daguin that was auctioned at Sotheby's for close to $10,000.

In 1974 and 1975, I got my BS and MA at NYU, and the program at the time was called (yes): Home Economics! I decided on my résumé that I would retitle the degree to describe more accurately what I had studied which was "Food Science and Culinary Arts." I told my mentor Cecily Brownstone, who was the food editor of the Associated Press, and she said: "Rose! You can't give your own title to a degree." I disregarded what she said, and within a few years, that's the exact title that NYU gave it!

JACQUES PÉPIN
1975 Jacques Pépin wrote his first of over 30 cookbooks, *A French Chef Cooks at Home*.

Several years passed. I had become a published author and had enough money to invite my newly remarried Aunt Ruth for lunch at Lutèce before she moved to Florida. The same maître d' was still in attendance and, to my amazement, remembered me from the Perles de la Volga incident. He congratulated me on my success and more than made up for my past caviar loss with many extra dishes. Aunt Ruth was duly impressed.

THE NEW YORK TIMES
1976 *The New York Times* Living Section was launched by food writer Patricia Wells.

8

Ladies' Home Journal

In 1975, after graduating from NYU, I knew it was time to move on and start working in the career for which I had studied so long. Maybe, it was luck because it was on my birthday, though I found out later it was my ambidexterity which I had taken for granted, but out of over 100 women trying out for the job in the test kitchen of *Ladies' Home Journal*, I got it. The test was to make an omelet (I seasoned their old pan first) and a recipe using ingredients most people would have in their pantry. My choice was spaghetti carbonara—still one of our favorite dinners. Sue Huffman, recently arrived from Chickasha, Oklahoma, where she was a journalist, was now the food editor. She was super smart and had great taste but knew very little about food. She learned fast!
RECIPE: Spaghetti Carbonara (page 248)

> ***LADIES' HOME JOURNAL***
> **1883** *Ladies' Home Journal* first issue was launched. Years later, along with its major rivals, *Better Homes & Gardens*, *Family Circle*, *Good Housekeeping*, *McCall's*, *Redbook*, and *Woman's Day*, they were known as the Seven Sisters, after the women's colleges in the Northeast. I eventually wrote for four of them.

In those days, it was a woman's job to make coffee for the executives, and as the newest employee, I was asked to take over this task. I took a strong stand saying that I did not go to college for seven years to make coffee. When one of the executives started flirting with the head of the test kitchen, asking how to make fish less fishy, before she could open her mouth, I responded with: "Make chicken!"

My first assignment was to do a tomato story from "soup to nuts." Sue wanted me to do a tomato surprise, which was a tomato stuffed with cottage cheese. When I told her I hated cottage cheese, her answer was a life lesson: "Make it so even you will like it." And I did, by adding lots of black pepper and scallions. A second important lesson happened soon after when everyone was gathered in my test kitchen cubicle. Sue asked me to add more salt to the recipe and retest. I must have looked surprised because she followed that with: “I’m tired of you looking so goddamn surprised every time I ask you to retest a recipe.” Determined never again to give her the satisfaction, the next time she asked me to retest, I maintained a poker face, except for one thing which prompted her to say: “And get your eyebrows off the ceiling!”

The lesson was that anything that changes in a recipe can and usually will affect the rest of it. Now, I always cringe when someone asks about substituting an ingredient in one of my recipes without having made it the original way first, unless they have a dietary issue.

Sue and I could have been great friends, but it was hard to tolerate her as a boss. I lasted about a year, having long practice in dealing with difficult women by not engaging them. Linda Foster, head of the test kitchen, became my friend. Once, when she was in tears due to something Sue had said, I told her to think of the homemaker in the Midwest who sees her name in the magazine listed as head of the *Ladies’ Home Journal* test kitchen. It made her see things in a new perspective, and I was amazed by her prophetic reply: “Someday, no one will have heard of me or Sue, but they will know your name.”

My first publisher, the late Irena Chalmers, once said that food editors were nothing better than a nest of vipers on a power trip. The exception was Margaret Happel who was loved by everyone. She was food editor at LHJ before my time, but eventually, I met her and fully agreed. I also loved Jeanne Voltz who was editor of *Family Circle*.

It was during my tenure at the LHJ that I became engaged to Dr. Elliott R. Beranbaum and moved into his Silver Towers NYU apartment.

Becoming a Dame

One day at work in 1976, I got a call from Anna Muffoletto, my former college teacher who now had a cooking school called Cordon Bleu. She told me that she and food journalist Carol Brock were starting a female society based on Escoffier called Les Dames d’Escoffier, and they wanted to choose their first Grande Dame, but neither had any idea who that should be. Without hesitation, I said M.F.K. Two days later, Anna

PHOTOGRAPH BY HUGH DILLON

Les Dames: Kathy Gold, Rose, and Fran Costigan

called to say that Carol Brock told her I could not be a member because "first I had to be someone!" (I channeled the days when my grandmother had two categories for people—somebodies and nobodies—and, clearly, I still fit into the latter.)

A few years later, the new head of Les Dames interviewed me, saying that half the dames thought I should be admitted, but the other half disagreed, and finally, they accepted me because no one had ever wanted so badly to be a dame, to which I replied: "I hate to tell you, but that's the way I am about everything!" They let me join anyway.

The first task they gave me as a dame was something they said no one else had ever been able to accomplish. It was to make a directory of the dames. What had happened was that they sent out forms, and of course, they got buried under the pile of work all these important dames had (which now I do, too). So, what I did was to call each dame and say that I understood how busy she must be, so I would take down her answers in shorthand. It worked, and that's how I got to know each and every one. (Years later, when *The Cake Bibl*e came out, I got so busy I had to let my Les Dames membership lapse, and through the years, now that I had become "somebody," Carol Brock kept begging me to rejoin. Many years later, I did.)

LES DAMES
1976 Les Dames d'Escoffier was created.

One of the dames was Barbara Kafka, the renowned cookbook author and food editor of *Vogue* magazine. She said what I later learned to be the classic New York polite society phrase: "We must have lunch sometime." A few months later, I took her at her word. Barbara suggested La Chanterelle which was a few blocks south of my home. She was known for her sharp wit and generous support of people starting out in the food profession. Toward the end of the meal, she asked: **"What are your three wishes?"** Not realizing that she was playing fairy godmother and delighting in what I thought to be a hypothetical exercise, I started off with my biggest wish at the time: **to have a baby.**

She looked a bit startled but quickly regained her composure and said, "I can't help you there, but I *can* tell you that when you're so busy you can't do *another thing*, that's when it will happen." Then, she prompted me for my second wish. **"I want to write a cookbook,"** I said without hesitation. "That's easy," replied Barbara. "I'll introduce you to my editor." My heart soared. "And your third wish?" asked Barbara. I took the leap and dared to reply: **"I want to have my own TV show."** To my total shock, Barbara's dry response was: "You and *der ganze velt*!" When she saw my quizzical expression, she translated it for me as: "you and everyone else" or literally "you and the whole world!" She misunderstood my questioning look. Growing up with a Yiddish speaking grandmother, I knew what the expression meant, I just wasn't expecting to hear it come out of so sophisticated a mouth! Then, this multi-millionaire food editor of *Vogue* magazine chose to go to the bathroom just before the bill arrived, so I paid for lunch and her advice.

I learned from this experience that people can help just by encouraging you to give voice to your ideas and to put them out into the universe. I ended up publishing 14 cookbooks. These books, and the many people who follow my recipes and share their ideas and responses with me, have become my children. And I did get a very successful PBS TV show, *Baking Magic with Rose*.

Fast-forward to 2025, Fran Costigan and Kathy Gold encouraged me to rejoin the Philadelphia Les Dames chapter. When it came time to decide on a book launch venue for my memoir *Ma Vie en Rose* published by 83 Press of Hoffman Media/*Bake from Scratch*, they both enthusiastically said, "Yes." I received the Les Dames d'Escoffier International Philadelphia Chapter Outstanding in Her Field Award, which was celebrated at their Heritage Dinner on September 13, 2026, and the book launch, in collaboration with the Philadelphia Free Library and Les Dames, was held on September 15, 2026.

THE SILVER PALATE COOKBOOK

1982 Sheila Lukins and Julee Rosso published bestseller *The Silver Palate Cookbook*. In 1989, they published *The New Basics Cookbook* and included my signature cake, the Lemon Poppy Seed Pound Cake, in the book. **RECIPE: Lemon Poppy Seed Pound Cake (page 224)**

9

The Beginning of My Solo Career:

Freelancing, Studying in France, and My Cooking School

While I had been at the *Ladies' Home Journal*, I had learned so much about food styling I started working as a freelance food stylist. I also tried to start a business making shortbread cookies. I put up a sign in my 30-story Silver Tower's building, and one person ordered for his mother who was from Scotland and missed shortbread cookies. She reported that mine were not the ones of her memory.

My New York Living Room/My Baking Kitchen

Next, I brought a sample to Dean & DeLuca, and Giorgio DeLuca wrinkled up his nose and said: "Needs salt; try Danish Lurpak butter!" I love salt, but this is one thing that I feel needs none. In fact, even one grain would be detectable in this pure and simple cookie. Nonetheless, I tried his suggestion but didn't change my mind. Lydie Marshall (she owned the renowned À la Bonne Cocotte Cooking School in Greenwich Village), who had been with me at the time, felt insulted on my behalf and said she'd never go back in the store! Those were the early days of Dean & DeLuca and the early days of my short-lived cookie career. Over the years, I grew very fond of Giorgio but still prefer my shortbread without salt.

My Illegal Baking Kitchen Renovation

At this point, I saw that I needed a separate work area apart from our small galley kitchen. Visualize entering our seventh-floor, corner apartment with the kitchen immediately to the right and then a "T." To the left was a bathroom and two bedrooms. To the right, behind the kitchen was a 16x20-foot dining/living room with a third small bedroom off its back side. This housed the three of us living there and now my daily home business that would require shelving, storage, and a workstation/counter. The living area had a couch and some furniture, and the dining area had a wood table for six, made by my woodworker dad and Elliott, which was also serving as my workstation.

I sketched some designs, opening up the kitchen to the living room and turning half of the living room into my kitchen workplace. My dad constructed an amazing 30-inch-wide by 7-foot-long marble-topped workstation on wheels. The elevator's ceiling had to be removed to fit it and done at night for its journey up to our apartment. I installed floor-to-ceiling, 8-foot-long Metro shelving with the workstation in front of it. The station's rear side had top shelves with metal bins for dry ingredients and more shelves for equipment. The front had doors for equipment. When Elliott and I moved 36 years later to our weekend home, the workstation moved as well to being used virtually every day.

After having done my student teaching at junior high level, and watching one of the girls put the canned tomato sauce in with the pasta and water when making spaghetti and tomato sauce, I decided that I wanted to start my own cooking school but with more advanced students. At this time, NYU asked me to step in and teach a microwave cooking class because the professor had decided she would prefer to leave academia for corporate life. I also had written a magazine article on microwave cooking, so my first plan was to teach it. In 1977, I did a freelance story about microwave cooking for *Redbook* magazine, which led to my wanting to have a cooking school with Gail Becker, who did the nutritional information.

It all began with Mimi Sheraton, restaurant reviewer for *The New York Times*, who came to interview me about my upcoming cooking school. When I told her I was planning to teach microwave cooking, she rose up horrified and asked how I, as the wife of a radiologist, would consider such a dangerous thing. I explained the difference between microwave rays and radioactive ones, but she shook her head, saying that *The New York Times* would never stand behind microwaving. (It was only a matter of time before Barbara Kafka had a column in *The Times* on microwave cooking. And due to her lack of knowledge about microwaving, writing that one could do deep-fat frying in the microwave, her book had to be pulled off the shelves because of reported explosions in the microwave and threats to sue the publisher.)

My Pivot from Savory to Sweet

When Cecily Brownstone introduced me to Lydie Marshall, she had invited me to a class at her renowned school À la Bonne Cocotte. She steered me away from teaching French cooking, saying that too many people were doing it and that what people really needed was cake decorating. But to me, taste and texture always came first, so I decided to teach baking to have cakes worth decorating. Lydie promised to help me by giving out brochures to her students. So, I pivoted to teaching cake baking and went to Wilton in Chicago to study cake decorating and sculpting flowers out of gum paste.

One day, Lydie told me that she was featured in a magazine article about coq au vin, which she made for her husband's birthday when they went to their home in Provence, France, every summer. She claimed to be using "*le vraie coq*" and not just any old chicken. So, of course, I had to make fun of her claims of grandeur by telling her that the title of the article should have been "Coq au Wayne" (her husband's name) or Wayne's cock. She did not think that was funny. I, however, still do!

This riff on Robert Frost's "Fire and Ice," was written by me for Lydie Marshall to cheer her up after she had a hysterectomy, which turned out to be a bad idea as it hurts to laugh with an abdominal incision. I found that out on my own years later.

> *Some say the world will end in goose fat, some say in duck.*
> *From what I savor of their flavor,*
> *I hold with those who don't give a fuck.*
> *But if it had to perish twice,*
> *I think I know enough of butter*
> *To say that for destruction*
> *It is even better*
> *And would suffice.*

Cleaner version: *From what I savor of their taste, I hold with those who favor flavor.*

Bon Appétit Saved My Life

In 1979, I had gone through several heartbreaking years of infertility at the end of which the miracle finally happened. But at four and a half months, I lost the baby and was at a loss as to how to go on living. I didn't want to get out of bed, but then the phone rang, and it was *Bon Appétit* saying they wanted to feature my cooking school in an article on a wedding cake. I knew this would have a huge impact on my career and life. I felt like the phoenix rising from the ashes and created the Dotted Swiss Dream cake. That simple and elegant design, contrasting with the ubiquitous and very elaborate decorations, went on to change the way cakes were decorated, although some pastry chefs were not happy being asked to pipe all those dots. I continued to write many stories for *Bon Appétit*, including my final one in 1995: "Fanciful and Festive."

ZAGAT RESTAURANT REVIEW

1979 The Zagat Survey was established by Tim and Nina Zagat. It collected ratings of restaurants by diners, and continued publishing for three decades until it was sold to Google. One of my favorite cousins, Ali, is married to their son John!

In the years that followed, I found salvation by putting my focus and soul into testing recipes, writing, teaching, and making wedding cakes and special projects. My books became my children, and I gave everything to them. My work gave me extraordinary joy and validation and lifted me from the despair of my loss.

Rose and her Campbell's Soup Cake

Lenôtre and My Love of France

I invited Mimi a second time to come for an interview about a possible cooking school. She complimented me on the mini cheesecake I made for her and the choice of coffee I served (I knew from reading her columns which coffee bean she preferred and where she got it), but she told me that my cake decorating needed to be more elegant and suggested that I study at Lenôtre in Plaisir, a suburb of Paris, France. My response was: "Now, I can tell my husband that Mimi Sheraton said I should study there." And I lost no time in enrolling for a class. Part of my rush was that, if I were pregnant again, it would be a long time before I would be willing to leave to go to France.

The class on *entremets* (cakes) happened to fall on the week before Christmas. French friends warned me that the French don't invite people for dinner and that the most I could hope for is a cocktail-hour invitation. They also advised me that, at Christmastime, there was no chance of an invitation at all. Happily, I ignored the advice.

The day of my departure, as I was rushing to leave, I got a call from Great-Uncle Nat, telling me I had to call his friend Nadège when in Paris and that we would cook together. I didn't have time to ask if this was a man or woman or anything more about his recommendation, but on arriving in Paris, I followed his advice. It turned out that Nadège was a married woman with three children and that she loved to cook. I was promptly invited to cocktail hour at their home on the Left Bank, a few blocks from Les Invalides.

The drawing room, with handmade lace curtains gracing the long French windows, was a study in elegance. I sat perched at the edge of my chair, trying to mind my manners and speak in the best French I could manage. Max, the husband, asked me a few polite questions, but things fell apart when he asked the inevitable one: "*Avez-vous des enfants?*" (Do you have children?) I started to answer, but to my horror, tears started welling up in my eyes, and trying as hard as I could, they would not stop. So, I explained that I had recently had a miscarriage. (I didn't know the French expression at the time, so in error, I said I had an abortion!) Max's response was immediate and gently compassionate. He said "*Je pense que vous avez des cafards*," which translates to "I think you have cockroaches," but actually means "I think you are homesick." And, to my total shock, he added that I should move in with them during my stay in Paris!

My grandmother, in all her wisdom, had taught me always to look to the wife, not the husband, which was my first response, and when I did, her expression changed from concern to compassion equal to that of her husband's. So, I said: "Oui!"

The next step was to write down their exact address to get there by taxi. I got out my prized Montblanc fountain pen, the size of a small cigar, and Max's eyes lit up with appreciation. "Ah, a Montblanc!" he exclaimed and asked me if he could use it to write the address. Now, I had been told never to let anyone write with my pen because the gold nib, which had softened to my handwriting, would be altered. So, I explained this to Max, and instead of his being intimidated, he exclaimed with delight: "*Une vierge!*" (a virgin). I weakly countered by telling him it was a bit scratchy to which he smiled and said: "I'll smooth it out." Realizing that I had just achieved the near impossible of being invited not only to dinner but to live with this French family at Christmastime, it seemed utterly ridiculous to withhold my pen, so I handed it over to him. And thus began a most valued friendship.

Here comes my favorite part of the story: I went back that very night to pack my things and took a cab from the humble hotel where I had been staying. The ride started out badly when I showed the driver the address, and he told me that he couldn't drive into that street which meant I would have to carry my heavy bags for several blocks. By then, the cab had filled up with thick smoke from a Gitanes cigarette the burley cab driver was enjoying. Timidly, I asked him if he would mind putting it out. The response was a wordless grumble of growling discontent.

I followed it up with: "Well, anyway, it's not good for the health." He spat out: "*Pas bonne pour la santé?*" (Not good for the health?) "You can't eat; you can't smoke; you can't drink anymore. What is left?" And as always, my sense of humor got the better of me, and with a smile in my voice, I softly replied: "*On peut toujours faire l'amour.*" (You can always make love.) Tragically, this theoretical compensation I had suggested also became bad for the health with the advent of AIDS. The driver stopped the car to turn around and scrutinize what manner of woman, with good French but an American accent, would have the nerve to utter those words. And then, he smiled and said in a resigned but amused tone: "*Oui! On peut toujours faire ça, Madame!*" (Yes! We can always do that, Madame!) I will take you wherever you want to go." This was a moment I will never forget. And with that, he drove me right up to the door of my new friends' apartment house—la famille Brossollet.

Max, Rose, and Nadège

A French Christmas

The plan of my visit was that I would return for a few days after attending the baking classes and stay for Christmas. In fact, Nadège asked if I would make a bûche de Noël based on what I was to learn chez Lenôtre. But though Nadège was a first-rate cook, she was not a baker, and her oven door did not close securely which would not have been suitable for baking. By the time I returned, however, just one week later, Max had bought her a new oven for my bûche to christen it! Nadège got out her collection of tiny toy buglers to decorate it, and we all thought it was a great success.

I think what meant the most to Nadège was that, as her teenage children were mocking the holiday and saying how bored they were and how it was "*toujours la même chose*" (always the same thing), I succeeded in giving them a different perspective by telling them how I had been warned not to expect hospitality of the sort I was enjoying and that I felt it to be a great honor to be included as part of the family at such a sacred time.

Watching the dinner preparations was a delight. I watched as Nadège spent hours forcing her stuffing, or *farce*, through a *tamis* (fine-mesh strainer)—so different from my fluffy bread stuffing which I prefer to the actual turkey. The Christmas dinner was served, and the farce tasted *dégutante*, but I was on my best behavior, so I tried to swallow it. The kids, however, were not, and none of the three would eat it. Nadège cried out in despair: "*Person mange la farce!*" (No one is eating the stuffing!) And all I could think of was: "*C'est un vraie farce.*" (It's a real comedy.) But, of course, I didn't dare to say it. I had trouble holding back laughter.

Nadège, Max, and I were close friends for over 30 years and many visits. Yes, Nadège and I did cook together, as Uncle Nat had predicted, and shared many intimacies and experiences, and Max, owner of the esteemed Belin publishing company and also publisher of the French edition of *Scientific American* magazine, was a fascinating conversationalist. When I thanked Uncle Nat for the introduction, his cryptic reply was: "I wasn't planning to send them a tenant."

I Opened My Own Cooking School

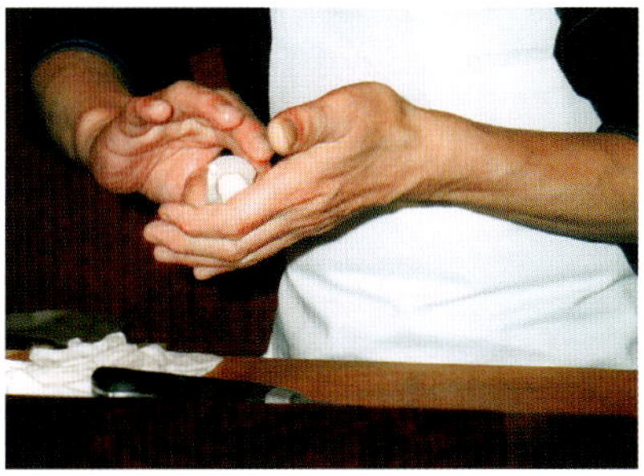

Chef Hiroshi Yoshikawa at Matsu Sushi

After studying at Lenôtre, I ran the Cordon Rose Cooking School for over 10 years out of my NYC apartment. I named it after the Cordon Bleu Cooking School but changed it from blue to pink! In the early years, I was also called upon to be a substitute teacher at the New York Restaurant School. David Liederman, creator of the famed chocolate chip cookies and brother to the owner of the school, decided that he no longer wanted to teach at the school. One of the students recommended that I put an advertisement in the Japanese newspaper. She said she taught many Japanese women English as a second language, and they would be much more polite than the students at the restaurant school. She was right, and it changed my life.

One of the students, Hiroko Ogawa, became my assistant. She was also responsible for my writing my first article for *The New York Times*. It was on the fusion of Japanese and French desserts, and she did all the research for me. Yoko Sakuma was another student I became close to, and she is still my dearest friend. Yoko took each class three times, saying she learned more English from my classes than at NYU! When she and her husband, Ushio, moved to Kyoto, Japan, she invited me to visit and went with me on a tour she arranged that was one of the best experiences of my life, including my meeting chef Hiroshi Yoshikawa.

IACP FOUNDED

1978 IACP (International Association of Culinary Professionals) is founded. It was initially called ACS (Association of Cooking Schools) for cooking schools and instructors, and later, it became IACP to include authors, publishers, and social media in the food world. I joined ACS shortly after starting my cooking school.

10

My Writing Years:

Publications as The Golden Age of Food Blossoms

Over the years, I wrote many baking and food articles for various magazines and publications. The following timeline includes some of the many highlights:

Making the White Swan Cake for *Chocolatier* Magazine

In 1977, at our weekend place in New Jersey, I was inspired to write my ode to the much-maligned state which got a large feature in *The Star-Ledger* with the headline: "I Love New Jersey." It was followed by a piece for *The Bergen Record* in 2001.

In 1980, Belmont Park, no doubt having seen my *Bon Appétit* pieces, asked me to make a large cake for their 75th anniversary. There were several other cakes, but mine was to represent the Belmont. Using a jig saw, my father cut wooden numbers "7" and "5" onto which I glued big rhinestones which sparkled in the sun. The cakes were paraded around the racetrack on horse-drawn carts. I overheard a woman in the bleachers say that mine was the most beautiful cake there. Wearing my antique ivory lace Victorian afternoon tea dress, I went to the manager to ask for my check, and he informed me that it was the ugliest cake there and that he preferred the cart. To his and my surprise, as if butter wouldn't melt in my mouth, I sweetly replied: "You deserve more than the cart—you deserve a kick in the ass!" I got the check.

The Cook's Magazine Cover Girl Oct. 1989

In 1981, *The Cook's Magazine* featured my first magazine article, "Understanding Génoise." In those days, no other publisher or editor would have considered doing such a scientific piece, even including weights! Little did I realize to what degree I spearheaded the movement toward quality baking and interest in science. It was so popular Chris Kimball offered me eight other baking assignments, including candy, a wedding cake, and "Understanding the Basic Layer Cake," over the next nine years.

It was through *The Cook's Magazine* that I met the talented photographer Vincent Lee, who worked with me on other stories and also on *The Cake Bible*. One day, while we were photographing, Vincent showed me the latest issue of *Cook's*, and I immediately called the editor, Mary Goodbody, to say how much I loved the stunning cover shot of Julie Sahni's mosaic of spices. Mary enthusiastically cried out: "Just wait until you see Richard Sax's nuts!" I heard uproarious laughter in the background.

The greatest high for a writer is seeing one's name in print for the first time. But when it finally happens, many colleagues agree that it is disappointing to learn how few people actually even look at bylines. My mother rejoiced seeing my name in print, and for a moment, it felt great. But then a cake customer cut me down to size by bringing the magazine and asking if I could make a wedding cake like it, blissfully unaware of the fact that it was my story and my cake in the first place. The most amusing example of byline avoidance was at a Kitchen Bazaar book signing in Washington, DC, when a man thought I had plagiarized the génoise in *The Cake Bible* from an article in *The Cook's Magazine* until I pointed out that I was the one who had written the article!

MARTHA STEWART BEGINS PUBLISHING

1982 Martha Stewart published her first cookbook *Entertaining*. She went on to publish a total of 100 books on various subjects. In 1987, she included my wedding cake in her book *Weddings*, and in 1988, she honored me by giving an extraordinary quote for *The Cake Bible*. In 2011, she invited me to be on her Hallmark Channel show.

From 1984 to 1987, for *Food & Wine*, working with my good friend, editor Susan Wyler, I wrote five major pieces, including

Martha Stewart and Rose

"Down with the Upper Crust" (pies without top crusts) and a piece featuring chocolate desserts. This wonderful magazine was created by Michael Batterberry, who went on to create *Food Arts*, a top food service magazine.

In 1984, I wrote two pieces for *The Confectioner* magazine: "Building the Better Mousse Trap," featuring my chocolate thermometer which I designed, and "A Swiss Confectionery Xmas."

In 1984, I wrote a major piece on Japan for *The New York Times,* continuing in 1985 with several other articles, including "Swiss Chocolate." In 1989, I wrote "Harvest," about foraging, and another big article on baking and its origins.

In 1984, I wrote a piece for *Chocolatier* magazine which almost destroyed the article I was writing for *The New York Times*. Here's why:

Behind the Times—A Story of Journalist Hypocrisy (that I never before published)
I've been wanting to tell this story for over 40 years, but the late Bert Greene, who was my dearest friend and a major food personality and journalist, had told me not to, saying: "Wait until you don't need *The New York Times*—and you still do!" A lot has changed, and it's not that I don't need *The Times*; it's that I don't need anything enough to allow this story to go unheard. The time has come.

The New York Times did a lot for me as an author. In 1988, when *The Cake Bible* was launched, Corby Kummer did a story that landed on the front page and seven-eighths of the next page of what was then called the Living Section (started by Patricia Wells). In one day, my book sold 18,500 copies which, at that time, was considered to be a best-selling novelist's lifetime earnings for a book. Ironically, the newpaper's front page also had a short article titled "Pavarotti Ends Diet" with a photo of Luciano Pavarotti holding up a wineglass. Consequently, it appeared that Pavarotti was honoring the pictured Chocolate Domingo Cake that I had intended to be his. It was against the policy of the newspaper to feature a person in this major way, and the editor in charge at the time was fired for having done it. Word had it that Corby was also reproached. And now, here's what the newspaper did to me and reportedly other journalists.

I had written several stories for the Living Section, but at one point, *The New York Times* decided that they wanted 100% ownership in perpetuity from all journalists. I refused to write under those conditions, and when Jacques Pépin and others also refused, the newspaper reversed their position.

Also, during this time, I had proposed a story about Swiss chocolate to the new *Chocolatier* magazine. They loved the idea but said that Fred Ferretti had also proposed a similar story. They offered the possibility of him doing the writing and me doing the recipes. They had already arranged with the Swiss Tourist Office to send Fred to Switzerland but were unable to fund another journalist that year, and they asked if I couldn't develop the recipes without actually going to Switzerland. My solution was to go on my own dime.

On my return, I realized that I had so much information it really deserved an article written by me, so I proposed it to Alex Ward, head of the Living Section at *The New York Times*. He liked it but said it was more suited to the Travel Section and forwarded it to his colleague Mike Leahy.

The Swiss Tourist Office was so beside themselves with joy that they would finally get an article into *The New York Times* they immediately offered to send me and a photographer to Switzerland to do more research. And on my return, I started editing the article I had already written before my trip for *The Times*, with one of their editors. In all innocence, I told the editor that the Swiss Tourist Office was so delighted that my article had been accepted by *The Times* they had sent me on a second press trip. Silence . . . then she said: "I'll call you right back." My blood ran cold. I knew something had to be wrong.

When she called back, she announced that she had spoken to her editor, Mike Leahy, and they were pulling my story. The reason: Now that I had gone on a "paid" trip, I could never again write for *The New York Times*! I was heartsick. I managed to restrain myself from saying that Fred Ferretti had taken the very paid trip for which I paid my own way, and he was a regular columnist for *The Times*. Instead, I said that I never should have told her, and she said: "Never regret telling the truth." Then, I asked to speak to Mike Leahy. I told him that I had no idea this was the rule and that I would repay the Swiss government for all the expenses of my trip. His response was that he would have to think about it. He said I should call him back in a few days.

I called the Swiss Tourist Office and told them of my plan to write them a check to reimburse them for the trip. To my astonishment and delight their response was: "Write the check. We'll cash it so you have proof and then reimburse you the full amount." And that is what I did.

I called Mike Leahy and told him what I had done. His response was that he still hadn't decided if he would accept it and run the story. He told me to call back the next day. This continued for several days, his playing the cat-and-mouse torture game. I asked my husband, Elliott, who ran the Outpatient Radiology Department at NYU Medical, that when Leahy came to his office with the inevitable duodenal ulcer, to give him a hard time. He said he would treat him like every other inflated ego patient—he would put him in the VIP room and keep him waiting. (VIP actually stood for "very impertinent person.")

Finally, Leahy decided that he would accept what I had done. But in an effort to humiliate me further he said: "This is a one-time thing. Don't think you will be the next Patricia Wells—you're writing is not of her caliber." So, I humbly asked him if he would be kind enough to tell me how I could improve my writing, adding that most of my writing was for magazines. After a short silence, he said: "Too many superlatives, but it's hard to be articulate about writing." Oh, how I was dying to respond with: "Even harder to be articulate about speaking." But I held my seemingly respectful silence, and the article ran in the Travel Section that Sunday, October 13, 1985, as the lead cover page story "Fare of the Country; for the Swiss, What Else But Chocolate?"

Years passed, and I read Pat Wells's story of her life in France in which she mentioned that her former editor, Mike Leahy, at *The New York Times* was a wonderful person. One wonders.

Albert Uster and Rose

Addenda: The article for *Chocolatier* ran in Vol. 1 No. 4, 1984, and I got the byline because I wrote the story and the recipes.

The New York Times now requires a writer to sign a contract stating that he or she will not take freebie trips.

I continued to take press trips to Switzerland, and they were so pleased with my stories they **knighted me**! I also developed a supportive friendship with Albert Uster, who was the major importer of many Swiss products and, in 1979, opened Jean-Louis Palladin's restaurant Jean-Louis at the Watergate in Washington, DC.

COOKBOOK AUTHOR GIULIANO BUGIALLI

1982 Giuliano Bugialli's *Classic Techniques of Italian Cooking* won the Tastemaker Award for best cookbook of the year under the International Category, and *Foods of Italy* won the Tastemaker Grand Prix as the best cookbook of 1985.

When I met Giuliano Bugialli at the Tastemaker Awards ceremony, I jokingly went up to him asking to see the award so I would know what mine would look like someday. Shocked, he asked if I thought I was going to win the award. My response was: "No, but I hope to write a book that is worthy of it." Five years later, we were both up for the award, and my prophetic comment turned out to be true for *The Cake Bible* which won book of the year!

When I told Martha Stewart that I had voted for that book, she thanked me. I asked why, and she said: "My husband, Andy, was the publisher!" When I met him a few years later, I discovered that he was the Andy Stewart who was my counselor at the Putney Work Camp when I was 14 years old. He ran the farm, so for all those years, I thought he was a farmer. A fellow camper, Carly Simon, became a famous singer/songwriter. We were both in the camp chorus.

In 1986, I wrote several stories for *Family Circle*, culminating with a cover story, "All-Star Cake," to celebrate the magazine's 60th anniversary.

SLOW FOOD ASSOCIATION & JAMES BEARD FOUNDATION

1986 The Slow Food Association was established. My relative Mina Givton, wife of Hanuch Givton, director of tourism in Israel, started the one in Israel.

1986 The James Beard Foundation opened its doors and became the home for culinary arts and a place to honor chefs. Over the years, I received six James Beard Awards including the Cookbook Hall of Fame in 2025.

From 1991 to 1997, the *Los Angeles Times* offered me a dream writing opportunity. Russ Parsons, editor of the *Los Angeles Times* Syndicate, emailed me saying "there are many recipes but very little good food writing," and offered me a weekly column. I asked the advice of my dear friend Marion Cunningham, who was writing a column for the *San Francisco Chronicle*.

Marion warned me that once a week would feel like every day and suggested once a month. Russ agreed, saying that I could write about anything I wanted and that one day a month, when I sat down for an hour to write my column, I was in heaven. In 1997, the most important feature I did was "Weigh to Bake" which highlighted the importance and advantages of weighing the ingredients over the far less precise cup measurement method.

THE FANNIE FARMER COOKBOOK

1979 Marion Cunningham revised the original 1886 *Fannie Farmer Cook Book*.

Importance of Weighing

Unfortunately, it would take more than a decade for other authors to include weights, and the reluctance of publishers to then include them even now. I wrote the column for seven years until another editor took over and admonished me to stick to my subject which he felt should be food and not wine. He had been a wine writer and took issue with my saying that Germany was the northernmost area in the world for Eiswein, insisting it was Canada. My husband, Elliott, was from Toronto and gave me the exact latitude which was indeed lower than Germany. So, I won the battle and lost the war.

From 1998 to 2022, I loved working with *Fine Cooking* magazine and wrote several pieces, including "Lemon Icebox Cake" and "Cheesecake."

From 1999 to 2022, I had the honor of being a contributing editor to the stellar trade magazine *Food Arts*. In 2000, one of my assigned articles, which Editor-in-Chief Michael Batterberry named "The Sugar Bible," won "The Best Food or Wine Article in the World" at the Gourmand Awards in Tasmania. I spent over a year researching and writing about sugar. When I turned the article in to Senior Editor Jim Poris, after his review, he proclaimed it to be "perfect," to which I replied: "I'm sure you'll find something to change." His response was: "Nothing—not even a comma!" This was a profound compliment from one of the most critical editors of my career. He also said that I was the most logical person he ever knew.

Food Arts Michael and Ariane Batterberry

SOCIAL MEDIA RECIPE BLOGGING STARTS

1997 The Chowhound website launches recipe blogging. Many food bloggers soon found supplemental money from advertisers and product collaborations, enabling them to work from home. Blogging became a major source of income. I chose never to have ads on my blog.

Shortly after writing this article, I persuaded Michael Batterberry to let me do a piece on the rare sugar called wasanbon. I paid my own way to go to the island of Shikoku in Japan to watch the amazing process of how granulated sugar cane is rubbed and washed to grind it by hand. The company did not usually allow visitors, but my dear friend Reiko Akehi, who had longed to go as well, somehow convinced the company that it would be an honor to invite me, and she accompanied me.

When *Food Arts* sadly closed its doors as a hardcover publication, I was given an online column which I named "Rose Nose." My friend chef Marcel Desaulniers, of Death by Chocolate fame, gave me a nose magnet from a museum in Williamsburg, Virginia, which I attached to the hood of my cooktop range!

One of my favorite pieces was about smell and taste, having verified by a simple test that I was a supertaster—which I had long suspected. The test involved counting the circumvallate papillae within a quarter inch area. Around 30 was considered to be normal, but I had so many I had to stop counting. Then, I realized that quantity was not quality, and having once been a smoker, surely some of them were damaged. I regretted every cigarette I ever smoked.

The Nose

FUSION CUISINE

Early 1970s Norman Van Aken coined the now ubiquitous term "fusion cuisine."

My First Article for "Rose Nose"

It is my belief that "foodies" are born not made. Of course, taste can be developed, educated, and refined but only up to a point. The ability to taste flavor subtleties is an inborn talent like any other. You know who you are—you who are led around by your nose, constantly sniffing out flavors. You are enthralled and captivated by a smell that delights you and equally put off and despairing of one you find odious and repellent.

Appreciation of food begins with smell. The senses each have a profound effect upon each other, but the two most intimately connected are taste and smell. Try smelling a gardenia while taking a bite of chocolate cake, and you will experience how the flower's aroma merges with the chocolate to produce a sensation that you are eating the flower as well. This explains why eating alfresco (outdoors) is such an enhancer of even the simplest flavors. It also explains why, when one has a cold or stuffed nose, one loses the ability to taste.

Smell is also the most compellingly poignant recaller of memories. What are the first smells you remember experiencing as a child? Mine are: the salty/seaweedy spray of ocean air in Far Rockaway where I was born; the intensely seductive aroma of freshly ground coffee at the A & P checkout counter where I went shopping with my grandmother; the yeasty, all-enveloping cloud of baking bread from the Silvercup factory as we drove over the Queensboro Bridge on Sunday nights—the last good smell of Long Island before returning to the city; and best of all, the enchanting perfume of summer honeysuckle in the early evening when its scent is most intense. Judith Kranz, in one of her novels, described honeysuckle as "the pure distilled essence of happiness," which totally captures it for me. I love the fragrance so much I want to consume it, and in fact, my Russian grandmother taught me as a little girl to bite off the end of the blossom and suck the drop of nectar from the end, a secret I love to pass on to delight other children.

KITCHEN CONFIDENTIAL

2000 Anthony Bourdain published *Kitchen Confidential* which stood the restaurant world on its ear! In 2001, we were both presenters at the Melbourne Food Festival in Australia. The organizer told me that my books sold much better than his, saying that it was because "we are serious cooks here."

The other day, I was sitting on my back porch enjoying a lusty sandwich of crab salad on brioche with tomato mayonnaise and a glass of cold Sonoma-Cutrer. The crab was fresh and sweet, and all was enhanced by the surrounding summer country air. But something was missing. Suddenly, I realized what: a whiff of ocean air. Perhaps, one day, aromas will be bottled as an added dimension to the meal, to smell as one eats, much in the way wine is drunk. One sure way to have enhanced flavor impact without the calories!

When I criticized the overuse of the f-word to the very refined and proper Ariane and Michael Batterberry, publishers of *Food Arts* magazine, I was surprised and amused by their response: "It is appropriate in this context."

From 2000 to 2008, I wrote about eight pieces for *The Washington Post*. I had two wonderful editors, Bonnie S. Benwick and Jeanne McManus, who wrote about my bread piece: "Good news: Bread memories will be in the November 8 edition. Let me tell you something: My staff is NEVER unanimous about anything. But they ALL love your writing in this piece. With your permission, I'm going to use it as an example of first-person writing at the Greenbrier next spring. It's personal and extremely relevant to the topic, which is rare in food writing." How invaluable to get such encouragement.

I was also invited by the paper to Washington, DC, to do "Chef on Call," where a reader is encouraged to ask a chef a question. The reader's question I was asked to address was how to make a great pie crust. My recipe became the most requested online recipe for several years running. **RECIPES: Perfect Flaky & Tender Cream Cheese Pie Crust & Cherry Pie (pages 236 & 238)**

From 2000 to 2010, I wrote for *Hemispheres* magazine. I met Randy Johnson, the magazine's editor, on a Swiss press trip, and we became close friends. He assigned me several articles for the United Airlines' in-flight magazine, including "Three Perfect Days in New York" and an article on bread. My bread recipes were added to the first-class menu! The magazine overlooked paying me.

In 2022, I did a feature article for *The Wall Street Journal* on holiday cookies to promote my book *The Cookie Bible.*

From 2025 to 2026, I have had the great pleasure of being a contributing editor to the best home baking publication, *Bake from Scratch* magazine, published by Brian Hart Hoffman of Hoffman Media. I was given the freedom and encouragement to write about whatever came to my heart and mind and was graced by working with the best possible editor, Amber Ryder Wilson. It is karmic destiny that Hoffman Media is the publisher of my memoir. I love being part of their family.

BAKE FROM SCRATCH MAGAZINE

2015 *Bake from Scratch* magazine was launched by Editor-in-Chief Brian Hart Hoffman and Hoffman Media. It began as a single test issue that quickly gained popularity, leading to its establishment as a regular publication. The brand celebrated its 10th anniversary in 2025. *Bake from Scratch* also publishes books.

The Major Food Magazines Overview:

1941 *Bakers' Helper* magazine

1941 *Gourmet* magazine, published by Earle R. MacAusland (He was a friend of my Uncle Nat, who gave me the 1962 13th printing of *The Gourmet Cookbook*, first published 1950.)

1956 *Bon Appétit* magazine, and **1976**, by subscription

1978 *Food & Wine* magazine, created by Ariane and Michael Batterberry and published by *Playboy* magazine's Hugh Heffner

1980 *The Cook's Magazine*

1994 *Fine Cooking* magazine

1994 *Saveur* magazine

1994 *Fine Cooking* magazine

2015 *Bake from Scratch* magazine

Booklets and Special Recipes:

I agreed to do the last three below to keep the products I valued on the market.

2001 I created a booklet of recipes for Sugar in the Raw.

Swans Down Cake Flour—Pro bono
I created a booklet of recipes using their flour.

Lyle's Golden Syrup—Pro bono
My recipe was on the bottle for years.

SIGNIFICANT EVENTS

2001 *America's Test Kitchen* magazine and TV show launched.

2011 *My Drunk Kitchen* YouTube platform inspired many to have home cooking/baking channels. Homesick Hannah Hart's comic video to her friend now has a channel with 2.5 million followers.

2018 TikTok, a short-form video app, took off as a platform for food demos.

2020 Amazon began selling food products, which enabled home bakers to make just about any recipe from around the world.

11

My Videos and TV Productions

Baking Videos and a Cake to Die For

Creative genius often comes along with the sort of temperament that engenders either love or hatred in others. One videographer, who was a renowned photographer, leading jazz agent, record producer, and a pioneer in the video "how-to" market, was an exception in that he inspired both emotions at once. My first view of him was as a crass, insulting egomaniac who questioned my authority in my field. He ultimately became my greatest champion, calling my editor regularly over the years with creative suggestions as to how the publisher could and should do more for my books. In the end, I saw his sardonic, sour side as a veneer which hid an exquisitely tender soul. Indeed, this videographer stormed against mediocrity and stupidity, but when encountering something of quality and excellence, he would lay down his life for it.

Rose's Heavenly Cakes Video at General Mills

In 1990, when he first approached me to do a video on baking, I conferred with colleagues who had done videos with him. To a person, they warned me that he shouted demoralizingly during production, so I agreed to work with him only on the condition that he would never shout. He was true to his word, technically speaking; rather than shouting, he whispered insults in a grim tone filled with venomous scorn. Having not slept for two days due to preparation requirements and stage-fright and feeling my blood chill, I suggested that I might give a better performance with a little positive reinforcement.

The videographer, so high-strung with the anxiety of a perfectionist persuaded of the fact that no one else could possibly care as much as he, just couldn't manage the requested encouragement. Others had told me that, during their tapings, he would swig directly from a bottle of Pepto-Bismol. Since none of the pink liquid was in sight, I figured things weren't going all that badly. His attitude, however, really got to me and made me determined, above all, not to let him get the better of me. The nastier he became, the more cheerful and smiling was my response. I never thought I could act, but looking at the video, I'm proud to say that nothing betrays my desire to strangle him.

At the end of the 18-hour day, after filming several demos of pies and cakes, much to everyone's relief, the videographer pronounced the immortal words "It's a wrap!" and strode out of the room with what seemed like disgust. The crew immediately formed a reception line and silently, with obvious respect, shook my hand. One said: "You are the only one who didn't scream or cry; I don't know how you took it." And I knew that my not breaking was their victory, too.

Part of what had helped me was the little voice in me repeating over and over "never again." And we never did make another video together, though we did become friends. What won me over were two things: the video was of excellent quality, and the videographer confessed that my chocolate cake had changed his entire attitude toward food. Prior to this experience, he had looked at food as nothing but a prop and had eaten only mass-produced cakes. He said that my cake, though three days old by the time he tasted it, was an epiphany for him. The way in which he talked about that cake revealed a passionate, open, appreciative side to the man where before I had seen only a hostile though talented tyrant. Again, out of character, he humbly begged me to make another cake for him. I was so moved that, before two weeks had passed, I baked him my favorite yellow butter cake. To my surprise, he was openly disappointed and not even tactfully grateful. Oh, he accepted the cake but proclaimed that it was the chocolate one he had been craving. I told him that, someday, I would bake that one for him, too.

Seven years later, I got a call from him from his hospital bed. "I'm dying," he proclaimed in his usual right-to-the-point, demanding directness, "and I want that chocolate cake you promised." He continued laughingly: "You can't refuse a dying man's last request!" But I knew him well by then, so I lost no time making the cake and messengered it right up to the hospital. He never thanked me personally, but mutual friends who talked to him afterwards reported that he ate it and shared it with great enjoyment. And that was reward enough.

The videographer died six months later. I know that it was only his ornery, fighting spirit that kept him alive that much longer. He needed the time to ensure that his video business would be taken care of and that the videos would live on. Ironically, our video, "Cookies, Cakes, and Pies," outsold all the others of famous chefs because, when I was in college, I became a member of HEIB (Home Economists in Business), and they would only write about members, so they promoted my video and none of the others!

MAJOR NETWORK EVENTS

1993 *The Japanese Iron Chef Show* aired on Fuji TV and was the first competitive cooking show.

1993 The Food Network started airing in the U.S. In 2010, I was a judge on one of Bobby Flay's baking segments.

Emeril Lagasse and Rose

My First Experience as a Spokesperson

In 1990, I became the spokesperson for the UDIA (United Dairy Industry Association) to promote the benefits of butter, when they heard what I was saying about butter for cookies in interviews for *Rose's Christmas Cookies*. They loved that I wanted one cookie made with butter rather than many made with margarine. A whirlwind tour, visiting local television stations throughout the country, backed up by a news print blitz, reached over 50 million viewers. I had become a natural on the air and hired for a second year. Years later, I was even asked to promote beef for the Brae Beef Company.

Shortly before Emeril Lagasse started his cooking show, Elliott and I visited his wonderful restaurant in New Orleans. Emeril told Elliott that he had developed neck problems due to the position of constantly leaning forward when cooking and that he was planning to leave the restaurant world and have a cooking show. Elliott suggested that he create a schtick that was his own and that was how the uniquely identifiable "BAM!" came to be. In 2023, Emeril and his son E. J. (Emeril John) Lagasse reopened Emeril's to great acclaim.

EMERIL LAGASSE SHOW AIRS

1997 *Emeril Live* airs on Food Network.

PBS's *Baking Magic with Rose*—Living the Dream

As for the third wish I made when Barbara Kafka asked me to make three wishes: Thanks to Marjorie Poore, brilliant producer of food shows for PBS, in 2004, with KitchenAid as the sponsor, I got my show-and-tell 13-part series *Baking Magic with Rose*. This was my golden opportunity to demonstrate many of the most important techniques in cake, pie, pastry, and bread baking. As the saying goes: "Be careful what you wish for as you may get it!"

The complexities and challenges of producing this show were unimaginable. First, we had to find an affordable location. My extraordinary friend and culinary archivist Barbara Kuck persuaded her dear friends, Susan and Bob Jasse, to loan us their magnificent kitchen at Alyson's Orchard in Walpole, New Hampshire. Another dear and generous friend, Madeleine Morris, who was a professional caterer in Las Vegas (and mother of my protégé David Shamah), offered to come and cook for the entire crew during the week of production. Renowned chocolatier Larry Burdick allowed us to borrow his top assistant. (Imagine having your makeup done by a chocolatier who understands cocoa butter!)

My beloved husband, Elliott, in an act of supreme moral support, took the week off from work and did what is most difficult for him to do: He sat silently and monitored the entire production process. There were untold behind-the-scenes activities and sagas too long to report, but here are the main bullet points: selecting and preparing all the recipes; amassing an entire bakers' kitchen in triplicate (both equipment and ingredients); preparing all the setups, from the mise en place of ingredients to various stages of the finished product, in more than triplicate; and choosing the wardrobe for 13 shows, not to mention, looking relaxed and refreshed when one is anything but.

Who would've guessed that there would be a heat wave in June in New Hampshire or that the audio would pick up the sound of the air conditioner so that we couldn't leave it on during filming. And I'm not going to delve too deeply into the nervous breakdown of one of the prep people, caused by Brett, or another of the prep people's psychotic episodes, making life difficult for all of us and lasting throughout the entire week. (Ignoring him was the greatest acting job of my life; my earlier baking videos [see page 83] were merely my dress rehearsal!)

When I frantically emailed my friend, Marcel Desaulniers, who had recommended Brett the saboteur, his response was: "He must have forgotten his meds." At first, I thought Marcel was kidding. He was not. But when all is said and done, it was worth it. No matter how painstakingly one writes or photographs step-by-step techniques, nothing comes close to having a video. This PBS series was the icing on my cake, my dream come true, my grown-up show-and-tell. *Baking Magic with Rose* ran on PBS stations around the country for three years, and it is also on YouTube, thanks to the persistence and effort of Hector Wong, for those of you who may have missed it.

Epilogue: *A year later, when taking a walk in another city, I ran into the trouble-making saboteur! He didn't notice me—he was too busy with the road construction work that was, evidently, his new profession for which surely he was better suited.*

Marjorie Poore also invited me to participate in their Rhode Island Johnson & Wales PBS series. When I arrived, the chef preparing my coffee cake said that, on baking, the streusel sank into the cake. It turned out that the range had been moved and not recalibrated, so the cake baked too slowly to set sufficiently. I asked if it took longer to bake, and the chef said they couldn't find any timers! So, I glued on more streusel with corn syrup, warning them not to cut into the cake. They didn't believe me, so when they got back to San Francisco, they had to re-bake the cake for the accompanying cookbook.

SATELLITE MEDIA TOURS

By the year 2000, the SMT (Satellite Media Tour) becomes a major component for promoting authors' books, sponsored by collaborating companies or events. Within a day, an author could go to a studio and connect via satellite with dozens of stations around the country versus extended days of touring.

My Inspiration for the First Video-Enhanced E-book Cookbook

Writing *Rose's Heavenly Cakes* gave me the inspiration for a cookbook with an accompanying video-enhanced e-video book. A collaboration with my book publisher and my website/blog sponsor, General Mills, they arranged to have the video shoot at General Mills Kitchen's home kitchen video set.

Since Woody lived just several miles from General Mills, he was able assist in directing the kitchen staff and on set. The dozen videos featured fundamentals for ingredients, techniques for baking, and equipment for cake baking. The finale video was my making Spun Sugar, for which Woody modified a balloon whisk for my Indiana Jones inspired whipping the sugar syrup into golden, long, fine strands of sugar. The video director, however, seeing that they would go into overtime, declared we had to skip this video. He changed his mind when I jokingly threatened him with my weapon, the whisk. The crew applauded when they saw the sugar spun into gold, nearly reaching one of the camera's lenses.

12

My Wedding Cake Years

Four Wedding Cakes

During the following years, while writing for magazines, I also made over 100 commissioned wedding cakes. One of the most special cakes was for my friend Rüdi Sprüngli of Lindt chocolate. At the request of his wife, Vera, I made two little mice to represent their pet name for each other—one pink with blue eyes and the other coated with Rüdi's couverture chocolate which I brushed on to resemble fur. I decorated the cake with cymbidiums, which are a member of the orchid family, not realizing that one is not supposed to put inedible flowers on a cake.

It didn't occur to me that anyone would actually eat them, but my husband came over and whispered to me that the Swiss ambassador's wife just ate one. Fortunately, I got no feedback about her feeling ill. Had it been lilies of the valley, she could have died. I made sure to add a list of edible flowers in *The Cake Bible*. Sadly, Carole Walter, in her cake book, wrote that lilies of the valley are not only beautiful but also delicious. Had she actually eaten one, she might not have been alive to write the book. The publisher had to recall the whole first printing.

I started developing recipes with chocolate and really needed to know the cacao percentage, but Rüdi was very secretive about it. When he returned to Switzerland, he invited me to visit his factory outside of Zürich. We were both given a chocolate tasting with the head technologist. He had us taste some chocolate that had been stored properly in a cool environment for decades, and it was surprisingly good. He also gave us a tasting of two chocolates—one made with pure vanilla and the other with the synthetic vanillin, to see the difference. The vanilla one seemed to rise up in the mouth like a musical note, but he told us that if we tasted three chocolates, we would not be able to distinguish the difference.

He then proceeded to ask me if there was anything I wanted to know. Hiding any possible hint of a "gotcha" smile, I asked for the cacao percentages, and he gave them to me. A few months later, I got a call from Rüdi, who was selling his chocolate in Montreal. He said the chef didn't want to buy it unless he knew the percentage of cacao! I was happy to help but couldn't resist saying that I was giving him the information he had made near impossible to get!

In those days, no one other than chocolatiers and producers had a deep understanding of chocolate. They didn't know what ganache was or even what the components of chocolate included. When working with chocolate, I often noticed a greyish-white appearance on the surface, so I called Jeanne Voltz, who was head of the Women in Food Science organization. Her answer was: "Rose, not everything has a reason!" I considered that to be the antithesis of scientific thinking. Next, I called the Nestlé company and asked to speak to the head of technology, and there, I got the answer. (The subtitle of this book could be *Pick Up the Phone!*) The film on the chocolate is called "bloom" and formed by cocoa butter that rises to the surface when chocolate is melted to above 90°F and goes out of temper.

On further research, I learned how to temper chocolate. I also learned that white chocolate is made up of one-third each: cocoa butter, milk solids, and sugar. This enabled me to create some wonderful recipes, using white chocolate as a sweetener instead of gritty powdered sugar for cream cheese buttercream, and in some cakes which gave them higher rise, moister and more even texture, and more melt-in-the-mouth quality. All of my wedding cake experiences became very useful, valuable "Rose Factor" charts in *The Cake Bible*.

Mr. Vancouver's Wedding Cake

"Mr. Vancouver" was Nathan Fong's pet name in Canada, given to him by all the chefs in recognition for his generosity raising a large amount of money to support AIDS victims.

Fifteen years ago, during a spirited conversation with Nathan, I told him: "If you ever get married, I will be glad to make your wedding cake." Fast-forward to December 2014, Woody and I were working on our computers when I received an email from dearest Nathan, to which my reaction was something like this: "Woody, Nathan is getting married . . . wants us to make his wedding cake . . . will fly us up to Vancouver . . . what? January 16th? We cannot possibly do that in less than a month! I'm emailing him right back, to say no!" Nathan quickly replied to my reply, with: "It's not January 2015; it's a year later!" Nathan's choices were a chocolate cake for his partner Michèl with the addition of raspberry for him.

He also told me that birch trees were to be the theme for the wedding decor. Woody and I decided to make the Deep Passion Wedding Cake from *Rose's Heavenly Cakes,* with the added enhancement of raspberry in the cake and the frosting, which would be ganache. For the birch theme, the cake was to be decorated with the Meringue Birch Twigs from *The Baking Bible.*

Michèl, in addition to having been a pastry chef, is also an event planner and talented decorator.

Nathan and Michèl's Wedding Cake

Making a wedding cake in Canada meant that virtually all of the ingredients and equipment had to be sourced by Nathan and his staff. Another one of the biggest challenges of baking in an unfamiliar location is always the oven. The commercial Blodgett convection oven always needed to be in convection mode, as we were told that the heat would not circulate without it. For the first cake, the savory chef advised us to bake at the same 350°F temperature that we normally use. This may work for savory cooking, but it was another story for the cakes. The porridge-like batter for this delicious cake, which magically mushrooms just a few minutes toward the end of baking, was instead getting blown to the back of the pan by the oven's convection circulation and higher heat. This made the baked cake lopsided. (We later discovered, after gradually decreasing the temperature, that the oven needed to be set a full 50°F under the usual temperature. This was confirmed by Jim Dodge, another of the pastry chef guests, unfortunately after the fact.) Our solution to the uneven layers was, when sandwiching the layers, to reverse the two.

Humidity is the enemy of meringue and, unfortunately, capable of turning crisp meringue columns into bending, collapsing spires. Our solution was to attach them to the ganache-covered cake the morning of the wedding, but in order to keep them from absorbing moisture from the ganache, we painted each of over 200 meringue twigs with melted white chocolate. We made double the number we needed not only to allow for breakage but also for plating along with the slices of cake from the sheet pans. To be safe, we decided to affix the birch twigs before the 11:00 a.m. wedding. The night before the twigs were perfectly crisp and firm, but on the rainy morning of the wedding, to our horror, we found them in a softened "marshmellowy" state. Fortunately, our assembly took place in the reception lobby where the room was air-conditioned. To dry out and stiffen the twigs to keep them standing tall, as they would be in a forest, on our three-tier chocolate "mountain," Woody acquired two fans from housekeeping.

When we were at the nearby church ceremony, I was summoned by the event planner, whispering in my ear, to take a phone call concerning the cake. We quietly but quickly left the church to attend to some of our falling timbers due to the air-conditioning and fans having been turned off. Though we had moisture-proofed the backs of the meringues, the fronts were still able to absorb moisture from the air. Even as the reception guests were arriving, Woody was running back and forth from the adjoining bride's room to replace some of the twigs, while I was uselessly wringing my hands. Then came the next unanticipated drama when a few of the guests wanted to touch the twigs. One guest even managed to pull one of them off, which Woody calmly replaced, as I shrieked NO! In order to be able to join the rest of the guests who were enjoying the delicious reception food provided by 20 visiting chefs from around Canada, who made everything from crispy pork belly sandwiches to fresh oysters and geoduck, we secured a hotel staff member to guard the cake with strict orders to slap any meringue-twig-seeking hands.

We breathed a major sigh of relief when Nathan and Michèl finally arrived in time to see the wedding cake still in perfect shape.

13

My Invaluable Experience as a Food Consultant

Prior to writing *The Cake Bible*, I was invited to be a consultant to one of America's top food companies, Procter & Gamble, in Cincinnati, Ohio. It was a life-changing experience. I was the first consultant ever to be hired by the company, with the sole purpose of improving their chocolate cake mix. I was told that, technologically, the company could do just about anything, but since they always hired from the top 3% of the top Ivy League schools, they had become too inbred, had lost the capacity for wildly creative imagination, and were looking for a different kind of creativity from the "outside world." They told me not to be limited by any technological restrictions.

I had to sign a nondisclosure contract that would last for seven years. The silver lining was that I was paired with one of their top engineers, Richard Walker III, and he was allowed and encouraged to discuss anything we chose to brainstorm. It turned out that, in addition to being one of the most intelligent people I had ever known, he was also one of the kindest and most gentle, and we became lasting friends. A few years later, he was given the choice of his ideal position in the company, and he became the first Black department manager of a Southern juice company owned by P & G, which was Citrus Hill. A few years later, he gave up corporate life to become a Methodist minister, following in the footsteps of his father and grandfather.

I learned many things during my tenure at P & G. Here is the most important one I learned and how I used it to address their question of how to create the best possible chocolate cake experience imaginable. I asked Richard if I could meet the company's chief technical expert, and he introduced me to the principal research scientist, an elderly man who had been with the company for many years. When I introduced myself, he expressed his delight at my interest in knowing more about chocolate. It seemed not many people chose to confer with him anymore.

I asked him how to maximize the flavor of chocolate, and what he told me changed the way I developed chocolate recipes to have the maximum flavor, the best texture, and even less cost. He started by saying that, for chocolate cake, it was better to use cocoa than chocolate because, when baking chocolate, many of the subtle flavor notes disappeared. Then, he explained that the flavor components in a cocoa grain were locked into its cell structure, so what was needed was to explode the cell walls to release them by adding boiling water.

The Best Secret for Unlocking the Full Flavor of Cocoa

Because I wanted to "have my chocolate cake and eat it too," I addressed the question of how to make the best chocolate cake imaginable by saying that cocoa makes the most chocolatey-tasting layer cake, but the best chocolate, mixed with cream (ganache), offers the fullest chocolate sensation. I would make an all egg yolk chocolate cake, which would have the most flavor, and use cocoa for the cake batter. Dissolving it in boiling water would release the flavor components, and after baking, injecting it with the best quality of barely heated bittersweet light chocolate ganache, made with double the weight of chocolate in cream, would maintain the full quality of flavor.

I added that I would store it in a room filled with chocolate because chocolate absorbs other aromas, so why not more of its own? Finally, I would have people eat it in the room filled with chocolate because what you smell profoundly influences what you taste. And that was my idea of the ultimate chocolate cake experience. They were genuinely surprised and delighted by the information I offered and, most of all, my "thinking outside the box" creativity. It was what they had been hoping for.

When I returned home to experiment with the simple but powerful information I learned, I created the cake I described and called it the Double Chocolate Sweetheart Cake in my books, *Rose's Celebrations* and *Rose's Heavenly Cakes*. I also used the technique of hydrating the cocoa, and I discovered that far less cocoa was needed to give flavor impact. This meant that the texture of the cake would be lighter and softer because cocoa tends to weigh down the cake's crumb. Initially, I was unable, however, to use the technique I later found is called "blooming the cocoa" for what became my favorite chocolate cake in *The Cake Bible*, the Chocolate Domingo. **RECIPES: Chocolate Domingo Cake & Wicked Good Ganache (pages 232 & 235)**

I loved the flavor that sour cream instead of water as the liquid component gave to the cake, but years later, Woody came up with the idea to sacrifice a little of the sour cream in order to "bloom" the cocoa with just enough boiling water to release the full flavor. And the result: Not only did the flavor intensify, but the texture improved as well. In the original version of 100% sour cream, there was always a little heavier dark line at the bottom of the cake layer, which disappeared completely when adding the boiling water to the cocoa. This is the cake I made as two sheet cakes for my 50th high school reunion.

Over the years, when people complained about a chocolate cake made with cocoa being dry, I learned the importance of telling people to cover the bloomed cocoa tightly with plastic wrap to prevent the rapid evaporation which was the cause. And for my chocolate chiffon cake, I scrape down the sides of the bowl and immediately pour the oil on top of the cocoa mixture which seals in the moisture.

High School Reunion

I was most fortunate to have had this extraordinary experience as consultant to a major corporation. I learned that being a consultant is more than advising—it is a mutual exchange of ideas, information, and learning.

A short while later, I had an enviable opportunity to take several P & G engineers on a chocolate tasting trip to France, no expenses barred. They were planning to develop a chocolate product. I took them to Valrhona, Bocuse Restaurant, Bernachon Chocolats, and also to Paris, where, disappointingly, it was the prêt-à-porter fashion week, and not a single high-end hotel was available. We could have stayed at The Ritz but ended up at a cheap student hotel. But we ate at the best restaurants, which were available because fashionistas don't eat much. Also disappointing was that the company didn't send the final product to me for evaluation, and when it finally hit the shelves, they told me that they had produced something wonderful. When I tasted it, I was horrified. It didn't last very long on the shelves, so I was not alone.

14

I Became a Writer of 14 Cookbooks

Julia Child once told me that she was going to stop writing cookbooks because it was so lonely. I think the reason I never felt that way was because of my love of classical music and especially opera, which accompanied me while baking and writing. Any possibility of loneliness was dispelled with the arrival of Woody as a partner.

1981: *Romantic and Classic Cakes*

I think of my first book, *Romantic and Classic Cakes*, as my dress rehearsal for *The Cake Bible* because it taught me so much about writing, editing, and proofreading. It was also Irena Chalmer's first venture as a publisher and was intended to be part of a series called *Great American Cooking Schools* to be marketed to gourmet stores rather than bookstores. Her concept was that the recipes taught at cooking schools would be thoroughly tested and that transferring them to book format would be easy for everyone involved.

This turned out to be far from true as, in those days, people tended to be very secretive, giving mere outlines of recipes and filling in the important details in class. I was not one of the withholders, however, my recipes were typed single-spaced on my IBM word processor, and no copy editor was willing to touch them. Poor Irena had to hire someone to retype the whole thing.

As an inexperienced book writer, I was unaware that a series had a format of a specific number of pages, so I overwrote—three times the size that would fit. My dream was to have everything I knew about cakes under one cover. Little did I know that, seven years later, I would write a book about cakes that was six times larger than my original submission. (Thank goodness by then I had a computer, or I never could have done it!)

Milton Glaser Cake

At first, I was upset to learn that I had to cut two-thirds of the book, and I stayed up all night ruthlessly cutting recipes. I had no choice, but Irena reassured me that I could eventually have everything under one cover in another book. That was until her senior editor, Jean Atcheson, warned me that there is such a thing as plagiarizing one's own copyright! Who ever heard of such a seemingly contradictory term? As I was planning to write *The Cake Bible*, I went to my husband, Elliott, in tears asking him what to do, and his wise reply was: "Nothing—just write the book, and by the time you finish, things will have changed." I took his advice, and by the time I finished the book, the entire *Great American Cooking School* series was remaindered (discontinued), so the copyright reverted back to the authors, and it was no longer an issue.

I had wanted to give credit to Paula Wolfert for inspiring one of the recipes in the book, but Irena said all the recipes had to look like they came only from me. Ever since then, I always gave credit and even put a photo of the styling team in my subsequent cookbooks.

The series had sold well enough to go into a second printing and had a charming design by the renowned graphic artist Milton Glaser, who went to High School of Music & Art (as did I) and then Cooper Union (as did my Aunt Margaret, who actually had gone on a date with him). Irena asked me to design a cake as a thank-you to Milton from all the authors, and I did two: one that was a delicious chocolate layer cake to eat and another that was made on Styrofoam as a display cake for him to keep. Inspired by his work, which reminded me of Matisse, I had a vision of each author being represented as a white goose flying against a blue sky toward Milton, whose name became the golden rays of the sun. I was tempted to have a golden egg dropping from Irena, head goose, but I decided it was a bit risky. (I should have done it!) The senior editor's husband, Richard Atcheson, who was a writer, created the perfect poem to accompany the cake, and on November 11, 1981, I presented the poem with the cakes:

High in the firmament is Milton's sun
Toward which Irena and her flock do run
In flight to celebrate their books' enhancement
By his design, for purpose of enchantment.
Thus, as it was in ancient lays,
We fly to honor genius give it praise
In token of which we present this cake, let Milton be our drake.

Richard saw the birds as ducks, probably because it worked better for his rhyme, but I thought of them/us as geese because of the golden egg!

Milton enjoyed the cakes and commented that he was impressed by my design which also reminded him of Matisse. I had wanted him to be reminded of himself, but that was close enough! When he praised my "artistry," I told him that both my parents were craftsmen—my father's medium was wood and my mother's was ivory (she was a dentist).

How I Connected with My Protégé

Romantic and Classic Cakes was a little book that had a big impact on my life. It introduced me to David Shamah who, at 17, became my spiritual son, protégé, advisor, and critic. He called to tell me about some mistakes he had found in the book. My first thought was "What does he know?" I quickly found out that each point he made was well-founded. David grew up with a

David Shamah and Rose at the Culinary Institute of America

passion for cooking, quality ingredients, and equipment. He taught me what mentoring can be. You see a spark and are compelled to fan it into a flame. You do it without wanting anything in return, like a mountain climber, "because it's there!" And as the flame grows, it warms your heart and soul.

I followed David through his education at the Culinary Institute of America, gave him his first KitchenAid mixer as a graduation present, and rejoiced in his career as a chef, which ultimately led to his first restaurant, Back to Nature, which was the first kosher vegetarian restaurant in Brooklyn, New York. He now owns a top catering operation in Nevada, specializing in Syrian and Middle Eastern kosher food. David is the best researcher I know, and through the years, he has given me invaluable advice about products, recipes, and trends. Recently, he wrote: "It's just so remarkable, the level of understanding and sharing we have." I couldn't be more proud of him.

How My Book Expanded My Horizons

The most unexpected thing happened when I was on a trip to Japan on a culinary tour sponsored by the Japan Society. It illustrates how even a little book can connect you to the world. An American, Barbara Adachi, who had grown up in Tokyo, and married a Japanese man, who had grown up in San Francisco, wrote a food column for one of the major publications. She invited our group to her home, which was a traditional Japanese house inside an apartment building. She generously suggested that we walk around to explore the rooms. When I got to the library, to my amazement, I saw my book! I immediately told her, and she was as thrilled as I was. We remained friends for life.

Barbara was an expert in the Bunraku puppet theater and arranged for us to go to a performance. On the way back to our hotel, I was sitting in the same cab as a senator, who was on the board of IBM, and God knows why, he asked if there was anything he could do for me. He was, no doubt, surprised when I said yes! I told him that I needed French keycaps for my IBM computer because French food terminology required accent marks.

He told me to call Jacques Maisonrouge at IBM and tell him it was a personal challenge from Bill (whose last name I don't remember). He told me that, even at the United Nations, they used paste-on accent marks, but I had tried that, and they come off! He sent me the keycaps ordered from France, but then, I had to persuade him to send a technician to replace the existing keycaps because they required a special tool. I was the only one in the entire country who had these keycaps, including IBM!

CUISINART FOOD PROCESSOR

1973 Carl Sontheimer introduces the Cuisinart to the U.S., and the food processor became a household staple. I was one of the early recipients.

1988: *The Cake Bible*—Establishing My Place in the Food World

It took seven years to write *The Cake Bible*. During that time, I had many culinary adventures and learning experiences. One of the most unforgettable was when I was perfecting chocolate génoise and received a call from Carl Sontheimer, father of the Cuisinart. He invited me to visit him in Connecticut and asked me to bring a cake, not telling me it was his birthday.

I chose the nearly perfected chocolate génoise. I made it the morning of my departure, wanting it to be as fresh as possible, and it was too late to bake it again even though I noticed that there were hard, little tan pellets of encapsulated flour that had dropped to the bottom of each layer. (I eventually solved this problem.)

Carl loved the cake and admired what he thought were the mysterious little "nuts," proving Julia Child's philosophy that, if you don't apologize for your mistakes, people are likely to think they were intentional! I told Carl that I wanted to write a column called "Make No Mystique About It." He was so impressed, he said that he would support my upcoming book and do everything possible to launch my career.

In the middle of the afternoon, he had what he referred to as an important meeting and asked if I could wait so we could continue our conversation after it. On the way home, I was so overjoyed, I stopped at my favorite restaurant on the Lower East Side, Sammy's Roumanian Steakhouse, and polished off three-quarters of a pitcher of schmalz! As it turned out, Carl forgot all about his promise until *The Cake Bible* was published. He wrote to me that he was so impressed by my thinking, exemplified in the wedding cake chart, where I noted that the total batter weight would not correlate perfectly for each size layer because it takes into account the amount of batter that remains on the beater, which is constant, and would not change for different amounts of batter. He said he had asked William Morrow publishers to give him a discount on the books so he could give one to every member of his staff. He then reported to me that they had ignored him, so he was going to do nothing for the book. It turned out that it did amazingly well without his help.

Finding an Editor

When it came time to submit a proposal for what was to become *The Cake Bible*, I approached the editor who Barbara Kafka had recommended—Ann Bramson at HarperCollins. I'll always remember her written response: "You throw the reader into a quandary of contingencies. You go over their heads and tell them more than they need to know."

I framed the address label, and it has graced my baking kitchen for all these decades. Instead of the name of my cooking school, which was Cordon Rose, it was written as "Condom Rose." My sense of humor got the better of me. I wrote a letter to the president of the publishing house saying: "With all due respect, I should like to point out that you really fucked up this time. The least you can do is send roses." I got a letter of apology from the secretary saying that I could just imagine how her name Sajit Katajian was messed up! (My first thought was that the Condom Rose was used to protect against it.) After having a good laugh, I cried. Then, I considered the criticism that I'd received and decided how I would use it to my benefit. I would still offer all the information I deemed necessary, but I would put it into sidebars so that the readers could choose whether or not they wanted to read it.

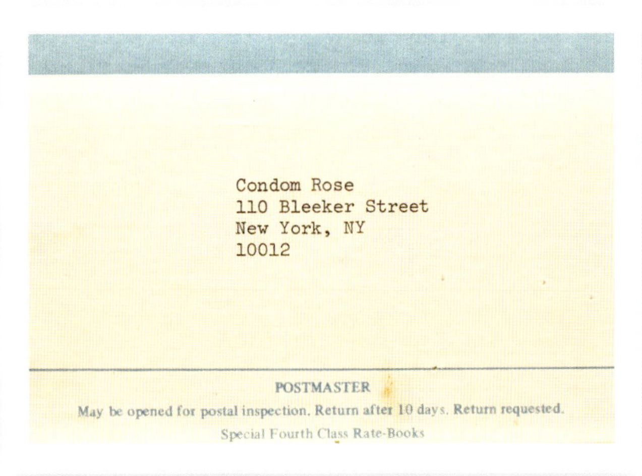

"Condom Rose" Mailing Label

Little did I know that Ann Bramson would eventually move to William Morrow and that she was the editor they would offer me to try to keep me from following Maria Guarnaschelli who was moving on to Scribner. And many books later, several of my books were published under the umbrella of HarperCollins.

Actually, my dream had been to have my book published by Knopf, with Judith Jones, who was Julia Child's editor and specialized in single-subject cookbooks. But I had a publicist at the time who happened to meet Maria Guarnaschelli, editor at William Morrow, at a party and mentioned my idea for the book, saying we were submitting it to Judith Jones. Maria insisted that she get a look at it because she loved baking so much. So, the publicist submitted a chapter, and Maria invited me to her office for an interview to discuss the book.

Before I had left the *Ladies' Home Journal*, the art director had given me advice that subsequently changed my life. He said to save the tear sheets of my articles. A portfolio of these photos was what I presented to Maria on my first interview for what was to become *The Cake Bible*.

The first question she asked was who my audience would be for the proposed baking book—the home baker or professional baker. My immediate answer was "both," to which she responded: "You can have both, but you have to focus on one." I chose the home baker. (But Maria later said: "You bring the home baker up to a higher level." A few years later, *The Cake Bible* was used as a textbook at the Culinary Institute of America, and in the years that followed, many graduates reported having started their businesses with my book.)

The next question was how much money I expected to make, and to her total amazement, I said that I would be happy to do the book without pay if I could have a color photo of every cake in the book. She said that she could not accept such a generous offer and that, besides, the book was so text heavy it would be a waste to have a "four-color book."

When I got home, I called my best friend Bert Greene and told him about my discussion with Maria. He was horrified and said that if I wrote the book for free, I'd regret it for the rest of my life. The irony is that, a few years later, after publication of the book, Maria told me that everyone comes to her expecting to make a lot of money and doesn't make any, but I, who was willing to do it for free, was the only one making money.

I had brought my album of photos from when I worked in the test kitchen of *Ladies' Home Journal*, and after a relatively short conversation, Maria said: "I'd like to take your album home and show it to my husband, John." My response was: "This is the only copy of my work that I have, and I've never left it in anyone else's hands." I had no idea that my next sentence would be: "But I'm about to make my first exception because, if I can't have you as an editor, I don't want anyone." Maria said: "I respect that you care that much about your work, and now, I wouldn't dream of taking it." But I insisted, and she promised to send it back by messenger the following day, which she did.

William Morrow had just published *The Simple Art of Perfect Baking* by the wonderful baker Flo Braker, and it wasn't selling, so they were not eager to publish another book on a similar subject. Maria suggested that I invite her and William Morrow publisher Sherry Arden for lunch to convince her that I was worth signing. I spent days and hours planning a menu which included homemade fettuccini with lobster and morel mushrooms and two desserts, one of which was chocolate. I also ordered my favorite champagne, Cordon Rosé, which had the same name as my cooking school.

The day arrived. Everything was in place. I was beyond excited, and Maria equally as much but also a bit anxious that everything go smoothly, so the first thing she did was to offer Sherry a seat, but the way it came out was: "Would you like to shit, I mean, sit?" I choked back laughter, seeing that neither of them seemed to register the hilarity of it. So, I opened the champagne and that was the next thing to go wrong. It was dead flat. I immediately called the SoHo Wines & Spirits store, and the owner, wisely realizing that if I was serving such an expensive champagne for lunch it had to be a very important occasion, offered to rush over with a chilled bottle.

Both women were very impressed that I got such service, and the tide started to change. They enjoyed everything I had prepared so much that Sherry announced at the end of the meal: "I want you." My response: "And I want you." The rest is history. Who but Maria would have had the daring to publish a cookbook with charts and weights and put her heart and soul into the work? My gratitude is forever.

Creating My Signature Style for Cake Baking and Recipe Writing

When writing *The Cake Bible*, I decided that **weights** would be my primary measurement for making my recipes accurate and consistent. While some authors had occasionally stated a few ingredients with weights, I preferred to list weights for virtually all ingredients. To establish charts for ingredients with teaspoon, tablespoon, and cup measurements, I bought a Mettler-Toledo precision laboratory scale accurate to 0.1 grams. For even more precision, for very small ingredients, I bought Mettler-Toledo's ultra-precision scale measuring to 0.01 grams for establishing weights for baking powder, baking soda, and salt, since these were core ingredients for softened butter/oil cake recipes. Kitchen scales for the home were just beginning to become available.I then created Excel-type lined charts for presenting the listing of a recipe's ingredients, which would become a hallmark with all of my books. I included volume and weights in both ounces and grams. Since grams are the most precise for measuring, over the years, the charts would be reformatted, listing ingredients followed by grams and lastly volume. Charts were also included for wedding cakes, with my "Rose Factor" charts for making virtually any size wedding cake layer.

Contrary to the established mixing method for home bakers with the standard creaming of butter and sugar, my numerous tests resulted in introducing a new way of mixing cakes with the reverse-creaming/two-stage method of mixing the dry ingredients first and then the butter and some of the liquid. In the late 1940s, the commercial industry was using the reverse-creaming method using shortening, since butter was expensive. For this method to work with softened butter, I discovered that the butter needed to be within a temperature range of 65° to 75°F.

This method gave the cakes a finer crumb, more even shape, and the velvety texture of a box cake mix. Oddly, to this day, I am surprised that many other authors have not adopted this method for their recipes. Also, their audience of home bakers, who bake from scratch, likely began baking cakes from boxed cake mixes, which have you adding liquids, butter, and eggs to the dry ingredients. What readers would repeatedly tell me that they liked about my recipes was the "Understanding" section that followed the recipes. In many cases, I explained differences between similar recipes.

When testing recipes for *The Cake Bible*, I always had lots of cake to give away. My dad would drive five miles down to where we lived even to get just one piece. And if anything in our apartment needed repair, I never had to wait long to have the handyman appear, sniffing the air for what I was baking and hoping for a piece of it. One of my favorite memories of recipe inspiration happened when I was playing tennis with my husband, Elliott, and suddenly, he stopped hitting the ball and yelled across the net: "I know it's not another man—just a cake—but can't you give me one hour once a week?"

It was the moment that I had come up with the idea to create the ultimate chocolate cake which I would call the tenor of chocolate cakes, and I dedicated it to one of my favorite tenors, Luciano Pavarotti. I wrote a letter to Pavarotti's impresario, Herbert Breslin, and received an immediate rejection, saying that Mr. Pavarotti was on a diet and did not want to be associated with anything sweet. I wrote a second letter, explaining the tradition of naming a recipe after a famous opera singer, such as peach melba and chicken tetrazzini. I added that I was sure that Pavarotti sang under my Great-Uncle Tibor Kozma's baton at the Met.

The second letter received no response, but my mental response back was: "To hell with you. I'll ask Plácido Domingo!" And his assistant said that Mr. Domingo loves chocolate and wants to know when he can taste the cake. I lost no time in baking the cake and bringing it Uptown to his apartment on the Upper East Side.

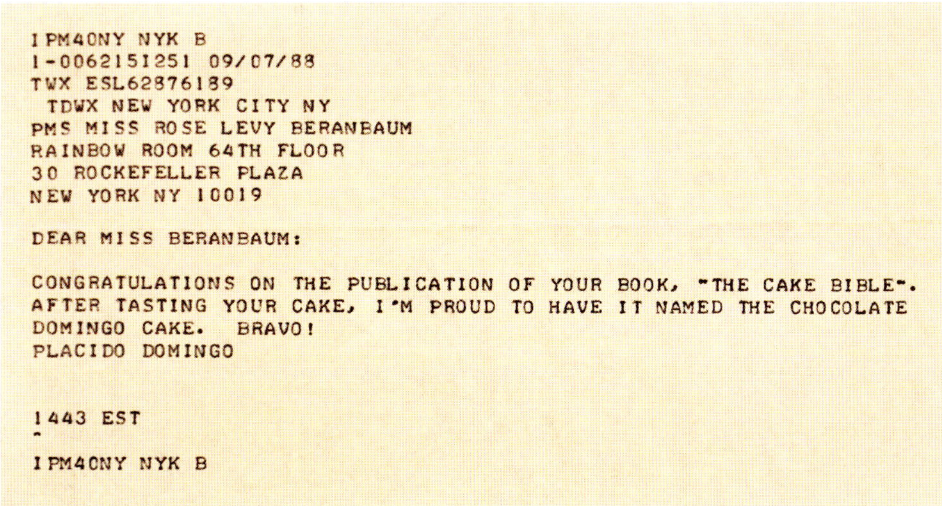

IPM4ONY NYK B
1-0062151251 09/07/88
TWX ESL62876189
TDWX NEW YORK CITY NY
PMS MISS ROSE LEVY BERANBAUM
RAINBOW ROOM 64TH FLOOR
30 ROCKEFELLER PLAZA
NEW YORK NY 10019

DEAR MISS BERANBAUM:

CONGRATULATIONS ON THE PUBLICATION OF YOUR BOOK, "THE CAKE BIBLE". AFTER TASTING YOUR CAKE, I'M PROUD TO HAVE IT NAMED THE CHOCOLATE DOMINGO CAKE. BRAVO!
PLACIDO DOMINGO

1443 EST

IPM4ONY NYK B

Plácido Domingo Telegram

When a two-page review of *The Cake Bible* came out in *The New York Times*, I received the following telegram: "Congratulations on the publication of your book *The Cake Bible*. After tasting your cake, I'm proud to have it named The Chocolate Domingo Cake. Bravo! Plácido Domingo." It's framed in my baking kitchen.

At the bottom right of the second page of the review was a photo of Pavarotti raising a toast which made it look like it was to the book, saying "Pavarotti Finally Breaks Diet." Several books later, when writing *The Baking Bible*, I was still burning to dedicate a cake to Pavarotti. He had recently died and so had his impresario Herbert Breslin. I asked permission from my lawyer, who said: "Go ahead! The dead have no rights—except for Elvis!" So, I created the Chocolate Pavarotti, adding white chocolate to a dark chocolate cake, which gave it a moister and lighter texture.

The Long and Complex Process of Book Production

Book production in the 1980s was not done electronically. After submitting the thousand-page manuscript, the publisher had to hire someone to input the material to create what was called page proofs. This required retyping the entire manuscript, and with all the numbers for weights and volume, the possibility of error was high, especially because the typist charged by the page. Bert Greene told me that he and his partner, Philip Schulz, always read back-and-forth to find the errors in transition. I didn't have a partner, so what I did was to dictate the entire manuscript into a tape recorder to play back against the page proofs. I found myriad errors. Realizing that, when it came to cake, an error in numbers would likely not be obvious and would spell disaster for the cake, I was determined that, in each stage of production, I would catch any errors that still remained.

My mother offered to proof the entire manuscript, and even the professional proofer didn't find the misspelling of the word dowels (used to support wedding cake tiers) that my mother had noticed. I realized that she had won gold medals in Latin but still wondered how she could've known about this misspelling since she was not a baker. Her answer was that, being a cabinetmaker's wife, she was familiar with the word! My sweetest surprise was when both of my parents started baking together from *The Cake Bible*!

Toward the end of production for *The Cake Bible*, it felt like being on a conveyor belt that kept increasing in speed and intensity. This was when my mother decided to give a party for her father's side of the family saying that I had never met them and that they were getting very old, so soon it would be too late. I explained how busy I was, but when she said "Cousin Henry looks just like Grandpa Max," of course, I had to drop everything and go. Cousin Henry was the same age as Grandpa when he died, and when I walked into the room, out of my mouth came "Grandpa!" He was the very image of him. It was as though my mother had given him back to me.

Then, there were his three sisters. Bertie had my mother's portfolio of my articles and photos on her lap and was looking through it with great delight and pride. She told me that her other sisters had all the best traits: One was beautiful, and the other was intelligent, but she had nothing. I said: "But you are the one with personality!" We exchanged several letters over the following year until she died.

As I got older, I've realized that, even though I am grateful for all the blessings in my life, the most enviable is my disposition, and it wasn't until I met my mother's cousin Bertie that I found from where it originated.

The Foreword

In 1988, when *The Cake Bible* was soon to go to press, Maria asked me to choose someone to write the foreword. She had approached Julia Child, even knowing that she never wrote forewords. I'm glad that she asked her anyway because I treasure the letter Julia Child wrote: "I'm sorry that I must refuse to write a foreword for the book because it is my policy not to do forewords or quotes. I'm being uncooperative, and it saddens me because this is really a splendid book, and I shall very much look forward to seeing it in print and having it as a reference. Rose Beranbaum is certainly one of our great practitioners and teachers. All good wishes for a resounding success."

Because Bert Greene was such a dear friend, I thought he would be the perfect person to write the foreword. He was the one who gave the book its title by suggesting that I call it "Beranbaum's Baking Bible." My response at the time was: "If you think it was such a great idea, why don't you call your book "Bert's Bible?" He said that he'd been wanting to use that title for years, but his partner, Philip, wouldn't let him because he was a minister's son. I told this to Maria who did a mock-up of the cover using *The Cake Bible* as the title. She told me that she was in the elevator at work one day holding the mock-up, and people could see it, and they all stood a little straighter.

I researched and found that the only other bible that was not a religious bible was *The Gun Bible*, so I said to Maria that if "bible" could be used for such a violent subject, it probably would be fine to use it for a gentler one like cake. And since that time, there have been many authors who included the word "bible" for their cookbook titles.

Bert's foreword arrived when I happened to be on the phone with the copy editor's office. She asked me if I wanted her to read it out loud, and after she read it, she asked me what I thought of it. My answer was that it talked more about him than about me. And her succinct response was just one word: "More!" So, Maria asked me to come up with someone else, and I chose an even more unlikely candidate than Julia Child.

Maida Heatter was my baking inspiration. I discovered her first book, *Maida Heatter's Book of Great Desserts*, in the early 1980s and was spellbound by her writing. No one described a dessert with greater appeal, in a way that makes one want to stop everything and run right to the kitchen to bake it. What a happy day it was every time a new Maida book appeared, and I bought them all.

I identified with Maida because we had so much in common in addition to loving baking. We both were born in Long Island and lived in New York City. We both were fashion designers who turned our love of craft to baking. But when my baking students encouraged me to write a cookbook, I thought: "Why bother? Maida is all that is needed." Then one day, in one of her books, I read something along the lines of "tempering chocolate belongs in a laboratory," and a bell went off in my head chiming *there's room for me!* My place would be to bring my passion for science and the way ingredients work to baking. And my goal became to build a bridge between the home baker and the professional baker.

I called Maida and introduced myself. She politely declined, saying that she had just written a foreword for a baking book that failed, and she didn't want to associate herself with another possible failure. My response was: "You are the only person I am asking, and if you don't write it, there won't be a foreword, so you can take as long as you need to look at the manuscript and decide." Her response: "Hold on a moment, and I will ask my husband, Ralph." Within seconds, she came back with a "Yes!" She would look at the manuscript and let me know in a few days. I ran to FedEx, and she received the book the next day. And the very day after, she called and said: "I see what you have done, and I will do it." (I get the chills of joy remembering and writing this.) I knew that Maida's blessing would put my book on the culinary map. But more than that, I had the approval of the baker I admired most.

Shortly before *The Cake Bible* was to go to press, my mother had hip replacement surgery and was in rehab at the Rusk Institute. I had retested one of the wedding sheet cakes and decided to bring it for the nurses and caretakers, hoping to correct my impression that my mother was being neglected. I was overjoyed when my mother called to tell me, that night, they massaged her feet, proving that there is nothing like cake to win people over.

My next challenge was my father. He chose her hospitalization as the opportunity to take off to his place in upstate New York. (He bought many acres with all the money inherited from his mother.) I called him and said: "Dad, this is the most important time of my life. It is the final stages of my book. I need you to come back and take care of Mom! If you don't, I will drive and get you and risk my life because I'm not used to driving on highways. I need you to do this." And he did. (Of course, at a later date, he left again one more time, and Elliott and I drove my mom to the Airstream trailer where he lived. She said, "Hi, Bob," and he said, "Hi, Lilly," as if nothing had happened, and they stayed together for better or worse for the rest of her life. She died at 83, and he died at one week shy of 98.) And *The Cake Bible* is still alive.

Planning the Book Promotion

Inspired by the 1988 book *Lit Biz 101: How to Get Happily, Successfully Published*, which advised the author to inform the publisher about everything they were doing to promote the book, I wrote an interoffice memo, copying the publisher's style of having everyone's initials at the top in alphabetical order and then circling them individually. The memo I wrote involved a potential press trip to Toronto. In it, I mentioned that my husband, Elliott, had over 100 Torontonian relatives, who were likely to buy and support the book.

A few weeks later, Maria called, saying that there was a rumor going around the offices that I was going to Toronto, and neither William Morrow nor Macmillan Company of Canada seemed to know anything about it. I asked if this had anything to do with a memo, and she said yes. I was surprised and amused that no one had read it well enough to realize that the memo had come from me! The happy result was that each publisher agreed to pay half of the trip. They were delighted when every library in Canada bought the book, and it became the best-selling cookbook of the year for the libraries. In short, I did everything I could to ensure the success of my book and hoped no one would notice I was doing their job. I went into bookstores, and if they didn't carry the book, I told them that *The Cake Bible* was an important book and, with difficulty, resisted admitting I was the author.

In the 1980s, the publisher did not hire an outside publicist for cookbooks; in fact, I heard that they were considered to be tax losses and write-offs. Lela Rolands was head of PR at William Morrow. Maria told me that she was very difficult and not likely to do much, but we should still approach her and asked me to bring flowers to the meeting. After talking about the book, I was stunned and overjoyed when Lela said to Maria: "She's not in it for the money but for the achievement. I'll do anything for her." It felt like a major victory, but one month later, she retired.

I asked Maria if she could somehow get the company to hire Lisa Ekus as an outside publicist. Lisa lived in Massachusetts, and I agreed to propose her as the publicist but was concerned about all the long-distance calls I would have to make. She assured me that I could call her collect and then proceeded to complain to Maria that I was doing that. I was even more unhappy when my brother's publicist, Tom Walton, offered to promote the book and work with Lisa without charging, and he reported to me that she accused him of stepping on her toes. (Years later, they actually did work together.)

I forgave Lisa everything when she got me on *The Charlie Rose Show*. He never interviewed cookbook authors, but she told him that there was a word in the book that was about **sex**. (It was "orgasm," referring to someone's reaction to the Triple Chocolate Proposal Cake.) Charlie's show usually had in-depth interviews with guests on politics, science, media, and culture. This was my first live video interview. Charlie was a good foot taller than me, and I started off looking like a deer in the headlights, but by the third segment of the show, he was so entranced by my Chocolate Pinecone Cake that he offered to be my janitor and sweep up after me, and instead, I asked him to marry me. (This was way before the #MeToo movement!)

That put a big question mark across his forehead. His response was that he thought I was already married to a doctor, but I told him he had the wrong name, and I always wanted to be Rose Rose! That show aired for years. Lisa's older daughter, Sally, who I knew since infancy, is now an excellent and successful publicist.

Another potential promotion that I arranged was with Warren Alpert, who I knew from the Chaîne des Rôtisseurs when we both were members. He looked just like John Wayne. Warren worked his way through Harvard and then returned to the university as a massively successful businessman to give lectures at their business school on how to succeed. He owned The Ritz-Carlton hotel in New York City. I met him at several Chaîne dinners, and he promised me, when my book came out, I would have "all the power of The Ritz PR behind me."

When I went to bring him the first copy off the press, Warren had me waiting for 30 minutes and then I got to enter his office where he sat behind a massive desk, wore a striped shirt and red power suspenders with his jacket off, and was still in the middle of what was, no doubt, a very important phone call. When he got off the phone, I handed him the book. He looked at it and asked: "What are you selling?" I looked at him in shock—think the artist-in-shock wounded look. He added: "What can I do for you?" And out of the depths of my spirit popped an answer with, unusual for me, forcefulness but resignation: "Probably *nothing*!" He was totally taken aback. It was somewhat gratifying to see his power deflated—suspenders, paunch, and all. He meekly said: "Never say that; there is always something a person can do for another." Then, he offered me a job producing cakes for one of his many companies, 7-Eleven stores, followed by the advice to think of whom I admired most as a mentor (Julia Child was my response) and try to follow her path. He then told me to write down everything I had learned from my session with him and then to return a few months later for a follow-up.

I lived about three miles from his office, so while walking home on Fifth Avenue, I kept stopping to jot down ideas until, suddenly, something rose up in me with a fuck-you message, and I threw it all in the garbage. I saw Warren years later when I was doing a story for *Hemispheres* magazine on New York restaurants. I was sitting at the bar at the Four Seasons hotel, having lunch with one of the owners, Alex von Bidder, and there was Warren, eating his lunch alone and dejected, as if all the life (if one can call it living) had gone out of him. He didn't seem to recognize me, but his eyes looked unseeing.

Another prestigious member of the Chaîne, the late Harry Knowles of The Manor, a historic wedding and event venue in West Orange, New Jersey, offered to give a book launch but only if it could be the first one in the state. At the time, states such as New Jersey and cities such as San Francisco did not support out-of-state authors, but since I had a residence in New Jersey and my brother had a major company (Pet Food Express) in San Francisco, they both made exceptions.

Then, Barbara Langley, our local neighbor on Pine Hill Poultry Farms, insisted on giving an event. Before raising and killing chickens, Barbara had been a top publicist and managed to garner editors from the tristate area. When Harry heard about this, he wanted to cancel his event, but I whined to him that it was only a chicken farm, so he relented!

The Book Launch

I turned 44 in April 1988 and was determined that the book should come off the press on 8-8-88. Knowing all the possible delays in production, I realized that the only way I could assure that it would happen was if I gave an "off-the-press party" for all the key members. The party was held at Union Square. I was certain that the head of production would not appear without the book, and sure enough, he arrived with the first copy still damp from the printer. Everyone signed the book, and we all enjoyed a lovely lunch.

I went home on wings of song, and my best friend, Paula Perlis, both brilliant and mystically inclined, arrived with a little silver bell that had a gold ball inside made by a famous bell maker in Switzerland. She said: "Close your eyes. I'm going to ring it over your head, and you will have a vision." Skeptically, I closed my eyes and had a vision of myself as a sphynx, sitting in the middle of the desert in Egypt, and as far as the eye could see were people bowing down before me! It turned out to be a perfect metaphor for what actually took place.

A few days after the official book launch in October, *The New York Times* came out with a two-full-page article, and that day, *the book sold 18,500 copies, making history.* (In those days, a successful novel sold that number in its lifetime.) William Morrow had to install a separate phone to answer all the phone calls about the book.

As a new author, it was up to me whether or not to have a book launch (and to pay for it). My friend Paula urged me to contact Roseanne Gold, who worked with Joe Baum at the Rainbow Room at Rockefeller Center that had just reopened. When I told my Aunt Ruth about the plan, she said to be sure to tell Joe Baum that it was our cousin who rescued him and his family many years ago when they first came to New York City from Florida. They had met for lunch at a restaurant, and our cousin declined going into partnership with Joe, saying he was too driven.

When the Baums went to get their car, it had been broken into, and everything was stolen. Our cousin gave him money to support himself until he got on his feet. I refused to use this as ammunition, but Roseanne generously arranged to make it affordable when she learned that the publisher would not pay anything to help. I only needed to pay for the service staff. At the end of the best party of my life, I thanked Joe Baum and reminded him about my cousin who had helped him. He looked at me gravely and silently bowed his head in response.

The Rainbow Room Party

For the party, I made four of my favorite large cakes from the book and 150 cupcake-size Grand Marnier cakes to give as takeaway gifts. I was allowed to invite up to 100 people, and just about everyone I ever worked with or for was included. But the party was on Maida Heatter's birthday, September 7, and she was unable to make the trip from Miami. My mother got to meet everyone because I gave her the job of signing them in. Having recently recovered from hip replacement surgery, she was able to be seated for a good part of the time.

It was like watching my worlds come together. My brother and his son, Alex, came from San Francisco. A good friend, Dominique, who said he believed in supporting his friends, came all the way from Gascogne, France. Eleanor Lynch, who had given me my first job in food and encouraged me to go back to school and get my degrees, appeared saying that she never went out in public "not having aged gracefully but wouldn't have missed this for the world." Monsieur Lamalle, importer of the best French copperware, and my dad connected because they were the only ones wearing berets at the party, and I got to meet Monsieur Lamalle's daughter, Cecile Lamalle, food editor of the *New York Post*. Jeanne Voltz, whom I worked with when she was editor of *Family Circle* magazine; Martha Stewart, for whose wedding book I had contributed a cake; and so many others came to celebrate my book.

When two strangers came up to me to congratulate me, I had to confess that I had no idea who they were. It was my agent, Ginger Barber, and her assistant. I hadn't seen or heard from her since signing the contract seven years before, and she had avoided my phone calls. Someone else came up to me saying I must feel like the bride, and my response was that I felt like the mother of the bride—the one who does all the work!

The most memorable moment of the event happened when I stood in front of the group describing the cakes that I made, and unbeknownst to me, my 4-year-old nephew, Alex, was running back and forth behind me and suddenly approached me screaming at the top of his lungs: "Congratulations, Aunt Rosie!" I had been speaking in my rapid-fire New York style, even faster than usual because I was nervous, but I was so charmed by Alex's nerve that I reached down to pat him on the head and said: "Thank you, Alex." I looked out at the sea of people, and it was like sunshine glinting on the waves because they were all smiling. And suddenly, I slowed down and was myself again.

While making the cakes for the book launch, Corby Kummer, who loved baking and was also a writer for *The Atlantic Monthly*, came to watch me bake and interviewed me about my process known as reverse-creaming which was featured in the book. With this technique, all the dry ingredients are first mixed with the butter and just a little of the liquid ingredients, evenly coating the flour with fat which minimizes gluten development before the rest of the liquid ingredients are added, and it produces a finer more tender crumb and more level shape than the traditional creaming method. Prior to this, it was thought that the method only worked with shortening and not butter.

The New York Times Two-Page Spread: 18,500 Books Sold in One Day!

When Corby's article in *The New York Times* came out shortly after the event, even he was shocked to learn that they had given him almost two full pages. My father ran to the nearest newsstand to buy the paper and read the whole article to me. Then, I ran out to get the paper and read the whole thing to Corby. My mother's comment astounded me. She said that not since she got into Cornell did she feel such pride. My response was: "Really, Mom?" I couldn't believe that anything I could do could begin to equal her success. But the success of this book was overwhelming.

My wonderful friend Paula Perlis insisted on taking over all the phone calls, saying that she hadn't encouraged me to succeed only to see me drowned by it. She mimicked my voice over the phone so that even my mother was fooled.

William Morrow's president, Howard Kaminsky (Mel Brooks's cousin), had his entire closet filled with the books to give as presents. Maria had snuck into his room when he was away and found them. She said that it was word of mouth that was selling the book, and I'm sure she was right. I think that people feared baking mostly because there was little understanding as to how it worked so that, when it didn't work, they got discouraged and gave up.

A failed baking recipe is close to impossible to fix, as one can't add things after baking to balance flavor or adjust texture. I got many responses from readers saying that, for the first time, they were able to bake a wonderful cake. Not only did the home bakers appreciate the book, but the professional bakers also valued it. On a visit to the Culinary Institute of America, Lyde Buchtenkirch-Biscardi, the only woman professor, dragged me into her classroom to explain why butter really works and how high-ratio shortening was not necessary or desirable. I had students come to my cooking school after they had graduated from culinary institutions because they wanted to learn a "higher quality" form of baking. **RECIPES: All-Occasion Downy Yellow Cake & Neoclassic Buttercream (pages 228 & 230)**

Working with Maria

Maria's vision for me was to be "the people's baker" and to "bring them up to my level" rather than underestimating their capacity to learn. We were always on the same page and loved working together. Working with Maria, however, was not all wine and roses. My favorite characteristic about Maria was her mantra of doing "whatever it takes," which, in her case, sometimes meant lying and cheating as well. She was known for verbally attacking her authors, but I never rose to the bait.

My second agent, Bill Adler, called her Machiavellian and told me that I was the only one who got the best from her because I didn't fight back. Years later, on a phone call,

Maria suddenly came out with: "I do all the shouting; you never raise your voice, and you are the strong one." She also told me that she wouldn't love me if I weren't so intelligent (now if *that* isn't a Jewish compliment!).

Maria seemed to think that genius and craziness walked hand in hand. She was very possessive of her authors. Instead of being a "connector," she was a "disconnector" born out of self-hatred and insecurity. She started out comparing me to Flo Braker, who had come before me, but in the long run, it didn't work, as I refused to be jealous of Flo. I loved her too much. We became dear friends and even sent each other Aries birthday cards every year.

Maria also did her best to put a wedge between Dorie Greenspan and me, telling me that she said to Dorie that she would never be like me and that she should write other people's books because hers would never succeed. History shows that Maria was entirely wrong. When Dorie and I ran into each other on the Boulevard Saint-Germain in Paris four decades later, we discovered how very much we had in common, and we became close, loving, and supportive friends.

Dorie Greenspan and Rose

There was more goodness and greatness than the dark side of Maria. There would never have been *The Cake Bible* if not for Maria and our collaboration. She dared to defy convention and included my ingredient charts and weight measurements. And when it came time to photograph the cakes, I told her that I had chosen the most elaborate ones because they were the most beautiful, but it was a pity not to show the more approachable cakes. She was so happy with the photos already taken that she gave me extra pages to do more and paid for all of them. Maria let me choose the cover of the book and participate fully, even reviewing the color separations. We were an incredibly forceful and effective team, together fighting to break a three-book contract to follow her when she left William Morrow. It brings to mind "dancing with the devil." It was magic. We were working on something larger than ourselves. The teamwork was seamless. If I had an idea, she would run with it. I remember Maria saying that everyone at William Morrow was involved because everyone wanted to be connected to building the pyramids. (Not sure we Jews would agree!)

Maria knew we had something extraordinary that had never been done before. Only the head of sales actually asked me what made it sell so well, and I decided not to tell him. It certainly wasn't him. However, Mark Kohut, who had a great intellect and was head of sales to the chain bookseller B. Dalton and Barnes & Noble, managed to sell the book to them, even though he knew nothing about baking.

They only took books with a first printing of 50,000, and our book only had a 30,000 first printing, but Mark stuck his neck out and guaranteed that the book would be a winner. So many things conspired to make the book a success, but above all, it was because Maria cared as much as I did. Later, there was only one editor, Pam Chirls, who cared as much as Maria, until I was blessed with Cassie Jones in 2021, when we started the revision of the 35th-anniversary edition of *The Cake Bible*.

Before the success of *The Cake Bible*, Maria called me "the bag lady" because I dressed down. But once the book was published and sold so amazingly well, she stopped calling me by that name. Little did she or I know how portentous it would be. Two books later, when I was testing recipes for *The Bread Bible*, part of my research was working with General Mills. After several years, the company actually put my recipe on their bread flour bag along with my image! I also used their Wondra flour, created for gravies, to create an exquisite texture and ideal flavor for sponge-type cakes such as génoise, chiffon, and ladyfingers. Wondra comes in a cannister, so I suggested they put it in a box for a larger size. When they resisted, I encouraged them to "think into the box" instead of "out of the box." It didn't happen.

It was a great honor, but the best part was when I heard from my father's caretaker, Shelly, that when she took him to the supermarket in their small town of Grafton, New York, he sat in his electric cart showing everyone that flour bag with great pride. One morning, I told Woody the story of my dad and the flour bag, and kiddingly he called me "the bag lady." That's when I realized for the first time how life had come a full circle.

After the Book Launch and the Opening of Many Doors

Life changed after *The Cake Bible*. It opened many doors, and the book defined me. At one point my husband, Elliott, reminded me that I was more than just the book. He also warned me that now people would listen to me despite my soft voice. And at William Morrow, I was looked at with newfound respect. One day, I was standing in Maria's office, and the publisher, Jim Landis, came in saying: "You won't believe what John Updike wants now—to be naked on the cover of his upcoming book!" Before Maria could respond, I came out with: "I suppose he wants to be renamed John Updick!" They both looked at the "butter wouldn't melt in her mouth" author in total disbelief and then roared with laughter. I wonder if Jim told Updike. I do hope so!

At the end of the year, Jim invited Elliott and me for lunch, and at the end, he said: "It is the social event of the year for me!" I thought he was being facetious, but he also went on to thank me for all I taught them about publishing, and he gave me an insight into myself I greatly appreciated, saying that I was a great connector of people. No wonder I valued how much this book connected me with people from all around the world. In press interviews, when people ask what gives me the greatest enjoyment in life, I always say that it is connecting with other people that makes my heart glad.

There are so many things that distance people: religion, culture, education, language. But if one can find just one thing with which to build a bridge, it is like magic. Once in France, while I was traveling with my friend and colleague Shirley Corriher, there was a businessman sitting at a nearby table with his worker wearing the traditional blue outfit. When it came time for dessert, he came over to our table and asked if they could join us. At the end of our conversation, he said that he enjoyed connecting with people and always tried to assess what size hammer he needed to "break the window of their resistance." Never have I been happier to be able speak French. We all said au revoir and felt elevated by goodwill.

After the book's success, my family looked at me differently as well. Aunt Florence, wife of the uncle who had tutored me through high school chemistry, called to tell me that, after reading about me in *The New York Times,* her bridge partners asked: "Whoever has heard of Rose Levy Beranbaum?" And with great pride, she said: "She's my niece."

People Magazine

One of the best press experiences I had was to be featured in *People* magazine. When I went to their photo studio, I didn't know that the photographer, Lois Greenfield, planned to dress me as an angel, wearing a white satin gown, wings, and a halo.

My black bra showed through the gown, so she had to loan me her white one, and it was two sizes too small. This was the female equivalents of "taking the shirt off his back!" I managed to smile anyway! I finally had fulfilled my wish to be the mythological Psyche, who had been given wings and immortality. Lois gifted me with a copy of the photos she took.

After the issue appeared, Maria told me that her daughter, Alex, was in the Columbia University library, taking a break and reading *People* magazine, and when she turned to the page with my photo, she actually screamed in surprise. On the back cover of *The Cake Bible* is a photo, taken by the same photographer, of me leaning on my beloved KitchenAid. I learned later that it sold tons of the mixers.

I am an Angel

New York, New York

New York has always been a very special place. It brings out unexpected things in people, from sarcasm to compassion. I remember the crowd in a movie theater yelling "louder" when the sound was too loud and how cars stopped honking for a while after 9/11. Here are a few more New York moments:

The most moving of all New York moments I remember was a girl in the subway who was crying while everyone looked away until the train stopped, and a woman about to get off, without comment or even staring, handed her a tissue. But perhaps more moving still was years before, when I was walking on Broadway with my mother, and we saw a girl who was standing by her car and crying because she had just been robbed. To my incredulity, my mother stepped up to the girl, raising her voice in seeming reproach, and told her to be grateful for her life and health which were the most important, and the girl stopped crying with the new perspective and caring from a stranger which she had received.

The funniest book-related New York moment happened when I was between cities on a book tour. I was in New York for just one day when Maria called and said: "You have to go to the old Scribner's building to photograph our book in the store window!" I told her I didn't have time, but she insisted saying that she would have her assistant, Maureen Haviland, accompany me. In addition to working full-time for Maria, Maureen was also working on her PhD on Cicero and was a very proper and polite young lady.

We arrived at Scribner's, and to our amazement, the entire window was filled with copies of *The Cake Bible*. In order to get a full photo, I had to step into the busy Fifth Avenue, and just as I did, a truck came wheeling around the corner, and the driver yelled: "Hey, asshole, get off the street!" And what was Maureen's response? "That's the asshole who wrote *The Cake Bible*!" I choked with laughter and took the time to take the photo.

Family!

Growing up, my favorite older cousin was Bill Howe. Ten years older than me, he was a top corporate headhunter. Clever, funny, and charming, he remains one of the most positive people I know, and I adore him. When I married Elliott, who was the same age as Bill, I couldn't wait to introduce them, hoping they would get along well. I listened to their first conversation, with Elliott doing all the talking and Bill listening with his experienced headhunter mind. Then Bill pronounced his verdict: "I get it; you have your own definition for words!" Now, it's true that Elliott, who grew up in Toronto, Canada, had a more precise use of the English language than most people in the U.S., but Bill's family also lived in Toronto, so I'm not sure if it was a question of definition. It was, however, the beginning of a fond though contentious relationship. Bill had Elliott pegged as a contrarian and never failed to push the button.

I also became very fond of Bill's wife, Joy, and the four of us met on a regular basis for many years. At one small Italian restaurant dinner in Tribeca, Bill went just one step too far, and my distinguished husband, with his grey beard and three-piece suit, stood up to his full short height and, at the top of his lungs, screamed at Bill: "Fuck you; fuck you!" Bill did not look at Elliott with embarrassment but rather amusement and enjoyment that he had gotten to him to such a degree that the refined Elliott would lose it in public. I was the one who looked at Elliott in stunned horror. But we were all outdone by the rest of the diners who all started to applaud!

One of Bill's most memorable expressions is: "I'm just trying to make the best move on the board." And the most moving thing he ever said to me was when we were having lunch at The Four Seasons in New York, and he quietly pointed out a distinguished executive sitting behind me and said: "I got that man his job as head of Time Warner, but I'm more impressed by you because his job description already existed, *but you created your own*."

My Mentor and Friend Julia Child

The greatest New York moment of my career was the victory ride back from the book's promotion in Trenton, New Jersey. This was where once I had worked in a brake lining factory and would go to Philadelphia every week to watch Julia Child's show in a dorm room at Temple University because I couldn't afford a TV. I never even thought I'd meet Julia in person. Twelve years later, I was invited to appear on ABC's *Good Morning America* show. When I returned home, the first person to call to congratulate me was my mother, and the second was Julia, warbling in her uniquely contralto voice: "Congratulations, dearie! I'm so proud of you."

I never, in a million years, would have thought that, all these years later after having traveled three hours every week to watch her on TV, I would not only be on TV myself one day, but also get a call from Julia Child, my greatest culinary inspiration, congratulating *me*. It was the most validating and best moment of my extraordinarily wonderful and always surprising career. Julia became a most supportive friend to me and to many others in the food writing community.

Julia and I were both at a book signing event. As I looked up after signing not even half of the 50 books each of us had stacked on our tables, Julia came over to my table, and I asked: "How did you sign all your books so quickly?" She looked down at me sweetly and said: "When people come up to me and say how wonderful it is to meet me, I reply, 'Thank you, dearie.'" She continued: "You, on the other hand, give them your whole life's story."

Live Television Demos

The success of *The Cake Bible* teleported me into doing live television demos. NBC's *TODAY* show, *CBS Mornings*, and innumerable news and lifestyle television programs in different cities wanted me alongside their trained personalities. Fortunately, my "deer in the headlights" persona evolved into my teaching students mode from my cooking school days. Even in first grade, I excelled in show-and-tell when I could talk about something other than myself.

I also made an appearance on the *Regis Philbin Show*, making my Chocolate Oblivion Truffle Torte, which is the most chocolaty cake in my repertoire, with only chocolate, butter, and eggs. Before the show went live, the obnoxious, rather well-known producer, commanded me to say that the torte was so rich it would give you a heart attack. I staunchly refused to say it. Co-host Kathie Lee Gifford was urged to take a bite, and while making a pained expression and sucking through her teeth, she said: "It's so delicious it made my teeth ache!" What does one register—the words or the facial expression?!

When on tour a few weeks later, I was on the morning show in Los Angeles, and there was that producer again. This time, he said that I had written such a wonderful book it was a pity I didn't have an exciting personality to go with it. I ignored him but did not forget.

I also taught a class in a cooking school held in a very hot commercial kitchen. When I began signing books, one of the attendees started fanning me, so I wrote in his book "To a Fan!" That was George Geary, who became a lifelong friend, even sharing his invaluable literary lawyer, Lisa Lucas, who became a close friend. George and I still laugh remembering his visit to our New York apartment, where I invited him to Sunday night pesto. He had the unfortunate experience of being seated in a chair that collapsed from under him. He felt terrible having broken it, but I thought it was worth the laugh.

For short demos, I chose a no-fail technique that didn't depend on electricity or a heat source. It involved melting chocolate chips in a resealable bag in a bowl of hot tap water and then piping a doily as a plate decoration.

Another great opportunity resulting from the book was when I was asked to make a nonedible presentation cake replica of the first new watch in many decades, created by the Harry Winston jewelry company. My father made me a large, angled presentation wooden board, and I covered it with black velvet. The watch consisted of concentric circles of diamonds which I replicated using fondant and rhinestones from the garment district. It was the only photo of the event that appeared afterwards in *Women's Wear Daily*.

The One That Got Away

I was offered a huge amount of money to make a 6-foot-long Hostess Twinkie and realized, just in time, that there would be no way to get it out the door since I lived in a corner apartment. Good I had the forethought!

In 2014, while promoting and touring for the book, I became a spokesperson for Davidson's Safest Choice Eggs. One advantage of my collaboration was my doing a SMT (Satellite Media Tour) to over a dozen television stations. Most of the stations were in cities that were not on our book tour schedule.

Best Book of the Year Award and More Awards

Before *The Cake Bible*, in 1986, I was one of the judges of the RT French Awards and had voted for Giuliano Bugialli. When he won for book of the year, I went up to him and asked to see the award, which was metal attached to a wood backing, jokingly saying I wanted to see what mine would look like someday. He looked at me in surprise and asked: "You think you're going to win book of the year?" My response: "Not necessarily, but I want to write a book worthy of it!"

In 1989, Giuliano Bugialli and I were both up for awards at what had become the successor to the Tastemakers Awards, the IACP/Seagram's Food and Beverage James Beard Awards, and *The Cake Bible* won book of the year over Giuliano's newest book. I was so moved that, as I was leaving, George Lang said: "Finally, quality has won the brass ring." In 2017, the book was inducted into The IACP Culinary Classics Hall of Fame, and in 2025, I was

IACP Member of the Year, honored for my "extraordinary influence on the culinary community and enduring contributions as an author, educator, and mentor. The 2025, updated edition of *The Cake Bible*—an IACP Culinary Classic—continues to set the standard for excellence in baking, inspiring generations of bakers and forever changing the way we approach the craft."

> **JAMES BEARD AWARDS**
> **1990** Conflicts between Seagram and International Association of Culinary Professionals had Seagram splitting off and becoming the James Beard Awards.

The Book Tours

Soon after publication, *The Cake Bible* was the Showcase Award Winner at the NASFT (National Association for the Specialty Food Trade, Inc.) for teaching about specialty ingredients. On the way to Atlanta, I used my frequent flyer miles to upgrade my flight to first class. Having just read Harvey Mackay's book *Swim with the Sharks*, published by William Morrow, I was motivated to follow its advice always to fly first class because one never knew whom they were sitting next to. I was already working on my next book, *Rose's Christmas Cookies*, and had told my husband that I wished I could come to the sales conference and bring cookies, the way I had brought cake before *The Cake Bible* launched, but it was no longer permitted as other editors thought it to be an unfair advantage. Elliott said I should reach out to the head of the Hearst Corporation, and my response was how was I supposed to do that?

On the plane, I was busy writing thank-you notes to all the people who had hosted me on the book tour. I had ordered postcards with the cover of the book pictured on them. I paid for the postcards myself, but all the salespeople wanted them, too, so Maria, as usual, generously reimbursed me for all of them. My thumb covered the name of the book, and I noticed the tall, austere gentleman sitting next to me was eyeing the postcard. I slowly moved my thumb to uncover the writing and then he asked me if there was any special meaning to the words "Cake Bible." My answer was that it was my book, and his response was "I own it!" He was none other than Gordon Jones, head of the Hearst Corporation! He immediately cried out to the two men sitting behind us: "We have one of our authors here!" Then, miracle of miracles, he asked me if I would like to attend the next sales conference for my upcoming cookie book and also to bring cookies!

I was on top of the world! The moment I got off the plane, I ran to the phone and called my husband saying something like "out of your mouth into my action!" Then, I called Maria. I found out on my return that Mark Kohut was standing next to her when I called. Mark told me that, after Maria and I hung up, she accused me of being a witch! I told him that, if I indeed had such powers, I would arrange with the airlines to seat people next to others that they needed to meet. The unfortunate ending to this story is that Gordon Jones thought better of his offer, and I didn't get to go to the sales conference after all. But it further convinced me of my psychic powers!

Once arriving in Atlanta, at the NASFT, I was asked to discuss trends. I had been so busy writing the book I had no idea what the trends were, so in a leap of inspiration, I put forth the trends I was hoping for, which were less sugar in desserts and a greater awareness in the science of baking (both of which did indeed happen)!

I continued to find a way to fly first class and once sat next to a man who was constantly being asked for his autograph. I figured it was either a sports person or politician because those were my two areas of extreme disinterest, and indeed, I found out once again that I was psychic. It was none other than the legendary New York Yankees baseball player Joe DiMaggio. Another time, the comedian and actress Joan Rivers was on the plane, and much to my regret, I was too shy to introduce myself, but I did have the opportunity years later when we were both on NBC's *TODAY* show.

I went on to promote the book at book signings, and one of the most memorable was when a chef asked me to sign his book which he had replaced because the original one was stolen. I endorsed it with this message: "Whoever steals this book will never be able to bake another cake." He was delighted saying: "We pastry chefs are very superstitious, so this will work." I ran into the chef in San Francisco years later at a book signing for *The Pie and Pastry Bibl*e, and he told me that it had indeed worked, and asked me to sign this book the same way!

Another book event for *The Cake Bible* was a class I did at Macy's De Gustibus Cooking School. I had invited Maria and her husband, John. I was demoing a banana cake, and a woman in the audience stood up and asked if I could substitute anything for the banana. Before I could respond, John answered: "Yes—watermelon!" A few months later, Maria, John, and I were at the NASFT, and we encountered a French version of feta cheese. John thought it was odd that the French were making a Greek cheese, and this was my chance to "get" him. I said it was a feta accompli (a pun on the term "fait accompli" which means after the fact or too late.) We all enjoyed the play on words.

Another book signing was arranged in Miami by Maida Heatter. Despite having had the honor of Maida writing the foreword to my book, I had never actually met her in person, so I asked if my husband, Elliott, and I could come to Miami for a short visit. It wasn't to get baking secrets though. The secret I was after was how, despite her celebrity, she was able to maintain a happy marriage. Maida arranged a book signing in a local bookstore. Someone asked if she was my mother (to whom she did indeed bear a resemblance), and she laughingly responded: "More like grandmother!"

After the book signing, Maida invited us to her home. I was so spellbound that, despite my rare ability to remember events as far back as my infancy, I don't remember anything except her utter delight that my Canadian husband idolized not her but her adored father, the renowned Gabriel Heatter, who was a radio commentator Elliott listened to as a little boy during WWII. As for the secret to her happy marriage, she reported that whenever her husband, Ralph, had the impulse to jump into the car and visit a friend, she would drop whatever she was doing and join him. I was blessed by Maida's support and belief in me. One of the recipes in my book *The Cookie Bible* was, of course, dedicated to her.

The Cake Bible Attack

I never received a negative book review until a few years after publication. I was signing books at the NASFT when a woman came up to me and told me that all my cakes were heavy and that she was throwing my book into the garbage. I asked her "what about the angel food cake?" She proclaimed herself to be a scientist and told me that my books told people more than they needed to know. I smiled sweetly and thanked her for saving my marriage. I told her that everyone so loves *The Cake Bible* that it's hard to remain humble, but thanks to her, I was helped. Her response: "Well! Enough about me!" she huffed and walked away. "About me" indeed!

People Whose Lives and Careers Changed

Over the past 35 years, I have received the most heart-gratifying testimonials from people thanking me for changing their lives by starting their careers as bakers. It moves me so much when I learn how *The Cake Bible* has touched other people's lives. Here are five testimonials by people whom I have come to know personally. The first is a story of one of the amusing ways in which it touched my life:

Many years ago, I stubbed my toe on my father's solid wood army chest from his time as a paratrooper in WWII. The next day, my throbbing toe was reddened, so I used my infrared point-and-shoot thermometer and discovered that the temperature of my injured toe was significantly higher than my other toes. I feared infection, so I called a foot doctor at NYU where my husband, Elliott, worked as director of outpatient radiology. That did nothing to get me the appointment, but I persuaded the receptionist that it was an emergency, so she allowed me to come and said she would *try* to work me in.

WOODY BAKES FROM *THE CAKE BIBLE*

1997 Woody chooses *The Cake Bible* for his birthday gift to enhance his cake baking for friends and family beyond recipes in *Joy of Cooking*. The Chocolate Oblivion Truffle Torte and All-Occasion Downy Yellow Cake become his favorite recipes.

Turns out, I didn't have long to wait, and it wasn't because the foot doctor knew my husband (which he did because Elliott's name was on every X-ray taken at NYU). When I explained to the doctor that I had assessed the temperature of the wounded toe with an infrared thermometer, he looked at me with a smile on his face and said: "I know who you are; I've been baking from *The Cake Bible* for years! Maybe, I should do a paper on toe temperature!" The toe was not infected, and I was much relieved, surprised, and amused that I had discovered another kindred spirit.

Mark Levy

At 25, Mark was selling books for a distributor when *The Cake Bible* first came out. He took the risk of recommending the book to all their accounts, and the first day, he sold 500 copies. A year later, he was promoted to sales manager. Later, he helped another book distributor sell over a billion dollars' worth of books. Mark went on to coauthor five books and became a consultant who has worked with the head of a division of The White House, a speaker to the United Nations, the former head of the Strategy Unit of the Harvard Business School, the CEO of Popeyes, the History Channel, and the co-creator of the longest one-person show in New York City. He told me that, for many years, when people asked how he got into his profession, he often said: "It started with *The Cake Bible*."

Jan Kish

Jan came from Ohio and took my week-long intensive baking class. She was a surgical assistant and was extraordinarily talented at cake decorating. She gave up her prior profession to open La Petite Fleur and made exquisite wedding cakes that were shipped around the world. Some of the cakes had the intricate lacey design of the bride's wedding dress. We have remained friends all these years.

Hector Wong's World Cake

Hector Wong

Hector grew up in Peru, and his first language was Spanish. When his family moved to Hawaii, his Aunt Lavinia gave him *The Cake Bible*, and he baked his way through the entire book, learning English along the way. He sent me a photo of the cake he did to honor and thank me. He signed it with: "For Rose, you brought me the world!" The cake was made up of cupcakes. The cupcakes topped with blue icing were the ocean and mango slices forming roses were the continents. Of course, Hawaii was located at the center of the world.

Hector is a gifted IT man, and he put all of my videos, including my PBS show *Baking Magic with Rose*, on YouTube. He also invited Woody and me for a once in a lifetime visit to Hawaii where his former partner, the astronomer of the Keck telescope, gave us an amazing tour. To top it off, he did all the prep for a baking class at Hayley Matson-Mathes's culinary school in Honolulu. Hector is also a poet. He explained why he had stopped baking with these eloquent words: "I've done and changed many passions; baking is one of them. Meeting you made me stop baking because I baked to meet you."

Hector and Rose

Paul Arguin and Chris Taylor

When I read an article by Kim Severson, in *The New York Times*, about Paul and Chris and how, on their first date, which was over a long-distance phone call, they made my challenging Scarlet Empress domed Bavarian custard cake from my book *The Cake Bible,* it made me long to meet them in person.

They happened to be in New York City a few days before our book launch for *Rose's Baking Basics*, and when I met their editor at another event, I asked her if she could persuade them to stay a few days longer to come to the launch. Paul, Chris, Woody, and I have been close friends ever since, and they have been happily married for 12 years!

In Chris and Paul's first cookbook, *The New Pie*, they included a recipe for a Purple Marbled Majesty pie. Its fruity swirls and creamy filling are a wink and a nod (in pie form) to the Scarlet Empress that helped bring them together.

In 2019, Woody and I had dinner with Paul and Chris at Gramercy Tavern. The pastry chef Sherry presented a large version of the Scarlet Empress for our dessert. Since then, we have continued to meet at IACP award ceremonies and conferences and at their Cape Cod home. And Chris made me a large, almost life-size, cookie portrait we could never bear to eat!

Chris Taylor's Cookie Portrait

Patricia Hampl

What better affirmation can an author have than appearing in another author's book?! Writer and poet Patricia Hampl devoted several pages to *The Cake Bible* in her memoir, *The Florist's Daughter*. She writes about making the White Lilac Nostalgia Cake from my book. My favorite part is: "The Lilac Nostalgia stood at attention, its lavender medallions fastened like so many medals for valor on its soldier chest. A cake in dress uniform, in service to a sweetness worth fighting for." I am grateful to friend, colleague, and poet Marcy Goldman for alerting me to this. The late Pat Conroy, my favorite author, once wrote that Patricia Hampl is the best writer in the English language today!

Candace Walsh

Candace's wonderful book, *Licking the Spoon*, was published in 2012. I only discovered it sitting in a pile of unread books that had been sent to me by publishers. And now, I know why it was sent. I hadn't a clue because there was no note with it—just a press release. Neither the publisher nor the publicist seemed to exist anymore. I tried to reach out to the author and posted a message on Facebook, but who knew if she would ever see it?

I had started reading the book because I liked the title. I continued reading because of the beautiful writing. And part way through, I got the surprise of my life! There was my book, *The Cake Bible*, from which she had baked my signature cake: Lemon Poppy Seed Pound Cake. As I continued reading through the book, other mentions kept appearing at many of the key stages of her life, terminating with making her wedding cake from the book.

I wish it hadn't taken me a decade to discover her book and finally having had the joy of connecting with Candace (thanks to the help of several people on social media). I extended my appreciation by sending her a copy of the revised edition of *The Cake Bible*, and we have become close friends and email-pals.

David Leite

David Leite of Leite's Culinaria is my dear longtime friend and one of my top favorite food writers and recipe creators. When he did an Instagram posting, in which he shared some very personal information about himself and featured my White Chocolate Whisper Cake from *The Cake Bible*, I saw something that I never before knew: #baking4mentalhealth. He also wrote about this in his memoir, *Notes on a Banana: A Memoir of Food, Love, and Manic Depression*.

I was stunned to learn that he credited my book for being such a large part of healing him and making him whole.

Erin McDowell and Rose at *Rose's Baking Basics* Shoot

Erin Jeanne McDowell

I first met Erin when she was involved in the baking and styling of the photographs for my book *The Baking Bible*. She first read *The Cake Bible* sitting on the floor of the Culinary Institute of America (CIA) library because, at that time, she couldn't afford to buy it. While writing her own very successful baking books, she has made the time to serve as the stylist for several of my books—*Rose's Baking Basics*; *Rose's Ice Cream Bliss*; *The Cookie Bible*; and, most challenging of all, *The Cake Bible, 35th Anniversary Edition.*

In the foreword of Erin's first book, *The Fearless Baker*, I wrote: "It is inspiring to see the fine and exciting work of this prized representative of the new generation of bakers. I am honored that she claims to have used my books as a launching pad to her baking education. And I am certain that Erin Jeanne McDowell will continue to march to the beat of her own drummer and rise to ever greater heights of discovery and baking excellence. She has become a lifelong friend."

Erin's assistant, Katie Wayne, on all of these books, is now a sought-after food stylist. Erin's *The Book on Pie* (2020) has established her as an authority for pie and tart baking. She also teaches baking in many areas of France.

Miro and Shilpa Uskokovic

This power couple also went to the CIA and baked entirely through *The Cake Bible*. We had the honor of their making our wedding cake as a gift. They now own the wildly successful Hani's Bakery and Café in New York City. Because I no longer make wedding cakes, and because they are two of our best friends, I gifted them with my beautiful stainless-steel 20-quart Hobart mixer, and customers enjoy watching it in action while they blissfully eat their pastries.

Miro Uskokovic and Rose at his Hani's Bakery Opening

Valerie and Bao Holding Banana Layer Cake

BethAnn Goldberg

BethAnn started her successful wedding and events baking business near San Francisco, learning from *The Cake Bible*. She contributed her White Chocolate Fondant recipe for *The Baking Bible*.

Valerie Lash of Bao Pastry

Valerie Lash reached out to us from Bao's Pastry in Valparaiso, Indiana, in 2024 about adapting recipes from *The Cake Bible*. Woody and I collaborated with Val to achieve her vision of a triple layer cake with ¾-inch-thick chocolate cake layers cut in 6-inch rounds from a sheet cake, and filled with ganache. Bao's Pastry has continued working with us, including a triple layer banana cake and other cakes.

Ron Ben-Israel

Ron credits *The Cake Bible* for teaching him to bake when he came to New York City from Israel as a ballet dancer. He became the leading designer of special occasion cakes in the country. Of course, I chose him to write the foreword for the 35th-anniversary revision! When I stopped making wedding cakes, I gifted him the many large wooden round cake bases which my father had made for me.

Ron Ben-Israel and Rose

An Unexpected Extraordinary Award

In 2025, I was inducted into the James Beard Awards Cookbook Hall of Fame. Woody and I were driving on the freeway going to New York City for an appointment when I got a call from an unknown New York City number, so I almost didn't answer. Then I realized it might be the person cancelling the appointment, but instead, it was a voice from the past, my old friend Dawn Padmore of the James Beard Foundation, saying that I was going to be receiving the ultimate James Beard award. I started to cry in disbelief, and Woody swerved to the side of the road. Due to problems with the airlines at the time, we drove all the way from New Jersey to Chicago to make sure we would get there in time for the awards ceremony. I used the drive as an opportunity to read the entire memoir manuscript to Woody as he drove.

1989 *The Cake Bible* United Kingdom Edition

A year after the success of *The Cake Bible*, Macmillan Publishers of London bought the rights to publish the book in the United Kingdom, and I was invited to come to publicize the anglicized edition. They had arranged with Heidi Lascelles, who was owner of a terrific bookstore called Books for Cooks, to put me up in the flat over the store. I remember vividly meeting the store manager, Clarissa Dickson Wright, who was introduced to me as a barrister who loved books. She struck me as a forceful, cheerful, exceptionally intelligent presence. I soon learned of her kind nature when I took sick. Not only did she give me a little tin of "tiger balm" to rub on my chest for my cough, but she turned up the heat in the flat after Heidi left for the day and came in extra early to turn it back down saying: "Heidi's mean and won't like my giving you more heat." I loved Clarissa, and she left a lasting impression on me.

Many years later, I was working late at night on another book and flicked on the TV just to see what was on late at night. It was the show *Two Fat Ladies*, and to my wild and joyful astonishment, one of the stars was my very own Clarissa. I had no idea of her talents as a performer but was not surprised to have found her to be a complete delight. I discovered that her father was a famous surgeon who operated on the Queen Mother, her mother was an Australian heiress, and Clarissa was the youngest woman in England called to the Bar. She wrote an autobiography called *Spilling the Beans*. If you look closely at her cover photo, you will see the humor, pain, kindness, and compassion in her eyes.

Translation of the Ingredients

For me to work on the book, which turned out to be more than a "translation" because it also involved different ingredients, the publisher rented a flat for me on Cathcart Road in London, and I spent over two weeks testing recipes from the book. The editor, Kyle Cathie, brought me her Kenwood mixer, many pounds of butter and flour, and all the things on my list essential for testing. It was delightful working with her and getting to know her family, but there were two things she could not accomplish. One was that Michael Batterberry of *Food Arts* magazine had encouraged me to meet Michael Aldridge, chef at The Connaught hotel. The other was to meet Paul Vegoda, the owner of a flour and grocery supply company in Sherwood. But once I was in London, I was able to reach out to both of them with great success.

It reminded me of a story my grandmother had told me when I was a little girl. An elderly Jewish man from the old country had received a letter from his son that was in English, and he couldn't read it. The first man he asked to translate it said something like: "Dad, I must have money, and you must give it to me." The old man was shocked because it didn't sound like his son, so he gave the letter to another man, and his translation was more like: “Dearest father, I am in great need of some money. I know it’s a hardship for you, and I wouldn’t ask if it weren’t so important.” This story came to mind when Kyle told me that neither contact was interested in meeting me. She was the “first man,” and I was the second.

I started with chef Michael Aldridge by bringing him an original copy of *The Cake Bible*. He came up the kitchen stairs, opened the door, and looked at me with such a startled and inquisitive expression that seemed to say “What do you want?” that I broke into a smile. I told him that I had made a reservation at the restaurant for the following night but wanted to bring him the book ahead of it. He immediately invited me to come down to the kitchen and poured a glass of champagne for each of us, and we had the most amazing conversation which revealed how much we had in common. He also had a microwave to reduce liquid and shared my scientific approach. He had been studying to be a doctor before he became a chef.

He invited me to tea at Brown’s Hotel the next day. The food looked exquisite, but we each sat at the edge of our chairs exchanging more thoughts and never ate or drank a single thing! He told me that he had stayed up all night reading the book. The first comment he made was that he was amazed by the continuity—that what I wrote on one page was consistent with what was in the book 100 pages later. It meant a lot to me because I believed it would lead to transparency and increased comprehension. As we were leaving, the maître d’ came running after him calling out: “Your tie, your tie!” The dress code required a tie, so Michael, who had dressed more informally, was given one on loan and had completely forgotten about it and everything else, except for the book. A few years later, he became the chef of the “Chunnel”—the train that went under the English Channel between England and France. I never saw him again, but I never forgot him.

Sourcing the American Flour

When I called Paul Vegoda, aka Mr. America because he carried so many American products, his secretary invited me to come for a visit. I took the train to Sherwood, which was near the English Channel, and on arrival, I saw a General Mills truck and a tall, dark-haired man standing by it. I had dressed in my best outfit which included a tight skirt, making it impossible for me to step into the high truck, so Mr. Vegoda had to lift me into it. That was the beginning of an unexpectedly delightful visit. I told him that I was born by the ocean and always wanted to see the English Channel, so he said he would take me to see it.

He stopped the car in the middle of a field with a view of the Channel and asked: “Are you Jewish (pronounced *jwsh*)?” I panicked, thinking that he was an anti-Semite and was going to harm me, but instead, he said: "Open the glove compartment!" I obeyed and then, to my surprise, instead of a pistol, I saw a black yarmulke—a clear indication that he was Jewish, too! He went on to explain that the Jewish population was very small in England and that he believed in supporting other Jews and would help me with my flour for my book project. When we got to his office, we continued the conversation and then he called his wife, Jilly, and asked if he could invite me to dinner, which meant forgoing their weekly tennis date. I don't remember the food because I was so entranced by this charming woman and all that had happened. Paul was an importer of the bleached flour which General Mills carried at the time and promised that, when the book came out, he would have a box of the flour arrive at the doorstep of everyone who had purchased it! And yes: Paul is related to the actor Abe Vigoda.

My introduction to the English "translation" expresses in detail what I had been up against to revise the original. And years later, the Cotswold flour company started to make their "heat-treated" flour, used in industry, which performed like bleached flour, available to the home baker.

Crossing The Atlantic by Cookbook—My Introduction to the Book

Cookbooks, particularly baking books, that cross the Atlantic have the well-earned reputation of being troublemakers. Differences in flour have long been suspected of being the culprit. When Macmillan of London bought the rights to publish my book The Cake Bible *in the UK, I was determined to get to the bottom of this culinary Tower of Babel. A British friend began sending me kilograms of the two basic flours available to British consumers: self-raising and plain, and I started baking. Much to my alarm, the cakes produced with the British flour were unrecognizable from their original models. It was hard to believe that innocent seeming flour could be responsible for such a dramatic difference. The logical way to conquer the problem seemed clear: to retest and redevelop the recipes to work as well as the originals, but with British ingredients. The only place to do this was in the UK with native equipment and native ingredients.*

Kyle Cathie, my brilliant British editor with pioneering spirit, made it possible for me to spend two weeks in a charming airy flat retesting recipes. She purchased a heavy-duty mixer, food processor, 12 dozen eggs and arranged a shopping tour to Sainsbury, a large British supermarket. I was delighted to discover that England is a baker's paradise: double cream with pure uncooked flavor, wondrous clotted cream which is divine simply spread on cake in place of buttercream, glorious golden refiners' syrup, flavorful marzipan, and nuts of every type and gradation imaginable.

The problem was indeed the flour. Bleached cake flour is indispensable for butter cakes. But the only bleached flour available was the "self-raising" variety which contained leavening. When a cake uses an acid ingredient such as sour cream, it needs to be tempered with baking soda. But when the flour already contains the maximum amount of baking powder, adding baking soda would make the combined leavening too high, causing the cake to collapse. Fortunately, the plain unbleached flour is just fine for all the sponge type of cakes.

The solution was first to assess how much baking powder was contained in the cake flour and then to create a blend of self-raising and plain flour in order to lower the overall leavening but still have the benefit of the cake flour. This necessitated other changes as well, such as replacing all yolk cakes with whole eggs and decreasing butter to strengthen the cakes' structure. With sour cream cakes, extra sugar was needed for aeration. Each and every cake had to be adjusted separately, sometimes as many as three times before it was exactly right. It was a night and day job, without much sleep, but well worth the effort because I can now be confident that when a British person is baking one of my cakes, it will have essentially the same flavor and texture as mine.

While in England, Kyle told me that the book could not be called *The Cake Bible* if it did not contain the beloved British gingerbread, a moist, spicy cake with an intriguing blend of buttery, lemony, wheaty, treacly flavors.

I developed the recipe while still on British soil but am happy to report that it works equally well in America, especially if you use the golden refiners' syrup instead of corn syrup. It is easy to make, not even requiring a mixer, and is a wonderful addition to the book. Regrettably, I didn't know to include it in the American version, but I did include it in subsequent books.

How I Got My Hirschfeld Caricature and How My Version Became Part of His Archives

Growing up as a New Yorker, I long admired Al Hirschfeld's amazing caricatures in *The New York Times* and joined the ranks of people searching for the name "Nina" hidden in the lines of his drawings. (Nina was the name of his daughter, and each of his caricatures always had her name written one or more times in it.) I never would have dreamed of having a Hirschfeld illustration of me, but when I became a cookbook author, my editor told me that fellow author Marion Burrows's husband had purchased one for her to use on the book jacket.

I called my mother and asked her if she thought I should commission a Hirschfeld. Her response: "Why would you want a caricature which exaggerates one's worst feature?" My answer: "I think of Hirschfeld as the poet of line drawing—that he sees into one's soul, and

I'd like to see how he would see mine." My mother's response: "If that's how you feel about it, then you should do it." No doubt that was in good part because I wasn't asking her to pay for it. But when I found out the cost of such a work of art, I was unsure whether to go forward with it.

How I Made Up My Mind

In 1988, when *The Cake Bible* had just come out to great acclaim, Elliott and I were invited to a New Year's Eve party at the Eldorado—the most elegant apartment house on Central Park West, home of the fictional Marjorie Morningstar, and actual home of David and Leslie Newman, screenwriters for the *Superman* movie. I didn't realize right away that the reason for the invitation was because Leslie was writing her first cookbook, *Feasts*, and planned to change careers from screenwriter to cookbook author. Her husband, David, seemed not altogether happy about her abandoning a lucrative profession for a questionable one, but since my book was such a success, he was encouraged to think that maybe he could divine my secret.

We rang the doorbell, and Paula Wolfert appeared, whisking us into the kitchen saying: "This is where the food people are." And there was Leslie, pulling out ingredients for the choucroute garnie midnight supper. I knew that my husband, Elliott, was none too happy to be relegated to the food people, so I nervously made a futile attempt at introducing him to Leslie. "Just a minute," she cried out, "I'm just taking out the sausage."

I don't know what desperation possessed me to offer up the following non sequitur, but here's what it was: "Well, speaking of taking out the sausage, I'd like you to meet my husband, Elliott." I was afraid he would walk out and leave me on the Upper West Side, but he had to laugh because so were Paula and, most of all, Leslie, who rushed out into the living room to announce what had just been said. I heard a roar of amusement and realized it had become our calling card for meeting all the non-food intelligentsia, such as Gay Talese and others of the literary circle.

On our way out, as David Newman ushered us to the door, I noticed that, in the foyer, there were myriad Hirschfeld pieces and other artists' caricatures of famous actors and celebrities lining the walls. I realized that this had to be the perfect person to ask for advice about the Hirschfeld I wanted. I got no further than saying that I was considering having one drawn of me when he cried out with eyes wide open in awe-filled admiration: "Hirschfeld wants to *do* you?" (I think at that moment he decided that his wife's defection from screenwriting just might be a good choice.)

It was a hard split-second decision: whether to let him think I was now that famous or to tell him the truth and get his advice as to whether it was worth the price. I chose the former with an emphatic "*YES!*" It was one of the few lies I ever told, and to this day, I do not regret it. And when it turned out that many people, when seeing the caricature, had the same assumption as David Newman, my husband admitted that he had been wrong to discourage me from spending all my savings to commission it saying: "Had I known how you would use it, I would not have objected." And the truth of the matter is that I had no intention of "using" it—I just wanted it for myself. I think . . . He probably knew me better than I knew myself.

In 1989, I was invited to come to Hirschfeld's top-floor studio in a brownstone on the Upper East Side to sit for the sketch. While he was drawing, I told him the story, ending with the word "*YES!*" Then, I asked if he had finished the drawing. He looked up at me and echoed: YES!

His associate told me on leaving that he had liked me, which is no doubt why he portrayed me as sweet. My Hirschfeld caricature became an icon for me to grace my business cards to writing paper. Woody placed it alongside his drawing of an Apple Macintosh computer for a banner page on our website.

How I Ended Up in Hirschfeld's Archives

The Cook's Magazine had its first-annual event honoring the "Who's Who of American Chefs." Julia Child was one of the first to be inducted, and I overheard Barbara Kafka saying in a dry voice: "So American." Craig Claiborne, formerly a longtime restaurant reviewer for *The New York Times*, who was still a frequent contributor, was in attendance. Alex Ward, head of the newspaper's Living Section, had told me that Craig was doing a duck story and that I should send the story I had proposed to him.

Weeks had gone by, and I had all but forgotten it, but when I saw Craig, I seized the opportunity and politely asked him about what had ever happened to my submission. His response was to put his hands around my neck in a mock choking position, saying: "I wish you would all go away and leave me alone." Edna Lewis, one of the most refined and polite of food writers, looked totally embarrassed and would have blushed if she could have. It was such a horrible feeling, and when I turned around to leave and the next person I encountered politely asked me how I was doing, I burst into tears.

Some time passed, and I was invited to participate in The Book & The Cook event in Philadelphia along with other cookbook authors, including Craig Claiborne. Shortly before the event, I received an invitation to attend a dinner at Le Bec-Fin honoring Craig. And the entire front page of the invitation was a Hirschfeld caricature of him. Yes! Hirschfeld fulfilled my prophesy of seeing into the soul of a person. He depicted Craig with his hands gleefully around the neck of a little chicken.

Here's what I was inspired to do: I shrank my Hirschfeld drawing to the size of the baby chicken. Then I created my own version of Craig's, replacing the strangled chicken with my image. This was prior to the completion of *The Pie and Pastry Bible*, and I promised myself that, the moment I finished this enormous and demandingly detailed book, I would send my amalgamation caricature to Hirschfeld along with the story.

Several years passed, and Hirschfeld was well into his 90s by the time I sent him the letter. And then, to my delight, I received a postcard (page 134) from Hirschfeld's wife, the archivist. I wish Craig could have known . . . I wonder if I was the only person ever to be sort of choked by him. Do let me know if it happened to you and what you did about it!

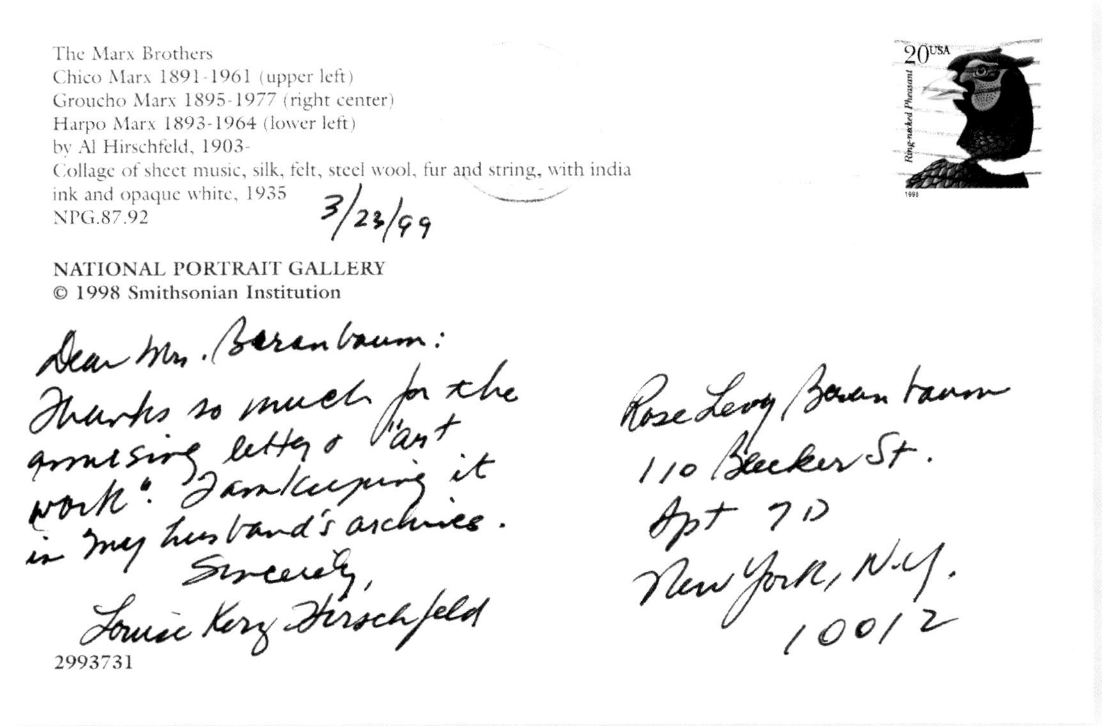
The Marx Brothers
Chico Marx 1891-1961 (upper left)
Groucho Marx 1895-1977 (right center)
Harpo Marx 1893-1964 (lower left)
by Al Hirschfeld, 1903-
Collage of sheet music, silk, felt, steel wool, fur and string, with india ink and opaque white, 1935
NPG.87.92

3/23/99

NATIONAL PORTRAIT GALLERY
© 1998 Smithsonian Institution

Dear Mrs. Barenbaum:
Thanks so much for the amusing letter & "art work". I am keeping it in my husband's archives.
Sincerely,
Louise Kerz Hirschfeld

2993731

Rose Levy Barenbaum
110 Bleecker St.
Apt 7D
New York, N.Y.
10012

The National Portrait Gallery Postcard/Smithsonian Institute

1989 *A Passion for Chocolate*

I was in Lyon, France, working with the Bernachons on the translation of their book *La Passion du Chocolat*. Maurice Bernachon, aka Papa Bernachon, invited me to lunch to celebrate its completion and asked me to choose between two restaurant chefs—Paul Bocuse or Alain Chapel. I was torn. Both were brilliant chefs, but Chapel, with his near military precision and passionate perfection, was the chef of my heart and soul, and his was my favorite restaurant in all the world. Despite this, and after some hesitation, I chose Bocuse because I knew that Maurice Bernachon's son Jean-Jacques was married to Paul Bocuse's daughter. Politesse won out over passion, not to mention the fact that I knew we would eat magnificently at either place. And I comforted myself with the promise that, someday soon, I would return to Chapel.

The day of the luncheon arrived. We folded our aprons, changed out of our whites, and drove off to what turned out, to my joyful astonishment, to be Chapel. The greeting Bernachon received from the maître d' was worthy of a king. But then, of course, he was considered the king of chocolatiers in France, and his neighbors in the food establishment were very proud of him. He was called Le Lion de Lyon! With his silver mane of hair and courtly gallant manners, I felt as if I were dining with the long fantasized French grandfather of my dreams. Chapel came out to greet us, and a serious discussion ensued (as only seems to happen in France) about our culinary fate (choice of food). I was so overjoyed I could have cried with pleasure.

The first course arrived, and from then on, the meal seemed never to end. We ate for four hours but so slowly I had the illusion of never being too full. (Afterwards, though, I went to my hotel and slept for five hours, and when I awoke, I was not hungry for dinner!)

I remember best the splendid regional Vacherin Mont d'Or, which was at its peak, the glorious burgundy that was the best I ever tasted and seemed like a musical note to rise at the end of each sip, and the *canneton à la vapeur* which was the best duck I ever tasted. (*Canneton* is a young duck which the chef poached in a flavorful broth and then the legs roasted to have the contrast of the crisp skin.) When Bernachon mentioned my appreciation to Chapel, as we were enjoying our digestif brandy on the porch, his answer was approvingly emphatic: "She is right. I asked my purveyor to find the best duck in France, and it turned out they come from Alsace." I felt as if I had passed an exam.

At some point, during the course of the meal, I mentioned to Bernachon how much I enjoyed the French facial expressions known as *faire la moue*—how you could see in their faces exactly what they are thinking. To my surprise, his response was: "You also have a face like that!" Finally, I knew how it was we ended up at Chapel instead of Bocuse! And a good thing, too, as it turned out to be the last time. My beloved Chapel died soon after.

San Francisco Book Tour Earthquake of 1989

My brother, with his young son, Alex, drove me to Capitola, south of San Francisco, for a book signing at Jones & Bones. The following day, it became the epicenter of a major earthquake. One of the owners posted a newsletter titled "Revenge of the Virgins," describing how the extra-virgin olive oil bottles twirled and crashed to the floor.

Back in San Francisco, making phone calls was a near impossibility, but I managed to reach my mother in New York to assure her that her only two children had survived. She brushed it aside to deliver the all-important news for my events that she had read in her dental journal that the acidity in chocolate prevents dental caries.

Shortly after the earthquake, one of the Berkeley, California, newspapers had a headline about my book that read: "Next Time, Leave Your Passion at Home!"

I was invited to the Smithsonian in Washington, DC, to give a talk about chocolate. I brought along a transparency of the cover of the book and my usual demo which involved melting chocolate chips in a resealable plastic bag using hot tap water. When I arrived, the person in charge informed me that the projector was running so hot it would melt the transparency and that the government turned off the hot water in the bathroom around 4 p.m. every day. Guess what I used to melt the chocolate? And I still got to show the transparency but only leaving it in the projector for a few seconds.

A few years after the book was published, I got a call from a Dr. Robert Steinberg saying that he had been diagnosed with lymphoma and didn't have many years to live. He had always wanted to be a chocolatier, so he was calling to ask me to put him in touch with the Bernachons to take him on as an apprentice for a short time. Papa Bernachon was a very generous person and took him on with open arms. When Robert returned to the Bay Area, he persuaded his friend John Scharffenberger to sell his champagne company and open Scharffen Berger Chocolate Maker. Robert went into remission for several years and created a wonderful chocolate. At my insistence, it was the first American chocolate to list the cacao percentage on its wrapper.

1990 *Rose's Christmas Cookies*

Jeff Smith, creator of *The Frugal Gourmet,* was contracted to do a Christmas cookie book for William Morrow but reneged at the last moment. Maria begged me to do the project, offering the assistance of fellow author Rick Rodgers so the book could come out in time. He was so much fun to work with we ended up collaborating on my subsequent two savory books.

My Brother Michael

Maria was concerned to have a Jewish name (such as both of mine) associated with a Christmas cookie book but was exonerated when a writer for a Rhode Island newspaper reviewed the introduction as the best writing about Christmas in the English language!

I loved putting together my favorite cookies and then Maria said there has to be a cookie house. The one I created was a rendition of Notre-Dame Cathedral, complete with flying buttresses and stained-glass windows made with melted candies. A few years later, I received a letter from a man who had been a food stylist for Miami's Williams Sonoma. Not only had he made this cookie cathedral, but he was also featured in the *Miami Herald Sun-Sentinel,* giving the cathedral to a local orphanage and starting a new career as a television food celebrity!

My mother's only cookie, Mom's Coconut Kisses, was included in the book. My brother, as the co-owner of Pet Food Express, persuaded me to include a dog cookie, as many customers bought them at Christmastime. At first, William Morrow resisted the idea, but when I pointed out that they had just published Barbara Bush's book, *Millie's Book,* about her beloved dog, my recipe for Bon à Fidos made it into the book and was later included in *The Cookie Bible.*

Meeting the Great Claudette Colbert

Most everyone loves cookies, so it was great fun promoting *Rose's Christmas Cookies*. Jim Melgren arranged a signing at Dean & DeLuca, even providing the lemon butter bars, my favorite recipe in the book, as samples for me to give out by the entrance to the store.

The door opened, and in walked a beautiful, elegant older woman who smiled while inclining her head slightly to the left. Her entire attitude was so reminiscent of Claudette Colbert that I could not resist calling out: "Has anyone ever told you that you look exactly like Claudette Colbert?" I thought that, at the very least, she would be flattered. You can imagine my surprise when she smiled sweetly, again inclining her head in that characteristic way, but this time with a mischievous gleam in her eye and said: "Maybe that's because I am!"

She continued walking toward the back of the store, leaving me with my mouth agape. A few minutes later, I began laughing again with delight at the sheer irony of having suggested that someone who looked like Colbert actually was the famous actress, when Ms. Colbert reappeared and said: "I see you are still amused. I must tell you a story of what happened to my friend Joan Crawford some years ago. She was walking down Park Avenue when someone stopped her with the comment: 'Didn't you *used to be* Joan Crawford?!'" This time, we both giggled with delight. Thank God, my comment hadn't had such overtones of insult.

I will always remember Claudette Colbert as a charming, gracious, and unaffected lady who was willing fearlessly to rise to the occasion, putting humor above self-protective anonymity, to share with a stranger one of life's most profound physical intimacies—laughter.

Media Training

One of my promotional lines for interviews about my cookie book was that I'd rather have one cookie made with butter than several with a substitute. This was noticed by the Dairy Council, and I was asked to represent them for a cookie campaign. They insisted that I take a Chicago-based course in media training given by the Silk sisters. I assured them I didn't need the training, but they did not relent, so off I went. At the end of the day, after the all-important lesson in bridging to get one's message across, I told one of the sisters how much I had learned from her, to which she said: "You didn't need any training!"

1992 *Rose's Celebrations*

I proposed doing a savories and desserts cookbook to Maria as she knew I was an excellent cook as well as a baker. (My philosophy is that bakers can cook, but many cooks can't bake because the required precision is not part of their makeup.) The successes of *The Cake Bible* and *Rose's Christmas Cookies* looked promising enough for Maria to take the leap. Julia Child advised me that it was very hard to cross the barrier between sweet and savory, though some have done it. She was right. My two savory books are the only ones that are out of print.

This book was so beautifully photographed and illustrated and contained some of my best savory and sweet recipes including Bulgur and Duxelles, Oysters in Beurre Blanc on Puff Pastry shaped on oyster shells, Copper Topper Cascade Mountain Cake, and Double Chocolate Sweetheart Cake. My nephew Alex came from San Francisco to be photographed for his birthday cake, The Checkerboard Cake, which was included in the book. The book's chapters were arranged by the seasons of the year with holidays and seasonal recipes as entire meals. Weights and charts were also included for the savory ingredients to complement the dessert charted ones. **RECIPE: Bulgur & Duxelles (page 247)**

Happy Birthday Alex Levy

1993 *Rose's Melting Pot*

This book contained some of my favorite ethnic recipes, including Tandoori Chicken, a recipe I brought back from India; Seafood and Chipotle Pasta that one reader said was worth the price of the book; and Tiramisù. Rick Rodgers and I shared a great laugh over my grandmother's P'tcha (calves' feet jelly) that would not gel. Turned out, he couldn't find two calves' feet, so he substituted one cow foot which lacked the necessary gelatin. The chapters for recipes here were presented by category, from soups and appetizers to desserts and beverages. Once again, savory ingredients had their weights and charts.

FIRST DEDICATED BAKING SHOW

1994 Debbi Fields, aka Mrs. Fields, hosts *The Dessert Show,* one of Food TV Network's first baking shows.

Pastry chef François Payard did such a wonderful rendition of my Dobos Torte at the launch party at Restaurant Daniel that Ariane Batterberry ate the second piece that Craig Claiborne left behind. Craig, entre nous, did not have the best reputation. Bert Greene told me about him and his buddies getting chefs to host parties for them. But I was charmed when he turned to me saying that my stuffed pork roast recipe was absolutely delicious, and I told him how for my 21st birthday I was given the money to make paella, and it was from his recipe. When Craig died a few weeks later, I called Yanou Collart, a powerful diva publicist in Paris, to invite myself to his memorial dinner. She said: "I didn't know that you and Craig were friends." My answer: "We didn't talk for years!" (Of course, Craig never noticed this.) I wasn't invited.

My Rolling Pins

1998 *The Pie and Pastry Bible*

Maria left William Morrow for a position at Charles Scribner's, and I waged a major fight to break a three-book contract to follow her. I was shocked to learn that my contract said any future book (not just cookbook) would have to be for them. I told my lawyer that I would stop writing and that I refused to be an artistic prisoner. I learned something important about negotiating: It works best if you're willing to go down with the ship. I succeeded in breaking my contract and followed Maria.

Over the years, I spent many vacations visiting my brother, Michael, his lovely wife, Mia, their daughter Mariella, and my cousin Joan, who was a very successful therapist in the San Francisco Bay Area. I once confided in her that, growing up with her and our twin cousins on the East Coast, I always felt less intelligent. Her illuminating explanations was: "I think because of all the drama in your house, you were a bit dissociated much of the time."

Marion Cunningham, one of the founders of Baker's Dozen West, reviser of *The Fannie Farmer Cookbook*, and longtime friend of James Beard, became one of my dearest friends. I also connected with many of the baker members.

One of my favorite stories is when Cheryl Lew, owner of Montclair Bakery in Oakland, California, told me how my brother would stop by the bakery after work every day and how, one day, he came after it was closed. He hammered on the door and told Cheryl that, if she knew who his sister was, she'd open. Her response: "Oh yeah—who is she?" When he said my name, she flung open the door saying, "Take whatever you want free of charge!" By the way, he never dared tell me this story.

Years later, I introduced Cheryl Lew to Emily Winston of Boichik Bagels and they became collaborators. The first time I tasted Emily's bagels I told her that when she opened her bakery they would blow all other bagels out of the water!

The Unique Relationship Between Authors and Editors

Marion Cunningham once recounted an incredible story about her relationship with her editor Judith Jones. Chefs and colleagues alike were awed by Marion. One day, when I was visiting Marion's home in Walnut Creek, California, we were comparing editors, with me saying that Maria will actually visit the author at some points in the editing process and her saying that, yes, Judith Jones comes all the way to California to work with her.

She went on to recount the story of how she is Catholic, and Judith wanted her to take Communion with her in a Protestant church. Marion explained that it is a sin to take Communion in a non-Catholic church. "So, what did you do?" I asked. "I took Communion with her," Marion answered. "Why?" I asked in incredulity. "Because I'm more afraid of Judith than I am of God!" she admitted. If that doesn't describe the author/editor relationship, what does?!

Toward the end of working on *The Pie and Pastry Bible*, Maria and I had the worst confrontation of our association. She had invited me for the weekend to her country house in Pennsylvania. Suddenly, without warning, her darkness and demons emerged. She screamed at me that she was tired of doing all the work and writing of the book for the authors who get all of the money and glory, which certainly was not the case with me. She went on to say that, though she always said she loved me, she really hated me—especially that I was like Pollyanna, never saying what I really thought.

Maria's modus operandi was to interrupt whenever someone started complaining, so I said that I would tell her what I thought if she promised not to interrupt me. She agreed, with hostility, and I said: "Working with you is like being subjected to toxic waste." This was the worst thing I ever said to anyone. Then, of course, I burst into tears. We had a long conversation, during which I said that there is always a grain of truth in everything, and in this situation, it was that she should get more recognition. I reminded her that I had always asked to put her on the book's title page, but the publisher refused, saying that other editors would ask for the same thing. So, I asked her to write the foreword. She said it would be an honor, and she did. The next morning, she removed her upper clothes, as if to bare her heart in apology, and it broke my heart. We went on to do one more book together, *The Bread Bible*. And as promised, she managed to control herself.

Learning the Art of Strudel and Other Pastry Doughs

To complete my research for *The Pie and Pastry Bible*, I accepted an invitation to travel around Austria to learn about making strudel. The young pastry chef at the Hilton hotel teased me by having me throw his pizza dough up into the air, and it landed on my chest. He started to cry when I left, saying he couldn't get anyone to help him because bakers were unwilling to get up so early in the morning. I also persuaded Denmark to invite me to study Danish pastry by letting them know that I had the same birthday as Hans Christian Andersen. I had asked Julia Child's advice, and she warned me that, those days, they were using shortening instead of butter and that I should instead take a class with Dieter Schorner at the French Culinary Institute in New York City. I did both, and they were wonderful learning experiences.

In 2015, the Austrian Tourist Office invited me to the event celebrating the 50th anniversary of the movie *The Sound of Music*. I was so proud of my strudel ability I went up to

Maria von Trapp, sharing with her that I was part Austrian and had strudel in my blood. When she stared at me in response, I asked her if she spoke English. The woman accompanying her said reproachfully, "Of course." I retreated silently to my seat.

The Pie and Pastry Bible was a great success and one of my largest, most comprehensive books. One of the groundbreaking techniques was a pizza recipe, in which I came up with the idea to stir the dough by hand, which was the first dough recipe to use a no-knead method! Another was the Churrant Pie, a variation on a sour cherry pie, which involved an optional stuffing of red currants into each cherry, to keep it round and bursting with extra flavor and juiciness—an idea of Elliott's. I also created many pie crusts, including the Cream Cheese Butter Crust which remains my top favorite. When I thanked the esteemed Harold McGee for creating the technique of rolling the butter into flakes with the flour mixture in a zip-seal bag to make a flakier crust, his response was: "You're welcome, but I got that technique from you!"

Promoting the Book

Maria invited me to inspire the sales force at the Cornell University's Cornell Club. For courage, I wore my mother's Cornell ring. Because she had much larger hands than mine, I had to wear it on my middle finger. I started the talk saying how, the night before, I was not nervous at the Toronto IACP talking to 1,000 people. But I was nervous talking to them because they were going to be the most important people in my life for the next year, and I was going to give them the tools to sell this book. To emphasize my point, I said that I was bringing my mother's ring home to Cornell, raising my middle ring finger without realizing the symbolism. Uproarious laughter ensued, and it served as a real icebreaker!

The Four Seasons Restaurant in New York gave me a press party where I demonstrated pulling strudel. The chefs all came up from the kitchen to watch as they had never seen this technique before. The most dramatic part was when, stretching the small baseball-size dough into a 48-inch round translucent sheet, four of my women friends/colleagues leapt to the table to help, and the sheet of dough ballooned into the air.

Chris Kimball reviewed *The Pie and Pastry Bible* saying that the apple pie was wonderful but not worth the extra effort of reducing the liquid. He went on to say that he agrees with Einstein (get this—Kimball and Einstein!) that the hand of God can be seen in the overall picture. I responded in a letter (he never posted) saying: "While I agree with you and Einstein, I sure know where to find the rest of *her* body—in the details." I prefer what *The Washington Post* wrote: "If God is in the details, as the aphorism goes, then Beranbaum must have one foot in heaven."

Woody and I have judged many a pie contest, but only one time did a contestant use my best pie crust, and that was at the Culinary Institute of America. Each student walked into the room carrying his or her pie, but only one had a sculpture on the top of a tree branch with a tiny pastry apple dangling from it. It was Lenny Liu, a Chinese neurologist, who planned to open a restaurant in Los Angeles. He was the one who used my pie crust and won the contest.

The only time we encountered my pie crust, but not as a pie, was a hilarious surprise. We were at dinner in San Francisco at State Bird Provisions in 2013. The guests included four pastry chefs, but only one was a man, and that was Woody. The others were the owner Nicole Krasinski, Michelle Polzine from 20th Century Café, and moi. The dessert plate was garnished with the best pastry I'd ever tasted which turned out to be mine. And the toffee pudding was Michelle's. What a bonding moment!

1998 Richard Adler and the *Queen Elizabeth 2* Ocean Liner

When I was a little girl, still in the high chair, I remember hearing my grandmother singing "everybody loves a lover; I'm a lover; everybody loves me." Many years later, I did two demos on the QE2 crossing the Atlantic Ocean, and one of the other "entertainers" was the writer of that song—Richard Adler! I offered to create a cake for him if he would write a song for me (the song just mentioned was for Doris Day). He said, "That's easy: Rosie, Rosie, Rosie; life with you would be so cozy." And Elliott, my late husband, who had tears in his eyes when Richard sang his own song with a voice damaged by throat cancer, responded with: "Is that the best you can do?!"

Rose and Elliott on the QE2

The Melbourne Food and Wine Festival

I had the honor of being invited twice to be a presenter at this Australian festival. The first time was to promote *The Pie and Pastry Bible*. I loved the Australians and also the fellow presenters, such as Anthony Bourdain. Interestingly, Anthony was a lot more charming than he seemed in *Kitchen Confidential*. For one thing, he never used his favorite word—fuck! The organizer told me that my book sold a lot better than his "because they are serious people!"

I loved Moshe Basson, who is originally from Iraq and the famed chef/owner of The Eucalyptus restaurant in Jerusalem. He was one of my favorite presenters and became a dear friend. When I asked him how to find the "Long Table" about a mile away, he pointed to some buildings and gave me very precise directions. When I asked him how he was able to do this, he calmly said: "I was a sharpshooter in the Israeli Army—I couldn't afford to make a mistake!" Some years later, he was chosen by Pope Francis to be included in the Netflix series *Stories of a Generation*. I also made a new and lifelong friend, Anna Schwartz, who had an extraordinary art gallery in Melbourne and now has another one in Sydney.

A few years before my second trip to Melbourne, I visited Dom Pérignon in the Champagne region of France. As a journalist, I was invited to join a group called the Young Millionaires Club. When one of the attendees, Bernice Tang from Singapore, asked about my books, she almost screamed with delight because her young daughter so loved *The Cake Bible* she refused to go to boarding school in California unless she could take the book with her! Bernice then invited me to come to visit her in Singapore.

Coincidentally, the airline partner of the second Food and Wine Festival just happened to be Singapore Airlines, and Singapore was the stop on the way to Australia, so I took up the invitation. It turned out that Bernice Tang was owner of the Tang Plaza Hotel and Tang Square. She drove me all over Singapore and made sure that I had a tasting of the famed fruit durian along with a fabulous lunch. I invited her to visit me in New York City but admitted that there was no Beranbaum Boulevard!

Unexpected Acclaim

The word got around that as well as being a precision baker, I also knew fine cooking, whether making it at home or enjoying it in a restaurant.

A favorite and humorous mention, stemming from my reputation for perfection, was in *The New York Times* magazine article "A Taste for Seduction" by Jonathan Reynolds: "Make something slightly ambitious. Although I prefer simplicity at a restaurant, the perfectly cooked chicken breast is not going to accomplish what you want unless your date is Rose Levy Beranbaum." This was published in 9-24-2000.

2003 *The Bread Bible*

Of all my books, this one was the most challenging due to my limited experience. But I love baking bread more than anything else and was determined to do a book on it. When Maria asked her husband, John, for advice, saying: "What does Rose know about baking bread?" His response was: "Whatever she needs to know she will find out!" And found out I did, which was a major learning adventure.

My Bread Journey

Many years ago, when I was a freshman at the University of Vermont, I met a bearded backwoodsman the students called "Bert the Beatnik." As he vigorously stirred his sourdough starter, he informed me that, "A woman should be able to bake bread." I received this as a great fundamental truth, and it aroused in me the feeling that I would never really be a woman if I hadn't at least made one loaf of bread. Seventeen is an age when girls ask each other how they will know when they are truly women. Some thought it would be when they lost their virginity, but I knew differently. Bread would do it. This was the early '60s, before hippies, before the Vietnam War, even before Julia Child became a major presence.

Keeping Your Mother Alive

I first fell in love with bread when my dearest colleague and friend, the late Flo Braker, brought me to meet Kurtis Baguley at his restaurant in San Francisco. She told me that his signature dessert, The Bostini, was based on my chiffon cake. It was so delicious I added the recipe to *Rose's Heavenly Cakes*. But it was his olive bread, the best bread I'd ever tasted, that had me begging for the recipe. Kurtis gave me some starter, saying to be sure to feed it flour and water. Another wonderful friend, Nancy Oakes, at her restaurant Boulevard, offered me some bread flour when I said that I needed it to feed my "mother" until I got back to the East Coast. The starter exploded through two resealable plastic bags in the plane's overhead bin.

There is a satisfaction derived from the art of baking bread that I get from no other kitchen activity. Not for me, a bread machine that would rob me of the pleasure of feeling the dough come to life under my hands. Just knowing that the bread dough is alive and rising in a warm spot in the boiler room fills me with unspeakable contentment. Often, when I know I will be forced to sit all day proofing a manuscript, I reward myself by making bread so that I will have an excuse to get up every hour to check its progress.

Perhaps the most exciting part about making bread is that the yeast is a dormant living organism that you bring to life, feeding it so that it will grow and expand, providing texture and flavor to the bread. It also seems utterly amazing that just flour, water, yeast, a bit of salt, and maybe sugar, judiciously proportioned, can be transformed into the most perfect loaf of bread.

Yeast is an amazing organism. A pastry chef friend once told me she had a yeast infection that wasn't responding to medication. I told her that yeast hates salt (avoid recipes that have you adding the yeast and salt at the same time) and that she should make up a super-saturated solution and use it as a douche but not to tell her doctor, as he'll surely say: "What does a pastry chef know?" Well, she did what I advised, and it was cured, and her doctor said exactly what I predicted as she only listened to one half of my advice and not the half that said not to tell the doctor! I've been hoping for a yeast infection for years now (to no avail) so I could try it in bread—after all—yeast is yeast. I would call it yoni bread.

My dad, who had the monopoly on bagel peels (long paddles used to move bagels around in the oven) throughout New York City, Queens, The Bronx, Brooklyn, Staten Island, and New Jersey, was visiting me when I was testing bagel recipes. Though he had never made a bagel in his life, working in wood gave him a sense of how best to shape the dough to develop the chewy texture of my childhood. He told me the story of how he had made a sourdough and was so disappointed that, when paddling up the Hudson River, during portage of the canoe, the container broke, so he couldn't use it. When I asked him what it looked like, he reported Technicolor, and I told him that if he had used it, I would never have been born because that was bad bacteria, and he might have died.

2000 The Creation and Care of My Now 26-Year-Old Sourdough Starter

I have never been a big fan of very sour sourdough bread and wasn't planning to include it, but Maria insisted, so I went about creating my own starter. As anyone who has done this knows, the moment the starter is at its peak, after many days of refreshing (feeding with flour and water), it suddenly bursts through the plastic wrap covering it.

The miracle happened on New Year's Day, and though it is very personal, I have to share it with you. My husband, Elliott, and I were making love, and at the exact moment for me, of what the French discreetly call "crisis," the starter exploded with a loud bang in the next room! At first, I was frightened, but then, I realized that the starter was ready and had to laugh! In the tradition of proud starter creators, I gave it a name—Billow.

I've been feeding my starter once a week with extra flour when going away for longer. My devotion to my starter was perfectly expressed in a conversation with my dear friend Erin Jeanne McDowell when out popped: "I need a nap but haven't fed the starter yet."

I gave some of the starter to Woody when he was still in the Twin Cities, and he fed it religiously for two years, filling his entire freezer but never daring to make a loaf bread. Eventually, he asked what to do with all the pucks of discard and ended up giving it to friends.

Finally, I persuaded him to make beer bread because it was a perfect beginners' bread, using the food processor, and also, because of his love of beer.

My Bread Education and Related Stories

I first met and fell in love with Kathleen Weber's breads at my first dinner at The French Laundry in Yountville, California. When the wait person told me that the bread at that time was not made in-house, I lost no time in asking my northern California friends to find out who was baking the bread. I was in the process of writing *The Bread Bible* and put in a call to Kathleen Weber, timidly asking if she would give me the recipe for her seeded wheat sourdough bread that I so loved.

I was stunned by her generous response. She actually said that she was honored and proceeded to send me a detailed recipe in addition to the flour and yeast she used for the bread, and she even offered to send the water! And that is how I fell in love with Kathleen, as a perfect reflection of the goodness, beauty, and integrity of her bread.

When an advance copy of Kathleen's bread book, *Della Fattoria Bread*, arrived at my home, I opened it up immediately and, to my amazement, saw my recipe for brioche! I had completely forgotten that, a few years before, Kathleen asked for permission to use it for the book, and of course, I had been delighted. I have to admit tears of joy came to my eyes that life seemed to have come a full circle. In the headnote, she wrote: "And to this day, Rose's brioche is the only one I've ever made. It looks like golden satin and is the softest most elastic dough I have ever worked with." I never visited the San Francisco Bay Area without a visit to, tragically now, the late Kathleen Weber in Petaluma.

As part of my bread education, Mark Fiorentino, super-talented bread baker, allowed me to spend several weeks doing a "stage" at Restaurant Daniel. I breathed in every second of the experience. He was so encouraging, supportive, and humble, and when I told him in despair that my breads never come out the same way twice, he said: "Neither do mine. Half the time, I don't know what I'm doing."

I also did a stage at the French Culinary Institute with someone born to bake bread, Amy Quazza, head of the bread baking department. Not only did Amy teach me to be unafraid of very sticky dough, but she also volunteered to help prepare bread for the photo shoot.

A True Visionary

Michael Batterberry, publisher of *Food Arts* magazine, was one of the most brilliant and eloquent people I've ever known. He gave me the profound compliment of my life, writing in the foreword: "If civilization were to fall, this volume could be used to help jump-start it." Each time I read what he wrote for *The Bread Bible* (and he only ever wrote two forewords), tears come to my eyes. The only two people for whom he wrote forewords were me and chef Suvir Saran, whose foreword to *Masala Farm* I wrote.

Michael gave me the assignment to write "The Sugar Bible," saying that he knew I was busy writing a cookbook, but I was the only one to do it, and he would wait for however long it took. In Tasmania 2000, it ended up getting the Gourmand Award's Best Food or Wine Article in the World. Two other favorites were "The Vanilla Bible" and a column I named "Rose Nose." He assigned two senior editors to my stories: Jim Poris, who said that I was the most logical person he ever knew, and Gary Tucker, who wrote my Silver Spoon Award and once told me that I "write in the sunshine." I loved them all, including Ariane Batterberry, and considered them family. Michael was fondly called "The Bat." He had a deliciously wry sense of humor. Once, I ran into him at a food show and shared with him an article called "Better than Sex Cake." I remarked that they needed a sex therapist. His response was that the Cool Whip was what put it over the top. It took years for him to give me the Silver Spoon Award because, in the words of Gary, I was too young—the downside of looking so much younger than I actually was.

Michael held a Sweets Conference at the Culinary Institute of America in Napa and invited me to do a presentation. Pastry chefs from all over the world were in attendance. Since one of the main sponsors was the California Raisin Board, I chose to do the panettone from *The Bread Bible,* which had golden raisins. The next morning, Yusuf Yaran from Turkey came up to me and whispered in my ear: "I couldn't stop thinking about you all night." I thought, "Uh-oh," until, to my relief and delight, he went on to say: "That panettone!" One of the chefs at the CIA made another of my panettones to give to the Batterberrys, who had been invited to breakfast the following day, but they confessed that, between the two of them, they consumed the entire pastry!

Best Bread Friends

The bread story dearest to my heart comes from my dear friend Angelica Pulvirenti, who grew up in Ragusa, Sicily. It was her responsibility to keep the rising bread dough warm under her bed blankets when she slept and then to take them to the communal baking oven. Each person would score their bread with a unique design so that it could be recognized when it came out of the oven. There was only one starter in town, and it was passed from home baker to baker.

I grew up across Central Park from Nach Waxman's Kitchen Arts & Letters bookstore and studied modern dance at the 92nd Street YMCA where my mother would continue to go for years to swim. It was just a block from Nach's bookstore, and on a regular basis, she would stop by to remind Nach, the owner, that her daughter was writing a cookbook and that she hoped he would carry it someday. One day, she tripped on a bump in the rug at the store, and according to Nach, he felt so bad when she fell that he promised he would carry my book when it was published. And that book was *The Cake Bible*. I once told him he should write a book on woodworking—Nach on Wood.

Nach had such a deep understanding of cookbooks and the industry that he was the one to whom I turned when I had a question about title, design, or subject. After *The Bread Bible* was published, he sent me this treasured letter which hangs on the wall of my baking kitchen. Not only did he take the time to write this letter, but he also called me a few weeks later when he hadn't heard from me. It turned out it had been lost in the mail, so he wrote it a second time!

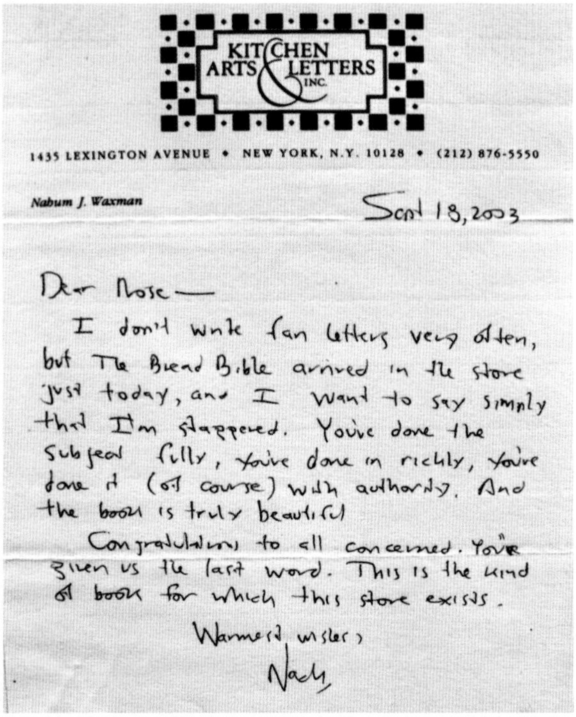
KITCHEN ARTS & LETTERS INC.

1435 LEXINGTON AVENUE • NEW YORK, N.Y. 10128 • (212) 876-5550

Nahum J. Waxman

Sept 18, 2003

Dear Rose—

I don't write fan letters very often, but The Bread Bible arrived in the store just today, and I want to say simply that I'm staggered. You've done the subject fully, you've done in richly, you've done it (of course) with authority. And the book is truly beautiful.

Congratulations to all concerned. You've given us the last word. This is the kind of book for which this store exists.

Warmest wishes

Nach

Nach Waxman Letter

Dear Rose,

I don't write fan letters very often, but The Bread Bible *arrived in the store just today, and I want to say simply that I'm staggered. You've done the subject fully, you've done it richly, you've done it (of course) with authority. And the book is truly beautiful.*

Congratulations to all concerned. You've given us the last word. This is the kind of book for which the store exists.

Warmest wishes, Nach

Three people gave us an incredible gift to make this book and the recipes most approachable.

Marie and Jim Wolf, in the Twin Cities, did an intensive bake-through after the book was published, with a group we called "Rose's Alpha Bakers." Marie baked her way through every recipe in the book, and Jim took photos of all the steps.

Matthew Boyer, in Texas, surprised us years later by baking every bread and having a stunning finished photo of each of them, enabling people to see exactly what the finished loaf looked like, all on the one page on our blog, www.realbakingwithrose.com.

I have long admired Jennifer Garner as an actress, but when I learned about her Instagram account Pretend Cooking Show, I discovered another dimension to her as a beautiful mother, baker, and supporter of children through her company Once Upon a Farm. In December 2018, I was on a train ride with my friend and colleague Marissa Rothkopf Bates, scrolling through Instagram stories, when I saw one by Jennifer Garner, praising my Chocolate Bread from *The Cake Bible*. My surprised response to Marissa was "that can't be THE Jennifer Garner!" Her response to me was: "It has to be her!" And it was! In 2019, she did another episode featuring my Multigrain Bread from *The Bread Bible*, saying that it was her kid-requested holiday favorite. Baking has connected Jen and me as close, valued, and loving friends.

Jen Garner Making Multigrain Bread

The Story of My Best Bread

Many years ago, Peter Kump and I organized an event at Café Beaujolais, owned by his son, Christopher, and daughter-in-law, Margaret Fox, in Mendocino, California. When I tasted their Tyrolean Sunflower Bâtard, which contained 10 grains, I pronounced it to be the best bread ever and asked Peter if his son might share the recipe. His response was: "I'm sure he would since he got the recipe from a little, old baker where we spend summers in the mountains in Austria." So, we asked Christopher, and I was disappointed to learn that he could not share the recipe because the bread was his top-selling item.

On my return home, I told the story to my protégé David Shamah, who came up with the perfection solution: "Buy the cereal mix which probably has the same 10 grains." So, I sent away for the cereal and counted out the grains. The bread wasn't quite the same, but I loved the version I created so much I also made a loaf variation by adding a bit of oil to soften the crust and crumb. I called it Tyrolean Ten Grain Bread

COVID-DRIVEN FOOD BLOGGING

2020 The COVID pandemic, and the need to work from home, resulted in a massive increase of foodies using all social media forms for providing their major source of income from advertising links. Thousands of people discovered the joy of baking bread, and sales of my book *The Bread Bible* soared.

Woody Testing in the Twin Cities

and now call it Multigrain Bread. It has long since been my favorite of all my breads. **RECIPE: Multigrain Bread Loaf (page 250)**

Several years passed when I got a call from Margaret Fox who was in Paris! She was calling to tell me that she and Christopher were getting a divorce and spending a last vacation together. To my astonishment, she went on to say: "And we think it's time to send you the bread recipe you wanted." What beautiful people!

Reading the recipe, I discovered that, instead of using equal amounts of the grains, they had added more sunflower seeds, which explained the name of their bread!

Of all the things I bake, I enjoy baking bread the most. I have a special place in my heart for bread bakers. And I will always be grateful for Margaret and Christopher's creativity and generosity.

I remember at the photo shoot for *The Bread Bible* where Amy, the gifted bread baker who taught bread baking at the French Culinary Institute, couldn't pull off the breads because it was on Riverside Drive by the Hudson River and a very cold winter. Maria came over to me and said: "Should we jump out the window right now?" Desperate for a solution, I finally appropriated the caterer's Styrofoam box, with a bowl of hot water as a proofer.

I love how the love of bread can connect people. When the book was translated into Chinese, I showed the photo of the cover to one of the waiters at the restaurant we had been going to for about 30 years. His eyes widened when he saw it. A few weeks later, we drove over to get takeout for the first time, as I had a bad cold. One of the other waiters (my favorite), who never smiled and barely talked to me in all those years, gave me a big smile and asked me how I was. When I told him I was sick, he smiled even wider and said that I sounded really good. I smiled back, pointed to my head, and said, "not from inside!"

In 2004, I finally was inducted into the James Beard Foundation's Who's Who of Food & Beverage in America. Michael Batterberry came up to congratulate me and said in his sonorous voice: "Long overdue."

2009 *Rose's Heavenly Cakes*

This is the first book that Woody and I worked on together. My dearest friend and esteemed colleague Lisa Yockelson, in Washington, DC, knew of my dream to have a four-color book with photos of every cake, so in an act of extraordinary generosity, she recommended her editor Pam Chirls, at Wiley, saying that I had paved the way for serious baking books and deserved a beautiful one.

Pam was a first-rate editor and friend and gave me the book of my dreams! Lisa wrote the exquisite foreword to the book, and I dedicated a cake to her I named The Pink Pearl Lady in the following book, *The Baking Bible*. We both cried when the publisher Wiley was purchased by Houghton Mifflin Harcourt, and Pam was required to stay behind because she edited the Culinary Institute of America cookbooks.

Lisa Yockelson and Rose

Woody and Rose Proofing *Rose's Heavenly Cakes*

Working with My First Full-Time Assistant Woody—by Long Distance

Since Woody was living in Minneapolis, Minnesota, he weekly emailed his test reports and photos. He soon was offering suggestions for fixing and for writing a recipe. We would have phone calls a couple of times a month. When it came to the critical "read through of the proof edits," he came out for a week for us to go over them together.

Along with Woody testing recipes came an unusual group of taste testers—Woody's fellow students from the Twin City T'ai Chi'uan Studio. Fellow students, Rondi Atkin and Lisa Strong, became our best evaluators. We used many of their suggestions. Also, Sifu Paul Abdella's observations resulted in our revising some recipes. Woody even used his tai chi sword to cut the cakes!

I had a vision for the cover of having a dark glazed chocolate cake adorned with bright red currants, but they were out of season and could not be sourced from anywhere in the world. Then the miracle occurred: When we arrived at the studio, the prior food stylist had not bothered to clean out the freezer, and one of the things she left behind were red currents. To my amazement, even after defrosting, they still held their perfect shape!

Ben Fink did the stunning photographs for the book. In 2011, he did his first video portrait as a gift for me called *A Moment with Rose*. It launched him into a whole new aspect of his career, making movie-style trailers for author's cookbooks.

Rose's Heavenly Cakes Launch and Awards

Caitlin Williams Freeman and her husband, John Freeman, made a memorable launch party in Oakland, California, which coincided with the opening of their Blue Bottle Coffee factory. She had asked permission to feature my white velvet cake as a component in her upcoming book *Modern Art Desserts*, and she served the cake at the event. I wrote the foreword for her book, and we are still dear friends.

Our book won Book of the Year Award at the International Association of Culinary Professionals conference and awards in Portland, Oregon. When it was announced, I was busy texting everyone about having won in the "best baking" category, and Woody had to urge me to get up to receive the Book of the Year Award which I was totally not expecting.

I'll always remember going backstage and seeing Thomas Keller who gave me a big hug. I said: "*You* should have won." And he said: "You deserve it." Not only is he a most extraordinary chef, but he is a beautiful, generous person I've long admired. He was up for the Book of the Year Award for his book, *Ad Hoc at Home*. Back on the East Coast, Gypsy Lovett, head of PR at Wiley, was the first to text "OMG OMG OMG," and our wonderful editor, Pam Chirls, texted that she went to sleep with her cell phone on her belly, and when it vibrated, she *knew*!

INSTAGRAM BECOMES A PLATFORM

2010 Instagram app launched to instant popularity. My total Instagram followers very quickly surpassed that of my website/blog.

The Story of Zach Townsend's La Bomba—All Because of Gelatin and a Japanese Chocolate Lacquer Glaze

In September 2001, I went to Japan to visit my dear friends Yoko and Ushio Sakuma who were living in Kyoto. On the way back to Tokyo, Yoko took me to a little jewel box of a pâtisserie owned by pastry chef Hidemi Sugino. We tasted a wide assortment of his specialties and marveled over how he could create such perfection in such a small space. What impressed me most was a chocolate glaze as shiny as lacquerware. We had one language in common which was French. Sugino-san gave me a copy of his book, which was in Japanese, and said that the recipe was in it and that all the recipes could be made with ingredients from a supermarket.

Yoko translated the recipe for me, but I will admit to having been intimidated by it. Five years went by, and in September 2006, an amazing coincidence took place. I got an email from Zach Townsend, a chocolatier living in Texas, asking me about gelatin and how to use it. My mind made the unlikely leap, and I wrote back asking if he was trying to make a shiny chocolate glaze. The answer was yes!

Zach had discovered a little cake coated with a shiny chocolate, called Le Valentin, at a pâtisserie in Paris called La Petite Rose. The owner had allowed him to watch her make it but would not give him the recipe.

I asked if she was by chance Japanese. When he said yes, I realized that she must have learned it from chef Sugino-san, which turned out to be the case! So, I proposed a deal to Zach: Since I had the recipe and he had the experience of watching it made, I would send him the recipe, and he would try to reproduce the cake, and I would put it in my upcoming book with credit to him. I also said that, someday, we should meet in Paris at La Petite Rose, and yes—we did! This glaze was the first "mirror glaze."

Zach Townsend and Rose in Paris

In May 2009, the year before *Rose's Heavenly Cakes* containing Zach's rendition of the cake and glaze called La Bomba was published, Zach and I met in Paris. We had many adventures and dinners while tooling around Paris, including the most amazing brunch at the Hôtel de Crillon. One afternoon, we visited La Petite Rose and ordered "the cake." To our mutual delight, we preferred Zach's version. We've been friends and colleagues, and Zach has been an invaluable proofreader for all our books since. He even hosted two press trips in Dallas. The most memorable event was given by Eleanor Roosevelt's granddaughter, Chandler. Our favorite chocolate cookie is from Zach and is included in *The Cookie Bible*. **RECIPE: Zach's Chocolate-Studded Truffle Cookies (page 244)**

Maria Guarnaschelli never forgave me for leaving her, but she took the high road saying that she was sure it was going to be a wonderful book. Then, at an event, I went up to her to give her a hug, and she raised her hand like a lion's paws snarling: "Don't kiss me!" I was so deeply hurt I was at a loss for words, and instead, I made the swiping motion of erasing her words like on a blackboard. I turned around and left. I knew I would always love Maria, but it was over for me. Years later, Maria's wonderful young granddaughter, Ava, and I exchanged healing emails, and in one of hers to me, she said that on her grandmother's deathbed, in 2021, she was saying how much she loved me and loved working with me.

After the book launch and touring, we thought it would be wonderful if there could be a bake-along featuring all the recipes in the book, excluding the wedding cakes, to extend the social media presence of *Rose's Heavenly Cakes*. Blogs were becoming the number one social media format. In 2007, I had launched my *Real Baking with Rose* website/blog, sponsored by General Mills. I also had the inspiration to have them produce a video-enhanced e-book which I presented to the publisher due to my affiliation with General Mills. It was the first cookbook to offer this.

PUBLISHERS' FINANCIAL SUPPORT

2015 Publishers minimized financial support for book promotion, expecting an author to provide it from social media financial sources.

I asked Marie Wolf, who blogged her bake-through of *The Bread Bible*, if she would lead a bake-along of this book, too. She gladly set up and administrated her own blog, *Heavenly Cake Bakers,* with fellow bloggers around the world posting their stories and photos of the recipe of the week from the book. Marie would later start another bake-along for *The Baking Bible*.

2014 *The Baking Bible*

After *The Cake Bible*, this is my best-selling cookbook. It is no doubt because it covers the entire realm of new sweet baking recipes, including, cakes, pies, tarts, and other pastries, cookies, candy, breads, and yeast pastries. Woody participated in helping me write the recipes. Shortly after reviewing the manuscript, Pam informed us that we had overwritten by 80 pages. Instead of cutting about 30 recipes, Woody suggested cutting the section with four wedding cake recipes. (The whole section of wedding cakes was later included in *The Cake Bible* revision.)

Testing, Writing, and Post-Production

Woody continued with testing and having the tai chi students as our taste testing group. He moved to be near our home in Hope, New Jersey, as post-production was beginning, for which I had added a new office addition so that we could work side by side. To save the expense of mailing printed page proofs of edited manuscripts, most publishers had now converted to using the Microsoft Word Track Changes function to make it possible to electronically edit queries by editors and author responses. When it came to the proof edit phase, we asked Zach Townsend to be one of the proofreaders because of his expertise. He would be our proof editor for our subsequent books.

The Photo Shoot

The book was also graced with stunning photos by Ben Fink. He rented Barry Wine's house, situated in the beautiful Hudson Valley, New York, for two weeks. Caitlin Williams Freeman, formerly of Miette Bakery, came all the way from California to be the stylist, assisted by Erin Jeanne McDowell, who also made us fabulous lunches. She had recently graduated from the Culinary Institute of America and would later become the stylist for all of our subsequent books. Most stunning was the Kouign Amann, photographed in Ben's black-on-black style and cut to show the pastry's flakiness; it appeared to be levitating off the surface against a black background. It was the perfect subject for the cover as it crossed baking categories of pastry, bread, and cake.

The styling and photography shoot involved eight of us with Caitlin and Erin as the main styling team, Woody and me as the second styling team, Ben and his partner on photography with a props designer, and Alison Lew from Wiley for design ideas. One afternoon, Stephanie Fletcher arrived to say that she was now our new editor because Pam was moved to a new division.

This was Woody's first photo shoot. He was so bothered that only portions of photographed desserts were eaten. This remote location did not give any options for donating.

One of my favorite cakes in the book is The Mango Bango Cheesecake—a request from Madur Jaffrey for which I'm forever grateful. She had asked me to create a mango cheesecake with swirls of mango in the filling. It was a challenge to keep the mango purée from integrating into the batter, but the solution was to concentrate and thicken it.

Faith Willinger, a brilliant American food writer living in Florence, Italy, introduced me to Vinnie Scotto when he was chef at Scotto's (no family relationship). I begged him for his Praline Pecan Meringue cookie recipe he used for his fabulous ice cream sandwich. He sent the recipe within weeks and then I lost it for years. Fortunately, his sister, Donna, had all his recipes on disc and sent it to me so I could put it in this book.

Faith suggested that I get Latini pasta from Vinnie because I used so much of it. For several years, he charged me wholesale and then refused to charge me at all. That was just the way Vinnie was—loving, generous to a fault, and a brilliantly innovative and capable cook. It was he who developed the recipe for thin crust pizza when he worked at Al Forno in Providence, Rhode Island, and when I was working on *The Bread Bible*, he invited me into his kitchen to teach me. I never ate dinner at any of his restaurants without a pizza appearing within minutes of arrival. And I never make pizza without imagining his reproach that I was overloading it.

More Awards

In 2015, the book won the Best Baking Book at the International Association of Culinary Professionals in Washington, DC. Alice Medrich, one of my most admired bakers, also had a book in the same category. When Anne Willan announced the winner, she referred to us as "clash of the baking titans." I looked up the definition of titans, and it was a perfect fit: "Titan Gladiator. Favored warbeasts of the skorne, the versatile titans can be conditioned and equipped for a variety of battlefield (sub baking) roles. The titan gladiator is armed with massive, spiked war gauntlets and uses its weapons and its armored body to pulverize enemy troops and warbeasts (sub pulverizing ingredients for enemy troops)."

2018 *Rose's Baking Basics*

For this teaching book, I was moved to use a quote from Colin Powell: "If you're going to achieve excellence in big things, you develop the habit in little matters. Excellence is not an exception; it is a prevailing attitude."

This is one of the most invaluable of all my books because it is the only one of 14 that has step-by-step photos of almost every recipe. It serves as a companion book to *The Baking Bible*. It is the first of four books that we did with photographer Matthew Septimus. I first met

Matthew Septimus and Rose

Matthew when Linda Angrilli, now retired editor of *Hue* magazine after 37 years at the Fashion Institute of Technology, approached me about doing a feature in this alumni magazine. To save everyone time, I had suggested using one of my existing press photos, but they wanted a candid shot.

Linda brought in photographer Matthew Septimus, a brilliant portrait photographer. He said that, someday, he hoped to work with me, but I told him that I was very devoted to Ben Fink. Then, Ben retired from cookbook photography to do video work and his own books. I wrote to Matthew that it would require several trips from far out in Brooklyn, where he lived, to Hope, New Jersey. His response was one of a true artist: "Whatever it takes." Woody and I made all the step-by-step recipes for him to photograph in my basement studio. Erin rented a studio in New York City to do the full-page beauty shots.

When Woody and I brought the book to Joan Hamburg's radio show on WABC, she asked us, as reportedly she had asked many bakers who appeared on the show, if they could reproduce her mother's marble Bundt cake that had pieces of chocolate suspended in it. Her mother had written the very sketchy recipe on a paper towel on her deathbed. Woody took on the challenge, by making chocolate curls, which suspended beautifully. When we brought the cake to her for approval, she called afterwards to say, to our delight, that her husband, on tasting the cake, exclaimed: "That's Mom's cake!" It became the Comfort Cake in *The Cake Bible* revision, and in 2025, we brought the book to her godson, Dan Barber, of Blue Hill Restaurant as a gift. I also brought him my dearest cousin Marion Bush who became an invaluable provider of wild harvest ingredients to the restaurant.

Dan Barber and Rose at Blue Hill

2020 *Rose's Ice Cream Bliss*

The title's inspiration was that I followed my bliss! I love ice cream more than any other dessert. The foreword was written by a fantastic writer and friend, Marissa Rothkopf Bates, who has now written a cookbook on her favorite subject, *The Secret Life of Chocolate Chip Cookies*. And I wrote the foreword for it!

As a sidenote, one day, Woody and I were on our way to the Culinary Institute of America to do a demo, and I had been rushing to get ready to leave. We stopped part way to have lunch, and when I went to the ladies' room, I discovered that the pants I had intended to wear were missing, and all I had on was pantyhose. Knowing that Marissa's house was on the way, I prayed she would be in, and, sure enough, when we arrived, she had a selection of three pairs of pants from which to choose. That is true friendship.

PHOTOGRAPH BY MATTHEW SEPTIMUS

Team RoseWood

Woody and I had the most glorious time testing the recipes and eating ice cream every day for lunch for many months. We didn't gain weight because that's all we ate for lunch, and we called it the ice cream diet. We also had such fun running over to help Erin and her assistant, Katie Wayne, who were doing most of the prep.

Erin had to keep the house very cold to ensure that the ice cream didn't melt, especially for the cover shot which involved myriad balls of different flavors. She had a whole freezer of extras as backup. Photographer Matthew Septimus said it was the best time in his entire life! It was the perfect team, so for the first time, we asked to include a shot of the team in the book. We continued with this team and included a team photo for the next two books.

2022 *The Cookie Bible*

My dear friend Rabbi Mendy Greenstein wrote to me that, since the cookie book was my 13th book, I might like to know that a rose has 13 petals! He also told me that one of the most important philosophical books of the century is *The Thirteen Petalled Rose* by a woman, Rabbi Adin Steinsaltz.

Although *Rose's Christmas Cookies* is still in print, I wanted to complete the quartet of baking books—cakes, pies and pastries, breads, and cookies—with a more encompassing cookie book.

My grandmother's pet name for me was "Cookie," and although she never baked any, it gave me a special feeling for them. This book contains all of my favorite cookies. It is the only one where we were not physically present for the photo shoot due to the COVID pandemic, but Erin called us via FaceTime all day for our input which made it almost like being there, and the results were spectacular.

2024 The Revision of *The Cake Bible, 35th Anniversary Edition*

When I was getting my college degree, I wrote a paper comparing the book *Joy of Cooking* to M.F.K. Fisher's *The Art of Eating*. Cecily Brownstone, my mentor, who was the food editor for the Associated Press, loved the paper so much she said: "You must send it to Marion Rombauer Becker because she is doing a laborious revision of *Joy of Cooking* and would enjoy hearing some encouragement from a reader." Doubting that my opinion as a student would be of much value, I agreed for Cecily to send it!

I was so grateful to her because I received a most gracious letter from Marion Rombauer Becker, a copy of which I pasted into the original *Joy of Cooking* which was the second cookbook I ever owned and was a gift from my ex-husband in 1963. The letter stated: "Cecily Brownstone just forwarded to me the super review of what you wrote for Food Preparation and Meal Service. It came as a great morale booster as we are working on revision—a long, long—and excruciatingly frustrating process! But with appreciation like yours, it makes our efforts seem more than worthwhile. With thanks and best regards, Marion Rombauer Becker, March 10, 1972."

I thought of this as I started my revision. I knew from my past experience in fashion design that altering a garment was more challenging than starting from scratch. This couldn't have been truer of a cookbook revision.

Cassie Jones became the beloved editor who took over *The Cake Bible* years ago after Maria Guarnaschelli left William Morrow. We had been talking about a revision for years, and I was reluctant because I knew all the beautiful and time-consuming photos would have to be redone, among other things. But when the book's 35th anniversary neared and it was in its 60th printing, my husband, Woody, urged me to go forward with a much-needed complete revision.

So much had changed, including ingredients, equipment, techniques, and technology, I knew it would be an enormous task, and indeed, it took three years for Woody and me to accomplish it. Cassie, at one point, had said the golden words: "Whatever Rose wants, I want." She lived up to that promise. It was worth every effort for the beautiful and informative book we all created, and it was my best publishing experience. An example of new technology is this improved recipe for lemon curd by making it in a microwave without any contact with metal. **RECIPE: Lemon Curd** **(page 227)**

Michelle Gayer, Rose, and Zoë François in Minneapolis

The first two copies were given to our dearest friend Sean Fellin, who invited us to an off-the-press celebration dinner, and to my ophthalmologist, Dr. Amit V. Vora, who patiently postponed my cataract surgery until the book went to press. The inscription was "To Dr. Vora, who gave me new vision to see my revision."

The book launch was held on October 22, 2024, by the Cambridge School of Culinary Arts owner Sean Leonard and his partner, Randy Freidus. There were over 100 attendees, including Suzette and Randy Owen of ThermoWorks, who came all the way from Utah. In gratitude for their generosity and as a gift to their students, we gifted Cambridge Culinary over 1,000 cookbooks from my culinary library.

Another special book signing was held in Woody's hometown in Minnesota at Barnes & Noble. Zoë François was our terrific moderator. The large audience really laughed when each of us admitted to once having been intimated by the other.

The Translations

The Bread Bible was translated into Czech, Russian, and Chinese. *The Cake Bible* was translated into UK English, Spanish, and Chinese.

When I started working with a Chinese publisher, which was a scientific publisher, I thought that the editor, Mia Tian, was doing an excellent job with the translation of *The Bread Bible* based on the detailed, in-depth questions she asked, but on first impression, I thought she was not a very pleasant person. I pictured a sort of stodgy, middle-aged woman with black glasses and no sense of humor. When I met her on her first visit to the U.S. as part of the delegation

Rose's Translated Books

meeting with their American publishing house for *Highlights for Children* magazine in Honesdale, Pennsylvania, the moment I saw her, I cried out in surprise: "You're beautiful!" She said: "So are you!" And we hugged each other.

We went into the conference room and couldn't stop talking for several hours. She brought a beautiful silk scarf for me, and I brought her my new Syn-Glas rolling pin in red, of course. We each pulled out our card case, and lo and behold, they were identical—from Japan. Neither of us had ever seen one like it before. Then, we discovered we're both Aries. A year later, she gave me the honor of naming her first child, and I gave her my mother's name, Lilly. She said it was perfect because her last name "He" meant "water." So now, this little Lilly Water Lilly creates the strongest bond possible in addition to our books together. The book got stellar reviews from every critique in China. And a Chinese friend told me that everyone who bakes bread in China has this book!

ChatBox AI Rose

Tai Blanche's Real Rose

THE IMPACT OF ARTIFICIAL INTELLIGENCE

2025 (and in the future) AI-generated photography and simulated writing style have become a creative and, at the same time, a dangerous tool. AI models already have impacted the styling/photography phase of book and other literary productions, endangering the careers of food stylists, prop stylists, and photographers. An author's writing style can be hijacked to be used by others for their own gain and potentially to discredit an author with fake text. Above is an example of a painting that my friend asked ChatBox AI to create. Without any input instructions, AI appropriated and modified the photograph taken by our portrait painter, Tai Blanche, to use as a reference for the front cover of this book.

15

Teaching, Book Tours, and Travel

Marcel Desaulniers, Standing Next to Rose

In 1979, I joined the Association of Cooking Schools (ACS) in its second year and went to almost every conference around the country and to regional meetings abroad. At the time, there was a divide between cooking school teachers and cookbook writers and chefs, but when chefs started writing cookbooks, the divide quickly narrowed. I encouraged my wonderful friend the late Marcel Desaulniers, of the Trellis Restaurant and also on the board of the CIA, to become a member, and he brought in many other chefs and aspiring writers.

ASSOCIATION OF COOKING SCHOOLS

1978 ACS (Association of Cooking Schools) was founded. It later became the IACP (International Association of Culinary Professionals).

Thanks to the IACP, I was invited to teach at several schools around the country, which brought many strange and interesting experiences and lessons learned as well as taught. My first venture was when I was invited to Norene Gilletz's school in Montreal, Canada. It also turned out to be somewhat of a baptism by fire as it was my first experience on television which Norene had graciously arranged. It happened that the guest who preceded me on that morning show was a professional stripper, so when the host greeted me, it was with a stunning question: "So Rose, have you ever taken off your clothes to earn a living?"

It was 6:30 in the morning, and still half asleep, I was shocked to find myself saying: "So far, I have found it safer putting the icing on the cake." I'm still not entirely sure what exactly about this statement made the host's mouth drop open and proceed, without further tormenting, to the rest of my demonstration. Aside from discovering that, as I was a foot shorter than Norene, I could not reach the demonstration counter and had to work on an inverted 2-foot marble slab she had ordered for my chocolate tempering, the classes went smoothly.

CIA AND JOHNSON & WALES

The Culinary Institute of America (CIA) opened in 1946 and Johnson & Wales in the early 1970s. At the time, it did not accept women, or that would have been first choice for my culinary education. Many students, like David Shamah, would tell me how my books inspired them.

I remember fondly a major ice storm in Dallas during which no one drove, except for the devoted students and cooking school director, La Verle Daley, who courageously braved the dangerous road conditions to take me to dinner at one of the top restaurants, Café Annie. She picked me up wearing a stunning silver fox coat and murmuring regretfully in the most relaxed of Southern drawls that she should have brought her sable coat for me, but it would have been down to my ankles. (I would have just hated that!)

One of my favorite experiences was teaching at Lee Barnes's cooking school in New Orleans. She was a good friend of chef Paul Prudhomme, who became one of my dearest friends.

Paul Prudhomme and Rose

I remember with amusement a student at a Pasadena, California, cooking school asking me how I stayed so slim, as she enjoyed the lunch I had prepared along with everyone else—except me, because no one had thought to offer me anything to eat, and the line of students wanting to ask questions kept me from getting any food.

Best of all, at a conference in Texas, the former IACP president, Nathalie Dupree, introduced me to Shirley Corriher, which led to many adventures and scientific discoveries about baking. At the time, Nathalie ran the cooking school at Rich's Department Store in Atlanta, Georgia, and invited me to teach a week-long class. She scheduled Shirley the week before so we could take each other's classes. I bought each of us a fake Oriental rug to stand on because a week of standing on marble would have been crippling!

There also was a minor earthquake in Anchorage, Alaska, during my stint as a guest teacher at the Saucy Sisters Cooking School. There were three major reasons I had been eager to accept the invitation to teach there. The first was a promise to see some of the scenic wonders of the area. The second was a promise to be provided with free-range eggs, a rarity for me living in New York. The third was a great headline I wanted to provide to the local press who was planning to publicize the classes: "New Yorker Brings Snow to Alaska." The "snow" referred to one of my favorite dessert recipes I was planning to teach.

The scenery was awesome. And I will always remember the chilling sensation of touching running water that was below freezing temperature. The free-range eggs ranged from peewee to jumbo, making it impossible to know how many eggs were being incorporated into each recipe. (From then on, I always offered volume and weight along with the number of eggs.) The Lemon Snow dessert missed the deadline due to the earthquake and never got into the local paper. But clever headlines aside, it is such a perfect dessert, be it summer or winter, Alaska or Florida.

Simca in Paris

IACP offered many regional meetings around the world. One was in Paris, where I met Simone "Simca" Beck. Simca was one of the culinary greats who devoted her long life to the enjoyment, knowledge, and teaching of food. It was she, together with Julia Child in *Mastering the Art of French Cooking*, who brought French culinary tradition to America, raising our culinary consciousness and changing forever the way in which we think about eating. I wish I could have had the chance to have known her better, because she possessed three of my very favorite qualities: passion, devotion, and irrepressible honesty. I only had the pleasure of meeting her once, many years ago at that regional meeting of the IACP in Paris, but that occasion was memorable.

One of the events was a dinner at the venerable restaurant Le Taillevent. I heard that Simca would be a guest of honor at dinner and hoped for the chance to meet this culinary legend, not imagining more than a short introduction at best, considering the large number of people present at the meeting, some of whom, no doubt, already knew her and would be anxious to talk to her. I arrived early and decided to take a seat at the dinner table rather than stand in the anteroom chatting with friends over drinks.

No one had yet entered the dining room, but for some unaccountable reason, I decided for once to sit alone and perhaps meet some new colleagues instead of gravitating as usual to the people I already knew. I remember thinking, "Let's see who I will attract," when in walked Simca, all alone. She looked around the room, and to my amazement, instead of reserving a table for friends or acquaintances, she came over and sat next to me. It was a gift from the gods and a lesson in humility. There was I, congratulating myself on my fearless courage of sitting alone, and there was Simca, more courageous still, coming over to sit next to a complete stranger!

Soon, other colleagues came pouring into the room, and we were no longer alone. It was a delightful evening. The food was wonderful, and the conversation still more delicious. Three statements of Simca's remain indelible in my memory. She said that, to remember the essence and taste of French food, it was necessary to come back to France at least every other year. When we all agreed that one of the sauces was far too salty, it was Simca who called over the maître d', crooked her index finger at him, and commanded him in no uncertain terms to tell the chef that the sauce was "*trop salé*."

Finally, at the end of the evening, she further warmed my heart by pronouncing that "most people in their lifetimes will never speak French the way you do, not having been born in France," thus divining my greatest pride. In short, after one evening, I was awed by her and trusted her integrity absolutely.

Our paths never crossed again, but when *The Cake Bible* was completed, I sent Simca an inscribed copy, and she wrote me a treasured letter with the ultimate compliment: "Not since our 'Bible' has one been written like this." The incredibly generous statement from her meant the world to me and now graces the back cover of *The Cake Bible* revision.

Sleeping Over Clinton

I had gotten to know my favorite author, Pat Conroy, when I contacted him asking for the recipe for duck and scuppernong grapes he had written about in his novel *The Prince of Tides*. We had a delightful phone conversation during which he told me that he learned something important about salting the inside of chicken from one of my savory books. And he invited me to visit him when the end of my book tour was to bring me to San Francisco.

I was on the book tour for *Rose's Christmas Cookies* in the fall of 1991, working my way west to San Francisco to do media events and also to visit Pat Conroy. It was the golden age of successful cookbooks where they put me up at top hotels such as The Ritz in Chicago. I had a suite on the eighth floor with an incredible panoramic view and a huge dining room which would never be used. I also had a budget to invite press people to dinner at the best restaurants in town, so every night, I dined royally and with interesting conversations. I was disappointed, however, that the food editor of the main paper, *Chicago Tribune*, opted not to come to see me at the hotel, sending someone under her with the following message: "My father is a rabbi, and I'm wondering why would you, a Jewish woman, write a Christmas cookie book?" My response was: "My great-great-grandfather was a rabbi and didn't tell me not to."

After several glorious days, I got a call from my editor Maria, who had seen some of the expense reports, asking why I couldn't be more like other authors and some nights just go to my room and have a hamburger. My response was: "If I were that kind of author, you wouldn't want my books!"

One afternoon, when returning to my room at the end of the long hallway, I was surprised to see a man wearing a dark suit and standing in front of the door. "You can't go in!" he said. "It's my room," I countered, "No, it's not—it's Mr. Clinton's." (Bill Clinton was, at the time, running for presidential election.) Apparently, my finger had hit the seventh-floor button instead of the eighth. I turned to leave, but never one to miss such a golden promotional opportunity, I took a few steps back to hand my business card to the man, who evidently was Bill Clinton's secret service agent, saying: "Please tell Mr. Clinton that I will be happy to make his inauguration cake." He smiled, and I went to my room to tell a friend what had transpired saying: "I'm sleeping over Clinton!" My friend warned me that this is politics, and people have been silenced for lesser claims.

I called Pat Conroy to tell him that I was frightened. He assured me that, if anything happened to me, he would take it to the press! But nothing happened, and I never heard anything back from Bill Clinton either. I did have a wonderful visit with Pat and his family. Coincidentally, his wife had also been a medical secretary at NYU. The most amusing part was, when leaving his home, his little girl looked up at me in wonder and said: "You're so famous." Pat and I exchanged amused glances because we both knew he was a lot more famous than *I'd* ever be!

Other Special Travel Experiences

On my first of many chocolate research visits to Switzerland, I had the amazing experience of riding a small train and seeing the Jungfraujoch at the continent's highest railway station. It turned out to be the source of one of my most thrilling but also funniest stories ever!

I was staying with my friend Charlotte in Zürich, and she insisted that I visit the Jungfraujoch because it was such spectacular experience. She sent me off to spend the night in Interlaken, in the Canton of Bern, and although it was summer, she suggested I take her down parka knowing how cold it would be so high up in the glaciers.

The train passed through beautiful mountain towns, stopping at Grindelwald, and then at Eiger Wald, and I was reminded of the Clint Eastwood movie *The Eiger Sanction.* The conductor explained to us that, to reach the final station, we would be going through a tunnel of rock and that there would be only one track, so on the descent, if there were a train mounting, our train would be sidetracked. (Finally, I understood the literal meaning of this word!)

When we reached the top, there was space for only about three people at a time to go out into the small open space, which revealed stunning views of a land of ice, glaciers, and snow-covered mountain peaks. I silently thanked Charlotte for keeping me warm in her parka while all the other tourists were shivering.

When we started the decent, at first everything seemed to be going well, until all of a sudden, the train started slowing down, the conductor leaned his head out of the window, and screamed out what sounded exactly like something my grandmother would have screamed in Yiddish had the end of the world been imminent: "Oy gavooooolt!" I exchanged a look of wide-eyed terror with the other two people in the car who, I could tell by their accent, were from Brooklyn and clearly were thinking exactly what I was thinking which was: "Oh my God—there's another train on its way up and our train didn't sidetrack." We waited for the impending crash, but nothing happened. Then, it dawned on the three of us, at the same moment, that what he was screaming, in a voice conductors the world over call out the stations for all to hear, was "Eiger Waaaald," and we burst into relieved laughter.

Many years later I attended a special Château Margaux dinner at the Four Seasons Restaurant in New York City and had the pleasure of sitting next to one of the owners, Alex von Bidder. Alex was the most charming and elegant man I knew, and I had never really gotten to have a conversation with him before. As we started talking, I noticed that he had the barest trace of an accent and asked him where he was from originally. His answer was Switzerland. By this time, I had visited the country at least six times and knew the regions pretty well, so I asked what part of Switzerland. His answer: "Oh, it was a very small mountain town—I'm sure you never would have heard of it." When I explained how well I knew Switzerland, he couldn't hold out any longer, and I heard the word my psychic soul suspected: "Eiger Wald!" How could I resist? I just had to say it: "Oy! Do I have a story for you!"

One of our most special recent book tour experiences was when Hanaa ElAzizi—a dearest friend, originally from Morocco, who had participated in our book bake-throughs—arranged for us to do a demo at Google in Sunnyvale, California, featuring a recipe from our newest book, the *The Cake Bible, 35th Anniversary Edition.* The cooking school staff did an impeccable mise en place, and the attendees were a delight. Hanaa and her husband, Toby, made an excellent Moroccan dinner that night which included a special cookie that was a family recipe. Crispy, chewy inside, and flavored with subtle orange blossom water, it is included in this book. **RECIPE: Hanaa's Moroccan Almond Cookies (page 242)**

Yotam Ottolenghi and Rose

In 1998, Israel was celebrating its 50th anniversary as a country, and my mother offered to send me to Israel saying that I needed to get in touch with my Jewish heritage which I had rejected when in college. Idealistically, I had wanted to be seen as me—not a woman, not an American, and not a Jew. Israel made me realize that the world was not going to see me the way I saw myself. On this trip, I identified 100% with Israel's spirit and struggle for survival.

The PR booklet for the anniversary sported a cartoon of an American couple—the wife fat and wearing a flowered dress, the husband wearing Bermuda shorts, and the tour guide with a belt of bullets crisscrossing his puffed-out chest and with his hairy arm pointing to a hill that only had one flower on the top, saying: "And all this we did in just 50 years." It mocked the usual arrogance and pride.

On landing at the Tel Aviv airport, there were so many people visiting and without reservations that we all slept on the floor! First thing in the morning, I was first in line to find a room with one of the residents who were hosting us travelers. By sheer and happy coincidence, I was given the home of the food writer for the major newspaper in the city.

I went on several side trips to explore the country. One was a visit to the Golan Heights. The tour guide, Shaoul (Hebrew for Sol), who for three prior days had been trying to seduce the seemingly naive young American me, had all of us gathered around him as he bragged about how he had fought in every war Israel ever had and had won. We were sufficiently spellbound for him to lean back on his little heels, arms outstretched, and say: "I feel just like mama goose!" I don't know what in me made me open my mouth to put him permanently in his place with: "You sound more like papa gander to me." His mouth dropped open revealing loads of gold inlays. Everyone including him (and me) roared with laughter, and I delighted in the change of expression in his eyes from lust to surprised respect.

On this same trip to Israel, I also had a great adventure going by cable car way up the mountain to the ancient fortress, the Masada. I was the only one in the tour group to wear an Arab headscarf, which kept me cool so that, in the extreme heat, I could walk up the mountainous paths to the very top. On the cable car ride down, for the first time in history, the car stalled. An Israeli airline attendant started screaming in fright that we were all going to die. Her boyfriend told her to shut up and that, as an airline attendant, she should be comforting people not scaring them.

My Great-Uncle Nat, whose wife's cousin Mina was married to Hanoch Givton, Director General of Tourism, gave me his office address to be used only in emergency. The first day in Jerusalem, I thought it would be a nice idea to disregard my uncle's advice and just stop by the office to say hello from his American relatives. I arrived before Hanoch and in a panic decided to leave my message with his secretary who kept insisting that "Mar Givton is arriving any moment" and arrive he did. He ushered me into his office to sit opposite him at his desk and asked who I was. When I told him, his response was: "I'm not big on *mishpacha!*" Not knowing what the word meant I asked him, and the answer was RELATIVES! I got up to leave, saying I was only there to say hello and I was leaving. The more I tried to leave the more he insisted I stay until finally he said: "My son Itamar is in the army, so we have an empty room, and I'm sure my wife, Mina, would love to have you stay." I proceeded to move all my belongings from Tel Aviv to their beautiful home in Jerusalem. I had the most amazing two weeks with the Givtons, and afterward, when Hanoch would come to New York, he invited me to dinners and plays. What started as a rejection turned into his falling in love with me. He offered me the dream job of flying around the world reviewing food for the Hilton Hotels if I would become his mistress. My Freudian therapist Greta Frankly suggested that it would be fine to do this as I would be giving him what he wanted and he would be giving me what I wanted. I asked if this wasn't tantamount to prostitution and didn't accept his offer, but we remained close friends, and I continued going to night school and getting my two college degrees.

BRIDGING TWO WORLDS
2012 Yotam Ottolenghi and Sami Tamimi connected two Middle Eastern worlds historically in strife through delicious recipes in their book *Jerusalem*.

The New Basics—Casting Cake on the Water

Sheila Lukins and I have a special history. My Uncle Nat had rented out his farmhouse one summer to Richard Lukins and told me that he liked him so much he would love to have him part of the family, suggesting that I call him for a date. By the end of the summer, I got around to asking for his phone number, but Uncle Nat said it was too late: Every weekend he invited a different girl until one smart cookie started reupholstering his sofa, so he had to invite her back every weekend. When I recounted this story to Sheila years later, she said that she wished she had known this because, at the end of every weekend, she cried and asked him if she should take her sewing machine back.

In 1988, when Sheila Lukins and Julee Rosso were writing their last book together, my recipe became one of the only three from other writers to be included in the 889-page book. When Julee had called to ask me for a recipe, I told her I would give her my signature one from *The Cake Bible* which was the Lemon Poppy Seed Pound Cake. She suggested I give her another recipe instead of my best one, but I insisted that, if I were to be represented in their book, I wanted it to be my favorite cake.

Peter Waldner Cartoon

Even a Cartoon!

Thirteen years later, my niece Joan Beranbaum sent me a cartoon that one of her assistants found in the *New York Daily News*, featuring my name and my cake. I loved it so much I wanted to have a full-size original, so I wrote this letter below to the cartoonist Peter Waldner c/o the Creators Syndicate in Los Angeles. I heard nothing for many months and then, one day, a letter arrived explaining that he actually lived on Shelter Island, New York, on the East Coast and that it took that much time for the Syndicate to send him my letter.

Peter also, in full disclosure, said that he had never heard of *The Cake Bible*, but as a political cartoonist, he always researched. He found the best-selling book of the time was *The New Basics Cookbook,* and the name Beranbaum struck a chord. He said he'd be happy to send me the original in return for a copy of my book! And his drawing is framed and has been gracing my baking kitchen for over three decades. (This more than makes up for my having taken the name Beranbaum which is invariably misspelled.)

December 19, 2002

Dear Peter,

I am the Rose Levy Beranbaum from your November 26th "Flight Deck!"

First, I want to thank you because it is probably the highest moment of my career (aside from winning the book of the year for The Cake Bible *in which the recipe appeared in the first place.) Thank you for giving me a thrill and exultation few people will ever experience in their lifetimes. When I was a little girl and got my first Little Lulu comic book to comfort me during my first nasty booster shot, I never in a million years would have known to dream of ending up in a comic someday. I'd love to know how you came to think of me and my cake. I thought I'd be lucky if people remembered the name of the book, let alone my rather complicated set of names—particularly the last one.*

16

The Birth of Interest in Food Science

I've often been described or introduced as a food scientist which I've always been quick to refute out of self-defense. That was because people, at least unconsciously, divided the world between science and art, and when it came to food, science was considered the antithesis—equated with nutrition and the absence of emphasis on flavor and devoid of humor. Gradually, I came out of the closet into which I really couldn't stuff myself for too long, given my excitement and desire to share what I was discovering about the way ingredients interact and the power this offers to create the best possible tasting things.

A marriage between science and art is the ideal. You have to know why, you have to know how, and you have to know what. By "what," I mean what is good, if not great. Elliott liked saying that I was not a "scientist," but rather, an "alchemist" and that scientists have theories that often are proven wrong, but I keep testing the recipe or concept until it is proven.

Evaluating Superfine Sugar Granules

I began to notice a growing interest in the underpinnings of cooking and baking to the point where books, like Harold McGee's *On Food and Cooking*, Shirley Corriher's *CookWise*, Robert Wolke's *What Einstein Told His Cook*, and my own book, *The Cake Bible*, had become bedtime reading and actual topics of conversation! Robert even had a popular column in *The Washington Post*; Shirley was featured in the *Los Angeles Times Syndicate*, and Harold was in *The New York Times*. In Paris, the esteemed Hervé This started writing a food science column when my friend Max Brossollet bought the *Scientific American* magazine for France and named it *Pour la Science* (which his friend, my Great-Uncle Nat, teasingly called "poor science").

In April 2007, The Experimental Cuisine Collective at NYU was organized by associate professor Amy Bentley, assistant professor of chemistry Ken Kirschenbaum, and chef Will Goldfarb. The mission statement was: "We seek to provide a venue for scientists, food academics, culinary and pastry professionals, journalists, and the dining public to gather and exchange knowledge and contribute to a rigorous scientific understanding of the physical basis for cooking processes."

A Demo and Lecture at NYU

In 2008, I volunteered to do a presentation on flour using angel food cake as the model for the NYU Experimental Cuisine Collective. By coincidence, several of the top people from General Mills happened to be in New York and were in attendance. I asked Woody to fly in from Minnesota to be my assistant, which turned out to be a really good thing! They had assured me that I would have a top PhD student in the food program assisting me. Not only did she not come up with a lapel microphone, which made it difficult doing a demo, she also didn't succeed in arranging to have the IT department provide a videographer.

Fortunately, Woody was able to be the videographer. He had brought his camcorder to film some extras while recording with the IT's camera. Sadly, the tape he used as a backup of the class overwrote the one he really had wanted to keep! The following week, his broomball team got to see me making a cake instead of the team's record-breaking previous game footage.

THE INCREDIBLE SHRINKING EGG YOLK

Early 2000s The egg production industry mostly uses younger laying chickens. Alarmingly, Grade A large yolks that were consistently around 19 grams, now range from 12 grams to 19 grams, and thus, an increase in whites per whole egg. Egg yolks are valuable for emulsification. With *The Baking Bible*, I started giving a range for egg yolks that may be required for an egg yolk-based recipe. Example: Cheesecake 6 (to 9) yolks.

The biggest would-be catastrophe was the slim glass bottle needed for inverting the cake. When I asked the organizer student for the bottle, she proudly presented me with a plastic Pepsi bottle, which would have immediately collapsed as the pan melted the plastic. I instructed her to go out and find a glass bottle and told Woody to put on an apron and take over baking the cakes. The class was a success, evaluating the flour of a supermarket's cake versus cakes made with bleached cake flour or Wondra flour.

Ken Kirschenbaum, in a thank-you note to me, wrote: "You are now a celebrity in the world of chemistry. Thanks so much, once again, for your contributions." He sent me this article from *Chemical & Engineering News Science & Technology*, Volume 86, Number 27, pp. 26–30, July 7, 2008, by Lisa M. Jarvis, writing: "It is the most widely read magazine in the field of chemistry. The article of 'Kitchen Chemistry' captured your contributions beautifully."

Kitchen Chemistry: Our Love of Food Is Helping Bring Science to the Masses

Rose Levy Beranbaum, author of The Cake Bible *and* The Bread Bible, *presented an amazingly comprehensive explanation of flour during the group's January meeting. Bread is about as basic as it gets in terms of its ingredients, but the baking process itself is quite complex. She went through the wide varieties of flour, how they differ in terms of protein content, which can range from 8 to 14%, and what that means in terms of texture, flavor, and lift. She threw out phrases and words like "phenolic acid," which is responsible for the bitterness of whole wheat flour, and "glutenin" and "gliadin," the two proteins in flour that form gluten. She went on to explain how the ratio of those proteins influences the density of bread because gluten can absorb three times its weight in water. In the end, she made the perfect sponge cake, weighing and timing the addition of ingredients with the precision of an analytical chemist. The roughly 80 audience members—some chefs, but many simply fans of baking and of Levy Beranbaum's cookbooks—were surprisingly well versed in the science of their craft. They also appeared genuinely interested in thinking about the chemistry of the baking process and how to apply science to get better results in the kitchen.*

FOOD-IMBEDDED MICROCHIP FOR IDENTIFICATION

Mid 2000s My cousin Richard G. Morris, as a biochemist, and his company made important contributions to the food world by developing and manufacturing scannable microchips about the size of a grain of sand for inserting into food products for ensuring authenticity of production dates and tracking distribution.

17

How I Became a Designer of Kitchen Equipment

Without realizing it, I've always had the sort of mind that wonders how I can improve on equipment design. My mother referred to me as mechanically inclined. And when my best friend's mother couldn't unzip her young son's jacket, because the zipper had gotten stuck, I was the one who was called to fix it.

My Thermometer and ThermapenOne

I found that almost all baking equipment at the time, at least for the home baker, was inadequate and inaccurate. No two sets of measuring spoons were the same, and most glass measuring cups were way off the mark. I worked pro bono with the POURfect Company to design accurate versions of both. I had been looking forward to OXO's measuring cups that presumably could be read even when not at eye level, but when they sent me one of them, I was so shocked to see how inaccurate it was that I called the company and asked to speak to the technical representative. The surprise validation was that it was his last day with the company, due to his disappointment of how his design was executed. One of the most positive experiences I had "picking up the phone" was when I called the Farberware Company saying that I was a food stylist and loved their round electric griddle to make evenly browned pancakes but would love to have it in a rectangular shape. The designer actually made one for me, which I have been using now for decades!

What Is a Prototype?

My Great-Uncle Nat was an inventor and industrial designer. His most famous design was the Movado Museum Watch with one dot in place of numbers. So, in the mid 1980s, he was the one I called to find out how to put an idea I had for an electric ice cream scoop into practice. He told me he had scooped ice cream as a kid and that all you need to do is wet the scoop in water. I told him that electric knives and even useless electric forks were very popular, so why not an electric ice cream scoop? He advised me to make a "prototype." That stopped me in my tracks, because I was sort of expecting him to do this for me and had no idea how to go about doing it myself. Discouraged, I gave up the idea.

A few years passed, and Charles Lamalle, the main New York importer of high-quality French bakeware and cookware, contacted me asking me to test two products, and guess what? One was the SEB electric ice cream scoop. I cried until I tried it out, and it didn't work well at all. The other product was a porcelain casserole by Apilco that was coated in gold. They said you could use it in the microwave. Given my understanding about microwaves, I was 100% sure it would not work, but Mr. Lamalle insisted I test it. Risking the potential of ruining my microwave, I tried it, and the inevitable arcing took place resembling a lightning bolt across the top. He let me keep it. I still use it, but not in the microwave, of course.

The Cordon Rose Thermometer

It wasn't until 1991 that I designed my first piece of baking equipment, and it was a major game-changer. The Cordon Rose Thermometer became the only thermometer on the market that was accurate to a fraction of a degree at all the critical points of baking and tempering chocolate. Here is how it happened: Ever since early childhood, I was intrigued by mercury. My dentist mother let me play with mercury when she was preparing amalgam fillings. And when I had a fever, a mercury thermometer was used to check my temperature. I still remember the day when I finally was able to see the mercury in the thermometer. I also remember walking by a laboratory class in college and seeing a student take the temperature of a syrup with a long laboratory thermometer, because it fascinated me.

My goal in teaching and writing cookbooks (which is also teaching) has always been to share my knowledge of baking and empower others. Temperature control is the most critical factor for successful baking. The road to success producing and marketing this product was paved with enumerable and unforeseeable obstacles and turned into an invaluable learning experience. Many years ago, I was making a classic buttercream, using an inexpensive candy thermometer—the one with the cute red wooden ball attached. Every time the syrup reached the desired temperature (or so I thought) of 238°F/114°C and when I transferred it to a measuring cup to stop the cooking and slowly poured it into the beaten egg yolks, it was disaster. The yolks curdled, and cooked instead of smoothly emulsifying. Out I ran to the corner supermarket to get more butter, swearing it would be the last time.

After three more times, it suddenly occurred to me to take the temperature again once the syrup was poured into the measuring cup, which made it deeper. I then inserted the thermometer, and with the deeper insertion into the liquid, the thermometer shot way up. That was how I learned about insertion point and the need for accuracy. It was an astounding discovery that thermometers, which I had believed to be infallible scientific instruments, varied widely in accuracy.

I complained that night to my radiologist husband, Elliott, that they made better thermometers for human beings than for baking, and he said: "Then why don't you use those?" My response was: "They only go up—you have to shake them to go down, and rising and lowering are both needed for tempering chocolate." He then suggested that I design my own thermometer to my own higher standards. "How would I do that?" I asked. He said to use the *Yellow Pages*, the telephone directory for businesses (no Google in those days), to search for thermometer companies and to design my idea of an ideal thermometer, without compromise, and compromise later if it was too expensive. I didn't like that part of his advice because, once I thought of an ideal design, I was not inclined to compromise. It turned out I didn't have to!

The very next day, I started calling numbers from the *Yellow Pages*, and on the second try, I landed on the company Miller & Weber, which made thermometers for the oil industry where precise temperature readings were critical to avoid explosion. By a miracle of coincidence, the co-owner Val Sauer was celebrating his 30th year there that day. Hearing that I wanted a short immersion thermometer, he was delighted to talk to me, saying that he was always trying to explain the importance of immersion levels, and that people just didn't get it.

He was also intrigued by my design of having the reading be engraved in opposite directions, instead of having Fahrenheit and Centigrade on each side in the same direction. The ideal thermometer should have Fahrenheit on one side being right side up and inverted on the other side, making it possible for someone who was right-handed to hold the thermometer with their left hand, while stirring with their right hand and also to be able to read it right side up.

He said it would be necessary for him to retool his shop equipment to make them, and he asked how many I wanted and if a gross would be acceptable. I had no idea what a gross was, but I said I only needed 24 for my class. Of course, this was way below the minimum—especially for a new design. But what won him over was the creativity of the concept.

He knew I was serious, and he agreed to give it a try. And that was how the Cordon Rose Thermometers—one for chocolate and another for sugar and deep fat—were born. Val and I became very good friends for years.

Persuading Chef Pierre Franey to Write About My Thermometers

The thermometers worked so perfectly and sold so well that, by 1996, I decided it would be a good idea to share them with other people, but I needed to get the word out. At the time, chef Pierre Franey had an equipment column for *The New York Times*, so I called him with hope that he would feature the thermometers. He arranged for me to meet him at Le Cirque after a lunch honoring the King of Spain. I arrived with my two thermometers and an eager smile. I was startled to find an armed guard standing at the door. I knew chef Franey was a national treasure, but this seemed a bit extreme. When questioned, Pierre looked at me as if I were crazy and explained that the guard was there, because the guest of honor was the King of Spain. I replied: "For me, it is you who are king and worthy of protection." He bowed his head modestly.

I showed Pierre the thermometers explaining what they were. He always looked like he was sneering, because the left side of his mouth turned down, but this time, it seemed to turn down even more than usual as he cynically asked: "Just how many people would buy a chocolate thermometer?" Defending my new "baby" product inspiration, I overcame my intimidation, and my playfulness and daringness got the better of me. As a true sarcastic New Yorker, I answered: "About as many as will buy the refrigerated marble top you wrote about this week!" And I tweaked his arm! His response was to explain, defensively, that his editor had asked him to write about the equipment he had in his kitchen. I went on to explain: "You see, people who are interested in tempering chocolate are failing and blaming themselves instead of the equipment. This thermometer will make it possible for them to succeed." Pierre made no promises but asked to try out the chocolate thermometer.

A few weeks later, the article appeared. It also included an H-B oven thermometer review. A testament to how people read it, I got many calls about the oven thermometer, which was not mine, and very few inquiries about the chocolate thermometer. So, I went on to send one to *Cook's Illustrated*, where I had written several baking articles.

A few months later, the review appeared, comparing my dead accurate mercury thermometer to one with red liquid rather than silver mercury and saying that the one with "red mercury" was easier to read. With total disgust, I told everyone who would listen, that they must have thought they had discovered a new element not on the Periodic Table of Elements. It was not red mercury; it was alcohol died red and wasn't even close to mercury for repeatability, speed, and accuracy. Soon after, *Cook's Illustrated* wisely hired a scientist on staff!

Learning How to Merchandise

I had no experience packaging or distributing products, so I asked a friend who owned Universal Foods—one of the largest companies in the country—and he offered to send samples of the thermometers to his top 10 distributors, claiming that his glass shipping expert would take care of them. Each and every thermometer broke, leaving me with no distributors. So, I did the distribution myself. Part of one of my rooms was filled with corrugated rolls of paper and boxes (the secret was clumps of newspaper between the rolls and the sides of the box). And never was a single one broken thanks to the advice from my friends at the thermometer company.

For several years, I sold both thermometers to Dean & DeLuca, Sur la Table, Broadway Panhandler, and New York Cake, and I made enough money to do a kitchen renovation. I brought a chocolate thermometer to a class in Switzerland where they were using one of those caged thermometers from France, which surprised me because I had learned about "stem correction" and how the metal cage or any backing would throw off the reading. The teacher admitted that, every time he received a new thermometer, he had to recalibrate it.

Perhaps Pierre Franey was right; my little thermometer business never made me a fortune, but it did gradually find its niche. And I had reliable thermometers for my own use (my main motive in the first place). Then, along came the USDA (United States Department of Agriculture) mandate in 2011 that mercury thermometers were dangerous if broken and subjected to heat, and were therefore illegal for use in the kitchen.

Along Came ThermoWorks

I was relieved and grateful when ThermoWorks started selling their Thermapen instant-read thermometers, whose speed and reliability was extraordinarily accurate and far superior to mercury. I learned another important lesson about technology: Never think anything is the best that ever can be! I was rewarded to know that my thermometers helped many people to become better bakers and to understand the value of accurate instrumentation.

ThermoWorks Owners Suzette and Randy Owen

Becoming part of the ThermoWorks "family," by working with them and participating in all of their conferences, I found many new invaluable products. The Square Dot, for example, led to my discovering that there is less fluctuation in a gas oven than in an electric oven.

I also created the "Reduction Spatula," a unique silicone spatula with graduated markings that enables one to see the amount of reduction when boiling a liquid in any size container, as part of their silicone line, now improved and produced by ThermoWorks. They also took on my silicone FastTracks and Mini Spatula.

Some of My Product Collaborations with Other Companies

In 2001, I worked with the POURfect Company to create accurate measuring cups and spoons. Regrettably, the company is no longer in business.

In 2015, I worked with American Products Group to create a Syn-Glas rolling pin, the material that requires the least amount of flour to prevent sticking, and silicone FastTracks, dough thickness guides, to ensure even rolling of pie dough. I had a patent for my product line.

Rose's Perfect Pie Plate, Cake Strips, and Reduction Spatula

In 2005, for Harold Import Company, I created my Rose's Perfect Pie Plate, which enabled people to make perfect crimped edges effortlessly. In 2008, as a spokesperson for Lékué Silicone of Barcelona, Spain, I was invited to Barcelona to do several lectures to pastry chefs. I met the renowned chef Ferran Adrià, and when I was introduced as the writer of bibles, I said to him that, while it's true I write baking bibles, in my country he is God. He kissed my hand.

Working with silicone, I discovered that it is a poor conductor. This inspired me to create silicone cake strips for surrounding metal cake pans, slowing down heating at the sides to produce moister cake layers that are flatter and more even in height.

I'm relieved that I no longer have to be my own distributor or shipper.

International Home + Housewares Show

For many years, I looked forward all year to the March International Home + Housewares Show (now called The Inspired Home Show) in Chicago. The magnitude of the show is enormous. It features 2,100 exhibitors showing thousands of new products, and it is also where my own products are presented by the companies that sell them. The show gives buyers the opportunity to see new products and make requests for placing orders. Most years, I will present my product line in the supplier's booth. I also get to see old friends and see what has evolved and what is new in kitchen products.

Rose and Photo Cop

In 2013, I was at the show representing a kitchen equipment manufacturer. Woody also came to attend the booth, and he baked 400 of his Pepparkakor cookies to provide an additional attraction for our booth. Most people noticed the incredible explosion of time-released flavors from the different spices.

The funniest moment of the show was due to Woody taking a photo for our blog at the Nespresso booth that we visited to get our daily cappuccino fix. Neither of us realized that photographing at the show required a special Press Badge. When a security guard walked up to us and informed us of this rule, I thought he was kidding. He explained that manufacturers will spy on their competitors' booths and try to take photos.

The following day, as I was standing at my booth, behind a display of *The Cake Bible*, a man came up to me extolling the virtues of the book and telling me how, before he was a policeman, he was a pastry chef and had learned everything from *The Cake Bible*. He looked oddly familiar, and I asked if, by chance, Woody and I had met him the day before. In fact, I queried whether he had been the one reproaching us for taking photographs. At first, he denied the possibility, clearly because he hated to think that he had done this to his mentor whom he claimed to idolize. Then, he actually got down on one knee to apologize.

When Woody offered him a cookie, he explained how he is not allowed to accept even a glass of water. It didn't take long for his beautiful spirit to overcome his qualms about breaking the rules, and he said he was going to make the first exception of his life and ask Woody to take a photo of me and him. I was beyond delighted. After the photo, out of the corner of his responsible eye, he spied someone a short distance away taking a photo of chef Cat Cora's booth. He excused himself before zooming over to read the person in question the show's party line. He came back to continue our conversation.

Here he is in the photo above, anonymity protected! Lesson learned once again: assume nothing—life is full of surprises.

18

Special Culinary Adventures and Highlights

Being a chameleon, I tried on many nationalities—the Italian me, the French me, the Indian me, the Japanese me, the Swiss me, the Aussie me, and the New Zealand me. Once in India, I referred to some neighbors as foreigners, forgetting I was one, too, and everyone laughed.

Charlie Trotter, Rose, and Emeril Lagasse at the James Beard House

The Beginning of My Love Affair with France

A food and wine lover never forgets her first pilgrimage to France. Mine was in 1971 when I was 27, and it served to crystallize in me the determination to devote my life to the pursuit of flavor. The expedition was shared by a friend, Elaine Kohut. We rented a typically powerless small car and tooled our way from Paris to Provence, enjoying many adventures, some of which included revelatory meals, and one that was quite unpleasant.

Chugging down the road south, we were in a traffic jam, and two guys in the car in front of us came over to suggest that we detour and go to a very charming inn called Le Saut de la Bergère in the Corrèze Mountains (The inn's name refers to the story of a shepherdess who jumped off the mountain to avoid being raped). Elaine was almost raped by one of the men, but the other one was more of a gentleman. I saw that he was wearing a wedding ring and mentioned it, to which he said: "*C'est un souvenir!*" As for the innkeeper, she had a coarse, florid face I later described as Rabelaisian. I also remember that the goose with chestnuts was excellent.

The next morning, fearing I would report her place (which apparently was a refuge for illicit affairs), the innkeeper asked me to hurry and then admired my use of the reflexive "*se dépêcher*," when I said I was hurrying. Then, she asked another guest—a doctor—to drive us down the mountain to our car. I still remember how he told me that American men didn't know how to make love and offered his services. It was not remotely tempting but, lesson learned not to follow strange men into the mountains.

The rest of the trip was without incident. One dining experience even brought me to tears of joy at its conclusion, and this was at Les Frères Troisgros in Roanne. I had read in awe about the degustation menu starting with lark's liver paté with an intriguingly bitter edge from the larks' diet of juniper berries, the velvety texture of which resulted from the gentle technique of heating the terrines and then removing them from the oven and wrapping them in heavy blankets to cook overnight by indirect heat. I anticipated that food so lovingly prepared would be extraordinary beyond anything I had ever experienced.

Nothing had prepared me for the thrilling intensity of the signature dish Saumon à l'Oseille (Salmon with Sorrel). The moist, rich salmon, cloaked in a fish stock-imbued cream sauce was magically lightened and enhanced by the most exciting counterbalance of acidity I had ever tasted—flecks of bright green sorrel (also known as sour grass). It made me more than gasp in astonishment; I was so overcome with pleasure I actually dropped my fork with a loud clang right into the sauce.

Within moments, the waiter appeared with both a large plate containing a clean fork and an amused if somewhat supercilious smile, charmingly informing me that there was no need for concern because there were many more forks in the kitchen. He seemed decidedly less amused, however, when I proceeded to subject the second fork to the same fate experienced by the first. I managed to hold on to the third fork long enough to polish off every last morsel of the fish and used an ideally flat sauce spoon, designed by Jean-Baptiste Troisgros, the founder of the restaurant, to consume every bit of the sauce.

Over the years, I have occasionally reencountered salmon with sorrel in other restaurants and wondered if it had been the newness of the experience that had made it so memorable, because no subsequent version ever caused me to come close to losing my grip on the fork. But when Jean-Baptiste's grandson, Claude, opened his restaurant CT in New York, I finally had the opportunity to rediscover and understand the dish, not only as it had been but side by side with Claude's updated lighter and even more brightly flavored version. When asked how this wondrous balance of flavors had been conceived originally, Claude explained that the Troisgros family has a particular passion for acidity. This was fascinating to me, because I realized that often I find something missing from an otherwise well-conceived recipe and that it is most probably the enlivening acid component.

I brought Claude my cherished signed menu from Troisgros, and we both laughed with disbelief when we saw the price of the six-course degustation menu from 23 years ago: 65 francs (about $13). Claude laughingly said: "It's gone up a bit since then."

In 1999, I gave the graduation address to the last generation of pastry students at the Culinary Institute of America Greystone. I was accompanied by my dearest friend Dianne Boate, who was known as "The Cake Lady" of San Francisco. The evening before the address, I invited her to an unforgettable dinner at the French Laundry. Every course was accompanied by a different wine, and neither of us dropped our forks.

Know Your Dinner Guests' Possible Allergies

The most memorable man I cooked for was chef Jacques Torres. I even wrote an article for the *Los Angeles Times Syndicate* called "Killing the Competition with Kasha," referring to the dinner I made for him, as described on the following pages.

As a food professional, I feel obliged to consider all foodstuffs in the edible category as being at least worthy of consideration for consumption. And I try not to flinch in disgust at other cultures' concepts of edible. I have, admittedly with difficulty, chewed and swallowed fried beetles in Mexico and just short of no-longer-alive-shrimp in Japan, managing in both cases to hide the horror that was threatening to engulf me. But I must admit that I am far less sympathetic to guests' food aversions than I am to their actual health problems.

The last time I remember catering to a food aversion was for a family party involving several garlic haters. I made two coleslaws, one with garlic and one without, clearly labeling each. Wouldn't you know that I was left with heaps of the one without, because everyone (despite their claimed likes or dislikes) went for the garlic version.

Another food sensitivity I have stopped catering to is cholesterol. This change of heart stems from a memorable occasion when a delightful chef friend came for dinner. I was in the mood for total dessert decadence, so out of concern for what I knew to be her health problem, I prepared a second dessert that was extremely low in fat. I made a mental note, as I watched her take ample helpings of both desserts, that, in the future, I would prepare only one dessert for everyone and cut smaller portions on request!

I respect caffeine sensitivity implicitly in the wake of my one test of the theory that, if you tell people there is no caffeine in the coffee, they will sleep. My mother forgave me, and I haven't tried it on anyone else since.

However, the oddest thing is that, when people actually have serious food allergies, they rarely seem inclined to warn you about them. Instead, they seem somehow to assume that no one is likely ever to serve them their one nemesis. For another chef, squid would have caused serious problems had she not informed me moments before the squid hit the pan, so I was able to eliminate them from her portion of the entrée.

I once invited my friend and esteemed colleague Jacques Torres, pastry chef at New York's famous Le Cirque, for dinner and prepared kasha varnishes (buckwheat groats). After his very first bite, he asked what was in the dish. I was flattered and thrilled, assuming he liked it so much that he wanted to know its every detail, but that wasn't it. Apparently, just having eaten one morsel of buckwheat, he could feel his lips tingling—a sure sign of disaster to come. Buckwheat can be an extreme and serious allergen, causing swelling of internal breathing passages and possible asphyxiation.

Jacques politely ate his way through the rest of the dinner, but it was only the next day, when his girlfriend, Kristy, called, that I found out just how much he had suffered due to the gradual swelling reaction and ensuing nausea. Even the following day, it was still apparent because, when he arrived at work, Daniel Boulud, noticing that Jacques's face was as puffy as the Pillsbury Dough Boy, asked him what was wrong. With characteristic goodwill and humor, his response was: "Rose Levy Beranbaum—she tried to kill me last night!"

Was it revenge when he told Michael Batterberry of *Food Arts* magazine that he shouldn't put me on a panel with chefs because I wasn't a chef? Ever loyal Michael's response was that I was "chef to the chefs!"

Going with the Grain and Fire at The Café des Artistes

In 1992, I hosted another memorable dinner that also features kasha! It is unfortunate indeed that such a splendid grain as buckwheat is burdened by the unappealing name of groats. In my family, it was known by its Eastern European name of kasha. But whatever it was called, I wouldn't have eaten it as it was prepared by my grandmother, who did the cooking in our family when I was growing up. Her kasha preparation was pale in color, soft and soupy like a cereal, and undistinguished in taste. Not for me! A friend, however, reintroduced me to it when I grew up, but her recipe was spicy with black pepper and oregano, and each grain was appealingly dry and separate. The secret was allowing the buckwheat grains to sit with the raw egg for at least 30 minutes, stirring occasionally to dry and keep them separate.

Over the years, I discovered other secrets such as browning the grains under the broiler after cooking to add crunch and deepen the color; adding sautéed mushroom slices, sometimes a little dried porcini mushrooms for extra flavor intensity; using stock instead of water; and making the bowtie noodles which constitute the classic kasha varnishkes. Goose fat is another fabulous enhancement. This dish has become my favorite grain dish and my traditional accompaniment to roast duck. The earthy, spicy, wheaty flavor goes so well with the rich crispy duck.

Several years ago, when I first made the acquaintance of a fellow food writer, immediately to become my beloved friend, Bert Greene, he asked me to make him my duck dinner. I had so loudly sung the praises of my special technique for roasting duck using high heat and boiling water that he wanted to write it up for the *New York Daily News*. Other guests included Bert's friend, Phillip Schulz, also a cookbook author; Jenifer and George Lang, owners of Café des Artistes; Blake Swihart, a food consultant; and Howard Solganik, also in the food business, who had flown in from Ohio just for the dinner.

I must admit I went a little crazy in the overboard department. I made the varnishkes (bowtie noodles) from scratch, using duck eggs and a pastry jagger to cut the shapes; prepared four ducks; and, for dessert, made homemade vanilla ice cream with hot fudge and brandied cherries, which I had picked and brandied over five years before. Never having made more than one duck at a time, I didn't realize that all that duck fat could ignite in the oven. Luckily, Howard arrived early and took over when I ran screaming from the kitchen, pausing only to hand him my safety goggles.

I suppose you could say the dinner was a success. Howard had saved the duck from cremation, and everything turned out just as I had intended, if not just as I had expected. The surprise was the guests, most of whom arrived with seriously diminished appetites for such a hearty dinner! Bert and Phillip had just come from a cocktail party with lavish hors d'oeuvres, and the Langs had just come from a preview tasting of everything on the menu of the soon-to-be-born restaurant Aurora. I was starving but felt a little funny going for second helpings when half my guests were having trouble with their first ones.

One thing was certain: The kasha varnishkes, not the duck, was the star of the dinner party. I discovered this when George Lang raised his glass of Jordan cabernet to toast the fact that if he, without appetite, could ask for a second helping of kasha varnishkes, the meaning was self-evident. And in a blind tasting of hot fudge, he chose mine over Julia Child's and even Schraft's! As he and Jenifer were standing by the elevator, I overheard him asking her why she never told him that I was three-quarters Hungarian. That's when I knew the dinner was a success because I had told him I was one-quarter Hungarian.

Oddly, though, the very next day, I heard on the news that there was a fire in the kitchen of Café des Artistes. At first, I was concerned that it may have spread to the dining room, graced by the famously glorious Art Nouveau murals. But when I learned that the fire was minor, with no significant damage, I couldn't resist calling to tease the Langs about having warned them only the night before that the special duck roasting technique only worked with a maximum of two ducks at time.

Bert never did write up that duck technique, but he did put the kasha recipe in his book *Green on Grains*.

Burnt Duck Is Best?

When my brother, Michael, visited from San Francisco, I wanted to treat him to dinner at Le Cirque—my then favorite restaurant in New York. We ordered duck, and it came burnt. When I complained to the wait person, his arrogant response was: "That's how the chef does it." My brother was disappointed in me that I accepted this answer. Sometime later, when I was visiting him and his soon-to-be-bride Mia in San Francisco, I chose a tasting menu at the Palace Restaurant, and the first course was foie gras. Mine was burnt. When I complained to this waiter, I got the same response as the one on the East Coast, but this time, my brother intervened with the perfect squelch: "Then, take ours back and burn them, too!" Yes—I was proud of him!

Years later, Elliott and I went to a new restaurant nearby our home in Hope, New Jersey. Once again, I encountered burnt duck, and guess who was the chef? It was the same one who had been at Le Cirque and had now moved to rural New Jersey! The restaurant closed within a year.

Charlie Trotter's Dinner and Writing "My Life on the Line"

In 1994, Charlie Trotter's restaurant was one of my favorites in the country, so when he invited me to participate in cooking a special dinner for invited guests, with 10 other cooks, who were all renowned chefs, I was thrilled. My personal challenge was to produce a dessert that would be both light and tantalizing after 11 other courses prepared by Charlie, Mark Baker, Elizabeth Terry, John Sedlar, David Waltuck, Geoff Felsenthal, Elka Gilmore, Christopher Gross, Jean-Louis Palladin, and Jean Joho. Whew! I chose an ethereal Lemon Snow with Golden Grand Marnier Sauce accompanied by my signature cake—Lemon Poppy Seed Pound Cake, baked as madeleines. I was blessed by the assistance of Charlie's pastry chef Michelle Gayer, who went on to open her own bakery, The Salty Tart, in the Twin Cities and has remained a dear friend for all these years.

Charlie's world-renowned sommelier, now vintner, Larry Stone, has also remained a lifelong friend.

My husband, Elliott, joined David Waltuck's wife, Karen, to greet and seat the guests. Karen was an experienced maître d', but Elliott had great powers of observation and ensured that a very overweight guest, who would not have fit into the standard chair, was given one of a wider size. He reported to me at the end of the dinner that my dessert was the only course that left nothing on the plate. Charlie had wanted me to make a chocolate dessert, but I considered that too heavy after so many courses.

Our Most Unique Dining Experience

A special memory was dinner at the late Vinnie Scotto's restaurant Scopa's preopening in 2008. There were only about four tables filled, and as we sat eating his glorious food, I said to Elliott: "The wonderful thing about Vinnie is that, not only is he a great cook, he's a beautiful person." I have the sort of voice that one has to be very close to hear it well, but apparently, one of the two women sitting at the next table overheard me. When she got up to leave, she came over and kissed me saying: "I'm Vinnie's mother." (I was glad that this hadn't been one of the times Elliott had chosen to contradict me—he often liked to play devil's advocate!)

A funny moment at the dinner ended up in a story I wrote for the *Los Angeles Times Syndicate* called "Adams' Ribs."

Vinnie Scotto has just soft-opened Scopa, and Elliott and I were poring over the menu trying to decide between pasta and grilled rib steaks. In an Italian restaurant, the pasta always tempts me most, but out of the corner of my eye, I discreetly (or so I thought) viewed the magnificently charred rib steak at the next table at a slight distance from ours. The man enjoying it looked over at me, smiled, and said: "Hello, Rose, would you like a taste?" When he introduced himself as Adam Platt (a favorite food writer for New York Magazine*), I explained that it was the rib I was after not the steak itself. He offered at once to hand it over to me as he didn't plan to nibble on it (or maybe he was just saying that to be a gentleman!). I told him I'd have to share it with Elliott as he too loves ribs, and to my utter astonishment, Adam replied: "Oh! My friend Adam here also doesn't eat the rib, so that one's yours, too!" It would have been funny enough with one Adam and one rib, but the amazing coincidence of two of each was staggeringly hilarious.*

Vinnie's second restaurant, Gonzo, was in the West Village. It was a family affair, with his lovely sister Donna as maître d'/manager and their dad as accountant. One New Year's Eve, shortly after he opened Gonzo, Vinnie showed me a white truffle the size of a tennis ball, saying that would be his New Year's dinner.

We ordered pasta with truffle, and he virtually showered it with the truffle. Vinnie was a giant of a man, handsome, talented, kind, and generous. He was only 40 years old when we lost him. I will always remember him, and I'm sure I'm not alone.

Marko and Rose in New York

Making Desserts for Marko Gnann

Of all my friends and family, Marko is the most critical but also the most appreciative of my desserts. After working together over many decades of testing recipes for my many cookbooks, when Marko and I both lived in New York, the moment a dessert was ready I would call him, and he would come racing over on his bicycle to try it and give his feedback. My favorite thing about Marko, even more than his love of desserts, is his love of traveling and people. We've met many times in New York restaurants, and even twice in Paris, and I've enjoyed many amazing dinners and meeting some of his fascinating friends.

Helen and Rose

Meeting Helen Goh

Helen Goh is a beloved English baker, author, and friend. We have been email-pals for many years, and Helen was one of the most supportive encouragers insisting that I write my stories. In June, 2025, we finally met in person at the James Beard Awards in Chicago.

SOCIAL MEDIA-DRIVEN KITCHEN PRODUCTS

These viral, social-media-driven products and Amazon generate hundreds of cheap, copycat, "beginners" cookbooks. Many of them are flawed with errors and less than 100 pages.

The Instant Pot, a five-in-one multi-cooker invented by Canadian engineer Robert Wang, was first released in 2010, gaining viral traction through social media and Amazon deals around 2016–2017. The Ninja CREAMi ice cream maker officially launched in July 2021 as a revolutionary countertop appliance using specialized "creamify" technology.

19

My 43-Year Life with Elliott—Moments of Our Marriage

Elliott

Dr. Elliott Beranbaum was head of outpatient radiology at NYU Medical Center. It was in his office where AIDS was first discovered in the U.S. When I reported to him that, at a Bastille Day Celebration, a famous French chef kissed me, sticking his tongue in my mouth, Elliott swore he would never touch me again—there was that much fear of contagion.

Elliott brought angiography from Sweden and perfected the instrumentation which saved hundreds of thousands of lives by avoiding the need for open heart surgery. He designed the mammography compression machine for Siemens, which required far less radiation and became the standard method. He also created the radiology language for Dragon software for voice dictation. In short, he was a genius.

We met at NYU Medical, introduced by a mutual friend. He was bald on top but had hair down to his shoulders, which turned me off. I had hair down to my knees, which also turned him off. On our first date, he was wearing a salmon pink jumpsuit, recommended by his cousin Merle who said women would like it. I wasn't one of them. We didn't date again until several years passed, but we kept bumping into each other at work.

Elliott was a Cancer to my Aries. He was also a contrarian and a realist to what he called my "rose-colored glasses." We were different in almost every way, except for our approach, which was exemplified on our second date when we discovered that we shared the same theory about sifting (mine regarding flour and his barium). We both agreed that sifting didn't uniformly combine ingredients, as was commonly thought. Rather, it promoted better hydration of a mixture. After a few months of dating, Elliott offered me a diamond engagement ring, but I preferred a commercial stove, which was fine with him. Elliott was concerned about our 10-year age difference and said that someday I might need to find a younger man but not to hurt him. I honored his request when the time came.

When we announced our engagement, Thelma, a fellow secretary who had worked at NYU for many years remarked: "He is the only doctor who doesn't gossip, and he will let you be free to be yourself." Elliott had a violently explosive temper, tempered by profound wisdom. The most horrifying of his temper tantrums was during a trip to Rome, when he couldn't find our way to the hotel at the foot of the Spanish Steps, so he fearlessly chose to drive down them instead! The temper came from enduring childhood dyslexia in the days that it wasn't understood, and bipolarity. I once heard him saying that he had no tooth decay because he had a base mouth. I couldn't resist responding with: "Base mouth but acid tongue." He was won over by my seemingly calm personality, but it didn't take long for him to discover that, under the calm exterior, was the high anxiety of a perfectionist.

Elliott told me that, when he was a young man in Toronto, his best friend was Catholic, so the two of them wanted to start an undertaking business, being certain of their success covering both of the major religions in the province. His father discouraged it, wanting him to be a doctor like one of his older brothers. I told him that someday I would write about this and call it "Elliott's Great Undertaking."

Our Second Married Life

We were married in July 1976 by the same Rabbi Kamenetsky who married my parents 32 years before. I had been warned that marrying a man with two teenage children would be a challenge, especially because they had tragically lost their mother when they were ages 5 and 3. Elliott asked me if I could handle it, and I said yes. One year later, he said:

"I thought you said you could handle it!" But how could I have known? The problems started just a few months after our marriage when he said: "The more we attack you the stronger you get." I felt backed into a wall and had to decide what was true and change it and what was not and ignore it, and I knew I was in for the battle of my life for years to come.

I once told Elliott that, if I had to marry a Jewish man, at least he wasn't a New Yorker, which would feel like marrying a relative. His response was: "I wanted to marry a Jewish woman from New York and instead ended up with a French woman." He had a theory that my mouth and nose were shaped like the French so that my words, even in English, came out with a French accent/intonation. I couldn't have been happier about that.

Elliott started complaining that food people always talked about nothing but food. He invited me to one of his medical conferences, and guess what they talked about? It wasn't medicine.

One day, he announced that, "words mean nothing—only actions count." You don't say that to a writer, so of course, my response was, "maybe yours don't!" Whenever we argued, it usually ended with his saying that, if he had to fight, at least it was with an intelligent woman. I absorbed and analyzed what he said and decided what part fit. But I never lost sight that I was married to a man who encouraged and supported me in my newly started career, and as Thelma had predicted, he did not interfere with my freedom.

Who was the smarter one after all—my late husband, Elliott, who had great wisdom and gave excellent advice, or I, who followed most of it?! He once posed the question why I asked for his advice and didn't follow it. My response was that I was not an automaton and that I needed to process and synthesize it and decide what part of it made sense to me.

One of Elliott's best pieces of advice was when he said that routine was a good thing and that doctors like himself, for example, who did things routinely, made fewer mistakes. I would have thought routine to be boring, but over the years, I learned otherwise firsthand. The best gift of routines is that, by virtue of repeating them over and over, they stay in memory, leaving the mind free to be creative about other things. And as people age and become a bit forgetful, the routines are the blessing that come to our aid.

It wasn't always easy living with a genius. One dinner conversation at a friend's birthday party included the subject of genius, and Elliott pronounced that I wasn't one. Moments later, I met the novelist Erica Jong, whose husband was my literary lawyer. Her opening statement was: "I know all about you—my chef friend says you're a genius!" My response was: "My husband was just saying that I wasn't one." Dismissively waving her hand to brush the thought away, she exclaimed: "Oh, your husband." When I asked Elliott who he considered to be a genius, he cited Einstein. My definition of genius is those who see things beyond the obvious.

I used to think that, someday, I would have a moment of enlightenment, when I suddenly would put it all together and realize something very important about myself that would make a big difference. What Elliott made me realize was that I've never been a consequential thinker and therefore never feared taking risks. I could never think of the consequences four moves ahead. When I played chess with my little brother when we were young, we each ended up with one king left on the board—a stalemate. Elliott often joked that, as a radiologist, he had X-ray vision, but his perception was always right on target. The most important advice he gave me was, "Don't worry and plan. It is a straight line between you and your goals, so don't even think about how to get there." That was my enlightenment.

My #MeToo Moment AKA My Mouth Is Mightier Than the Sword

With the advent of the #MeToo movement in the news, I remembered that, shortly after we were married and prior to birth control for roaches that virtually eliminated the problem, there was an infestation of roaches in the apartment. I hired an exterminating service for three sessions, called Myron the Helping Exterminator. At the end of the second session, 6'3" Myron decided to try helping himself to me. He grabbed me and put his mouth on mine and wouldn't let go. When I was finally released, the first thing that popped out of my mouth with vehement conviction was: "I'd rather have roaches!"

I'll never forget the hurt look on his face. He took it in a way I never had intended and with devastating effect. What I meant was that I'd rather have roaches than be overpowered and assaulted. What he clearly thought I meant was that I'd rather have roaches than be touched by the likes of him, and that as a man, he disgusted me that much. I wasn't about to let him enter the apartment again, but I needn't have worried. He honored our financial agreement for the third session but sent one of his workers.

Vignettes of Our Long Marriage

When I needed a new general practitioner, Elliott referred me to his own doctor (Dr. Mitchell Charap) saying that I'd like him because he collected wine. Always one to look for "bridges," when Dr. Charap was doing his routine questionnaire and got to the part about what line of work I was in, my unthinking response was, "the pleasure giving business." You can imagine his shock that his patient, colleague, and former professor, the distinguished Dr. Beranbaum, would have a wife in what pleasure business usually refers to. He looked up, his eyes expressing total disbelief.

Dr. Charap and I had much to laugh at ever since. Elliott told me never to leave Dr. Charap because he was his most gifted student. But he forgot to tell Dr. Charap never to leave me, and he retired a few years ago. On my last visit, I gave him the 60th printing of *The Cake Bible* and inscribed it as: "To the other person who Elliott admired the most." I will always remember him.

Elliott and I bought a weekend house near Blairstown, New Jersey, and my friend Cecily told me that Ann Seranne of *The Blender Cookbook* moved to that town to raise Yorkies. Cecily warned me that Ann was a very difficult person which proved to be true. One day, when shopping at a supermarket, I overheard a woman calling out the pharmacist in a very cranky voice. It had something to do with generic medications being less expensive. I asked her if she was Ann Seranne, and she demanded to know how I could possibly have known. I said it was a lucky guess.

Elliot and I had some funny moments, including our weekly tennis date. One day, I missed a ball and shrieked "*merde*" in French, but Elliott thought it was murder and called me "Killer Rose" until he found out the true meaning which was "shit!" I had thought it was a compliment!

Elliott disliked traveling, and my boss and his associate knew it. My boss's note congratulating Elliott on our engagement read: "Now, you'll be traveling around the world!" It was prophetic. Elliott accompanied me on many trips, including wine trips to New Zealand and Germany and other trips to France, Switzerland, Sweden, Sicily, Hawaii, Brazil, Portugal, and different parts of Canada, the country of his birth. When eating out in New York City, he cringed when I was recognized because we invariably were given myriad desserts.

Fall from Grace

As I was leaving for one of my European press trips, I hugged Elliott goodbye and told him that I was really going to miss him. His response was "life goes on." It did. I was so hungry for love that, when I met the arriviste Mr. Wolf, who was indeed a wolf in sheep's clothing, I succumbed. I saw his true character too late when we met back in the U.S. and took a shower together. The scalding water hit my back, and he said: "Better you than me."

I once read him the poem *The Sick Rose* by William Blake which fit to a tee, though his response was that he "wasn't into poetry."

O Rose thou art sick.
The invisible worm,
That flies in the night
In the howling storm:
Has found out thy bed
Of crimson joy:
And his dark secret love
Does thy life destroy.

At the end of our short relationship, he asked me to put him on a list to receive food samples. I guess he got on the list by himself because, thanks to social media, I discovered years later that he had become very fat. In that same conversation, he used the phrase "now that I've had you . . ." It was a short route from "love of my life" to that ugly phrase. But my revenge was sweet: I gave his best friend my editor. And the silver lining was that the poison of this experience kept me from making the mistake ever again.

Elliott's Retirement and Living in Hope

After over 50 years of working at NYU Medical Center, Elliott was forced into retirement, which meant losing our NYU affiliated apartment in New York. We moved to our weekend home in Hope, New Jersey. I turned the entire basement into a baking kitchen and loved living in the mountains along the Appalachian Trail. Sadly, this move was very bad for Elliott, who had so loved his work and living in New York. He was at a loss, not having any hobbies other than tennis, which he could no longer play. This started what he referred to as his rapid decline.

After four decades of marriage, I learned the true meaning of the marriage vows "for better or worse." An incredibly deep bond was formed. I realized that all either of us wanted was

Mountaintop House in Hope

Hope, New Jersey, Baking Kitchen

to be loved, and we had spent our life together at cross purposes. What was happening to him felt like it was happening to me.

The last year of his life, while I was writing *The Cookie Bible*, I devoted my primary attention to his care. And finally, we gave each other great gifts of love. One of mine to him was when we drove into New York for my annual mammogram at what used to be his office. Elliott couldn't find a parking spot, so he sat in the car. I asked the person at the desk to tell Rosina, the woman who ran the office, that Dr. Beranbaum was outside in the car and that Rosina would want to see him. She informed me that Rosina was in a meeting to which I said: "I didn't say he wanted to see her; I said she will want to see him." Rosina went out and sat with him in the car for a whole hour!

Taking Care of Elliott

After an angiogram procedure by a referral doctor kept him in the hospital for weeks instead of the projected three days, Elliott, who had advanced Lewy body dementia, had the presence of mind to ask to see the MRI. He saw that the surgeon had gone into his vein on an angle, which he had taught thousands of medical students never to do. I was moved to write the following letter to his cardiologist who was from India.

October 30, 2019
Dear Dr. Talati,
I want to thank you for taking such good care of my husband Dr. Elliott Beranbaum. It has moved me to share with you some details about your patient which I think will be of interest.

Dr. Naresh Trehan, who was Frank Spencer's fellow, did a rotation with Elliott, who considered him to be a gifted surgeon. Naresh returned to India many years ago and opened the first cardiac and transplant hospital which is now an entire village.

Elliott was a vascular radiologist at NYU Medical Center for over 50 years. During many of those years, he ran the Outpatient Radiology Department. Two of his major contributions to the medical field were bringing angiography from Sweden and perfecting it for this country and designing the Siemens mammography diagnostic machinery to compress the breast and significantly reduce radiation.

I met Elliott 45 years ago when I was secretary of the tumor service at NYU Medical, which paid my way through college and graduate school. Coincidentally, Naresh and his wife Madhu were my best friends. And also coincidentally, I had just written my master's thesis on sifting flour and how it does not uniformly incorporate ingredients, which changed the way in which cakes are now mixed. Elliott had come to the same conclusion for the barium for his GI studies and had gotten a blender before creating the banana flavored premix that is used today.

The next appointment, Dr. Talati came up to me, bowed, and shook my hand. I never told Elliott about the letter, but he knew.

I also took Elliot to all his specialists. One day, his general practitioner offered him a second pneumonia vaccine saying that he would never have to have another one again. I calmly stated that he had said the same thing two weeks before. I kept a chart of all his visits and showed it to the doctor who had to acknowledge that it was true. I also had a 106-page record of my texts to Elliott's two children, keeping them up-to-date with his medical care.

At the rehab center, I fought to have them retest for a major heart disease which he was diagnosed as having. They had lost the test, and we needed to know if it was hereditary. I insisted saying: "He's dying, and you can't test a cadaver." It worked—and it was not the hereditary type, much to the joy of his offspring and me.

One night, Elliott had talked about dying and the type of person I should choose as my next husband. I went into his room, kissed him goodnight, and said, "I love you," to which he responded, "Are you going to bed now?" And I said: "No, I said I love you, you stupid shit." He laughed and said: "Yes—I am a stupid shit—what can I say?" I said: "You can say you love me, too!" So, he did—a bit jokingly, but he got it out!

A few weeks before he died, Elliott told me two things for the first time: that I was a wonderful writer and that he loved me very much. And he thanked me for taking care of him. I also overheard a phone call with his daughter saying that I was amazing. Two weeks before he died, Elliott spoke to me and Woody separately, telling us that Woody, my associate and also his caretaker, should move in to take care of me after he was gone.

On 12-21-2019, the shortest day of the year, after 43 years, I lost my husband Elliott. He had been, in his own wise words, rapidly deteriorating. Some of his last words to me were never to give up my work, and it was my salvation during the months before and after so many losses. Although my heart was still heavy with loss, it was also filled with love, support, and gratitude for all my husband had given me. And I gave him what he wanted most for the ending of his life. When he was a resident in medical school, he was almost kicked out for saying, that when a patient is at the end of his life and in great pain, he should be given "morphine ex mortis" (morphine until death). I was able to activate hospice care so that he could be given morphine to dull the pain of dying. Woody was also able to give him his last verbal request which was to have a gin and tonic.

It was at Elliott's deathbed, when he had just died, that his daughter asked what Elliott's wishes were for his ashes or a memorial. I said that he didn't care what happened with his ashes; he didn't want a memorial and had no last wishes. Then, it occurred to me that he did have one, and so I told them: "His only wish was that we stay together as a family." He did not get his wish. Not only did I lose Elliott but almost all of the Beranbaum family.

Five weeks passed, and I stopped crying all the time but felt deeply wounded. There were so many moments when grief descended lowering me to the ground of despair. I could not have survived living alone in the mountains with all this pain, if not for Woody. He never once told me to stop crying. And he printed out our colleague Crescent Dragonwagon's list of appropriate responses to widows, even though he didn't need them. (She was twice widowed.)

20

Woody— Return to Paradise

Grandma's Favorite Expression Was: "Someday Someday"—Someday Is Here

6-5-23: Woody's Haiku Number 2216
living our dreamed life
how beautiful to live,
in harmony with work and play

My response: "You don't have to write anymore haikus; that is the perfect one."

PHOTOGRAPH BY TAI BLANCHE

Woody and Rose

Woody Is the Myth That Became a Reality

The mythology of one person being divided in two and searching for their other half is most prominently found in Plato's *Symposium*. Plato's dialogue presents a story where humans were initially created with four arms, four legs, and two faces, but they were split in two by Zeus as a punishment for their arrogance. Each half then spends their lives seeking their missing other half, their soulmate.

Woody and I are both Aries. He is stronger, but I have more endurance. People confuse what they think is my strength, but it is only determination despite my lack of strength. Intensity of this sort has to be part heredity and part example.

It's never a decision who does what—we both do whatever meets the eye and needs doing, only I can't open bottles without seriously hurting my fingers, and it's totally effortless for Woody. We are both incurable "completionists" and can never stop until the task is done. I never would have imagined such total compatibility could exist. That's not to say that we don't find some things irritating about each other, but they aren't the fundamental base things that damage a relationship.

Conversation with Woody during the COVID pandemic confinement, after I had a sudden influx or should I say outflux of memories and wanted to share them with him:

> **Me:** You don't seem to have been very interested in my stories.
> **Woody:** Well, sometimes, you talk too much.
> **Me in a huff:** Well, you ALWAYS talk too much.

This was a rare exchange. We usually get along as perfectly as I've ever experienced with any human being. I guess it's the confinement that sometimes took its toll. Our mutual friend, Lisa Strong, wrote to us: "You two are twins with your own language." I have and could have told Woody anything, and he encouraged me to write this memoir, taking notes for years as I told him my stories. Woody has also, in his words, become my "governor"—as in a car's governor to help me at times slow down or keep on track.

How We Met

In December 2003, when the only social media I had was my website, Woody and I communicated for the first time. His question was about the Mousseline Buttercream from *The Cake Bible*, which was the most challenging buttercream recipe. Several years later, together, we worked out a way to make it foolproof by reversing the addition of butter into the meringue.

In his first email to me, he introduced himself by saying: "You may not believe it, but your favorite fans in the Twin Cities are broomball players and t'ai chi participants." He often brought cake samples to their events; I had never before heard of either activity. Their favorite cake was The Chocolate Oblivion Torte. This was the start of what was to be a long-distance Minnesota-to-New York exchange on baking-related topics.

Several months later, I was invited by General Mills in Minnesota to do a cookie video news release, and that was when Woody and his wife met me in person at a coffee shop.

He brought two cakes: the Chocolate Oblivion Torte and the All-Occasion Downy Yellow Cake, filled with raspberry purée and frosted with buttercream, that he had baked from my book. I was so impressed that I asked him if he would like to test some recipes.

The first recipe test I gave him was for a white chocolate version of the Chocolate Oblivion Torte. It failed because it needed the cocoa solids of dark chocolate, so on second thought, we turned it into the most sublime white chocolate buttercream. I then gave him several other recipes that I had researched and written for *Rose's Heavenly Cakes* and was pleased with his detailed reports. For seven books, I had worked alone for virtually all testing, writing, book production, and promotion, except for valuable researching advice from David Shamah.

A year later, I invited Woody to come to our New York apartment to see if he could become my assistant. When he met me, he had recently changed careers from commissioned sales to be an on-site condominium maintenance manager. Woody's baking was self-taught and limited mostly to cake baking. He had baked a few recipes from *Joy of Cooking*, until he got *The Cake Bible*. The softened butter cakes and the Chocolate Oblivion Torte were his main repertoire. He also had done some baking from *The Pie and Pastry Bible*. Being on a budget and never having been to New York, Woody booked a hotel which he thought was the Hotel Stardust in Woody Allen's *Stardust Memories*.

Woody is actually his nickname that was given to him by his post-college stereo store manager, because Woody liked Woody Allen movies and had a similar sense of humor. After Woody spent one night in the YMCA-like hotel, I rescued him, inviting him to sleep on our living room sofa. As you can imagine, he was awestruck to be working side by side with his favorite baking author and standing behind the same workstation pictured on the back of *The Cake Bible*. We baked a couple of recipes. When Elliott observed us and saw how Woody gracefully would take items from me or hand me a spatula, he commented: "He knows exactly where to put his hands." We worked as a team like an operating room surgeon and a nurse. When it was time for Woody to return to Minnesota, I was in tears waving to him as the shuttle bus drove away.

The Beginning of an Initially Long-Distance Marvelous Partnership

Our relationship enabled me to write my books faster, better, and more accurately and gave Woody a platform to use his extraordinary mechanical, artistic, and technological abilities to test and video recipes. It was having a blank baking slate on which I could teach my methods and which he followed with devotion. For Woody, working with me fulfilled a hope he always had: "To be able to touch other people's lives, without necessarily meeting them." In addition to his emailing reports, he also made a couple of visits to New York to go over things.

For these trips, Woody would bring me over 20 pounds of superfine sugar, because he could buy it in bulk. He got quite accustomed to the airport's TSA staff flagging his sports duffle bag, thinking he was dumb enough to try sneaking cocaine through. I would send chocolate back with Woody. On a later trip that we were taking, his duffle bag was flagged. When we asked why the five pounds of dark chocolate had been the culprit, the TSA agent smiled and informed us that the chocolate's composition was similar to plastic explosives.

During this time period, Woody had divorced his wife due to ongoing irreconcilable differences. He said he would never marry again, and I said that I wouldn't be unfaithful to Elliott. A few years later, Elliott had a hip replacement, and the surgeon damaged a nerve that rendered him impotent. One day, he suggested that I have "what's his name" as a lover. I said: "Are you referring to Woody? You must be kidding!" But the idea slowly seeped in. It was almost biblical: Seven years from when we first communicated, Woody told me that he had been celibate since his divorce, so I should really take him up on his desire to be lovers while he was still 100% disease-free. That wasn't a very persuasive offer, but then a while later, he said that, no matter how long it took, he would wait for me, and that was the deal maker! Also, I felt that it wasn't fair to him to wait any longer.

Even though I thought sex was over for me, we were driving to Portland, Oregon, for the International Association of Culinary Professionals book awards (our book *Rose's Heavenly Cakes* was nominated), and I said: "If we win, we can become lovers." The night before the awards, I decided not to wait. The clincher is that not only did we win the Best Dessert Book, but we also won Book of the Year. Though it hurt at first from inactivity, I rediscovered the joy of sex from this most considerate and loving lover. Prior to then, we had traveled together for several years, sometimes sharing the same bed and always remaining chaste!

The Motivation for Woody to Move

We had completed the manuscript for *The Baking Bible* and had scheduled the styling photography shoot for the fall of 2013. Woody wanted very much to be part of the shoot but was conflicted because, at the time, he had been an instructor for over 20 years and had been rising as a disciple/legacy. His T'ai Chi Sifu Paul Abdella told him that working with me was his dharma and to feel free to follow me and move to New Jersey.

Woody made the move to a small townhouse in the nearby Delaware Water Gap, Pennsylvania, to enable him to work with me every day on *The Baking Bible* and two more books. He was also invaluable in taking care of Elliott and the household during the last year of Elliott's life. It was one and a half years later that Woody and I were married.

A Marvelous Cast for Our Wedding

On 6-21-21, the longest day of the year, it was the most perfect wedding day of my life! Woody and I got married in front of the county seat courthouse in Belvidere, New Jersey, in the park with towering 300-year-old trees. Shortly after the ceremony, Woody's amazing daughter Maran, who came for the first time from Minnesota, and our photographer Matthew Septimus, who drove in from Brooklyn and gave us a day of photos as a wedding present, signed the witness forms.

Our Wedding Ceremony with Maran

PHOTOGRAPH BY MATTHEW SEPTIMUS

Before the wedding, we asked Maran to arrange Woody's collection of hundreds of dried roses for Matthew to photograph with us lying beneath them, channeling the photos of Julia and Paul Child nude in a bubble bath and of Yoko Ono and nude John Lennon on the cover of *Rolling Stone* magazine. (I had long fantasized lying on a bed of soft rose petals, but these were prickly!)

My dearest friend Paula appeared as a surprise. I wasn't expecting her to come to the brief ceremony. We all went for dinner to our favorite New Jersey restaurant. We had a whole separate room to ourselves for our party of 10. Each cherished friend talked about how they met me and us. There was so much love; it wasn't just about us—everyone was included fully.

The wedding cake was our favorite Deep Chocolate Passion, made by our dearest friends Miro and Shilpa Uskokovic, who returned early from South India to make the cake but were still quarantined from exposure to COVID, so sadly, they were unable to come. Matthew drove all the way from far out in Brooklyn to Queens to bring us the cake. And then, when Woody went to pay the bill, he discovered that Paula had already paid for the entire dinner as well as offering a bottle of the finest champagne! As the best wedding gift of all, though I never wanted to have a stepdaughter again, I got Maran, who is one of my favorite and most admired people.

Shortly after the wedding, we made it into the *New York Post*. When writer Angela Barbuti asked me how I knew that Woody was the man for me, my response was: "I saw right away how he always knew just where to put his hands, twice the size of mine, but he was so skilled. He had such a delicate loving touch." Of course, I was referring to baking, but how could a tabloid resist such a play on words! Angela also wrote an article for all the newspapers, available in newsstands throughout the city.

Team RoseWood

Over the next five years, we continued to work and live as an inseparable team, producing three more cookbooks, and now this memoir. In a review by *Publishers Weekly*, we were given a new moniker: "Partners in Crème!" We were each gifted an apron as a wedding present from our dear friend Marina Padakis Lowry with the moniker embroidered on it. Woody used his extraordinary construction skills to enhance our home, while I worked on writing articles and this memoir. He also read through the memoir, editing and adding valuable text, having spent over 20 years listening to me telling my stories.

BIBLE IS THE WORD

My having included the word "bible" for *The Cake Bible* and subsequent books, by the year 2026, it has inspired around 100 cookbooks to include "bible" in their titles. Flavor bibles and barbecue or grilling bibles have over a dozen authors each. All are hoping the holy word would trigger a buyer seeing the success of *The Cake Bible*.

The Cake Bible 60th & 35th Anniversary Editions

On April 29, 2025, we were driving into New York City for my annual mammogram exam and received a phone call with no caller ID but the same area code as the hospital, so I risked taking it. It was instead from Dawn Padmore of the James Beard Foundation giving me the most joyful news imaginable: I was to be the 2025 recipient of the James Beard Awards Hall of Fame, the Oscars of cookbooks. I cried with joy remembering decades ago studying with James Beard, and years later, in 1989, winning the first James Beard Book of the Year for *The Cake Bible*. Life had come a full circle.

21

Miracles in My Life:

People Whose Lives I've Saved Including My Own

My life often feels like miracles and circles of coincidences, so I began to keep track of some of the miracles that have occurred over the years. Here are eight of the top ones, but other ones are throughout the book.

Near Drowning: The beach was my first preschool playground, and my father brought me some of the sand for my sandbox that he made for me. Following the example of my mother, the ocean was my friend, even though I nearly drowned when I ignored her advice and followed my Great-Aunt Polly into the area where the sand broke. I wrongly assumed that, being older than my mother, Polly knew better. I was able to do the dog paddle, so I managed to stay afloat. I remember looking down, seeing Polly's white legs deformed by the water, and her saying, to my disappointment: "I can't save you."

Then, a nearby swimmer paddled up to us, and I was relieved to think she intended to come to my rescue. To my shock, she hit me on the head and then grabbed me around the neck and raced me to shore. We sat on the sand surrounded by onlookers, and I listened to her boasting about how in life-saving one is taught to hit the victim first so that they don't resist. Five-year-old me thought two things: I wasn't going to resist and why is everybody paying attention to her, when I was the one who nearly drowned?!

The Perfect "O": When I was in the second grade at Public School 93 learning cursive penmanship, the teacher asked me to draw a capital cursive "O" on the blackboard, and somehow, magically, I drew an absolutely perfect circle. Everyone gasped, including the teacher, but then she said: "You have to put a loop through it at the top." I resisted and was heartbroken when she insisted, because it destroyed the perfection. I wanted to cut out that piece of blackboard and save it forever. When I got home, I told my mother, and she said that she too could draw perfect circles, so I guess it was genetic!

The Four-Leaf Clover: On one of the first dates with David, the man who was to become my first husband, we were walking in the Vermont mountains, and I jokingly told him that I could find a four-leaf clover easily. I swooped down to pick one of the many clovers in the grass. Amazingly, it was one that actually had four leaves. I think it scared him.

The Attack: When I was 24 and living alone in a two-flight walkup in the West Village in New York City, a stranger started following me up the stairs. Part way up, he grabbed me and tried to put his hand over my mouth. When I screamed, one neighbor came down the stairs carrying a sword, but Bill Winkler, who was closer, appeared sooner. The mugger shrugged and walked out the door. I followed him and kicked him as hard as I could, calling him the worst name I could think of. He just kept walking. I've never since walked into a place, which was occupied by only one man.

About 10 years later, I ran into Bill. We were both married and had moved to opposite sides of Bleecker Street. I thanked him for saving my life, to which he said: "My wife says yours was a life worth saving!"

A Special Namesake: It was a Rose Levy (not a relative) who brought the Bundt cake pan from Germany to Nordic Ware.

Flying Champagne Corks: Twice, a champagne cork zoomed by me, a few inches from my eye. The first time was at the famous pastry chef Yves Thuriès's restaurant in Cordes-sur-Ciel in the South of France. They offered me nothing but an apology. The second time was at Picholine in New York City. They offered me a dessert wine when I really would have preferred a little of the Dom Pérignon after its cork had near blinded me. I now always avert my face when I see anyone opening a champagne bottle. At home, Woody warns me and even goes into another room.

A Butterfly Fell for Me: At Vinexpo in Bordeaux, I was having lunch at the German pavilion when someone cried out: "There's a schmetterling on your head!" Not knowing what that meant, I reached for it and felt what I thought to be a squishy bug. The amazing thing is not only did it not move or fly off, but it remained there for over an hour until I stood up. Someone took a photo, so I can prove this!

Falling Backwards Down the Stairs: I missed a step, fell backwards, and my head crashed onto what fortunately was a fault line corner of an inherited antique coffee table by the famous Devon Dennett. When I saw the broken piece, at first, I thought it was my skull! The miracle was that I wasn't hurt, and the coffee table has since been repaired.

LEVI AND LEVY

In 2025, I was enchanted by this 4-year-old cooking prodigy on his Instagram show "Cooking for Levi." His wisdom, skill with language, and loving spirit were extraordinary. This inspired me to invite Levi for a baking class to make the Chocolate Domingo Cake and Wicked Good Ganache from my book. I learned that Levi means "united." It was destiny.

I was grateful that Jack and Emmy Zhang trusted me to teach their son, and taped it for the show. Of all the many students I have taught, Levi is the most memorable.

Levi and Rose on "Cooking for Levi"

Lives I've Saved Other Than My Own and a Baker's Validation

Elaine Kohut, who was wearing stacked sandals when we were walking on Le Pont d'Avignon in the South of France, tripped near the edge, and I risked my life grabbing her.

Paula Perlis turned her head to talk to me while crossing Eighth Street in Greenwich Village, and I pulled her away from an oncoming small truck.

Bill Liederman, owner of the New York Restaurant School where I was teaching, was talking to me while crossing the wide 14th Street in New York City. I pulled him away as a bus was about to hit him. He thanked me for saving his life, but shortly afterwards, he fired me. He must have thought that no reward would be adequate.

Squarespace Validating Comment: Chris Lehrich

This comment was especially meaningful to me because my purpose for giving information about what ingredients contain not only gives the reader the freedom to create but also helps them fix something that may not be working. In this case, Chris became a hero to his young daughter.

I just wanted to say thank you—you're my kind of lunatic!

My daughter started baking lussekatter, a Swedish Christmas bun-roll-bread thing. She got ¾ of the way into the initial process and then discovered that we only had 50g of sugar and she needed 67g.

I could see the signs: meltdown on the way. Fortunately, she told us what the problem was before the meltdown happened. And I remembered: In The Bread Bible, *there's a discussion of substitutions, including sugar and honey.*

Okay, so I calculated the necessary quantities—up 168% in honey, remove 17.2% of that in water—and we moved on from there.

Guess what? It worked perfectly. (I expected this, but my daughter and my wife were amazed that a little calculator work plus a decent scale could solve the problem.)

Thanks, Rose!!!

Epilogue: "I want you!"

Fall of 2025, we gave a baking retreat class with Erin Jeanne McDowell at *Bake from Scratch* test kitchen in Alabama. Owner/Publisher Brian Hart Hoffman also invited us to the celebration launch of his new product line at Williams Sonoma. When I told him that I was searching for the ideal publisher for my memoir, he nearly screamed: "I want you!"

I looked so astonished he repeated it! I realized immediately that since *Bake from Scratch* magazine is the only magazine devoted to the home baker, and as a contributing editor, I had found the perfect publishing home for this book of my heart. As icing on the cake, I absolutely adore kindred spirits, Brian, Editor Amber Wilson, and Editorial Director Rachel West.

Brian and Rose

TILIT

My Recipes

Lemon Poppy Seed Pound Cake
(page 224)

Lemon Curd
(page 227)

All-Occasion Downy Yellow Cake

(page 228)

Neoclassic Buttercream
(page 230)

Chocolate Domingo Cake
(page 232)

Chocolate Domingo Cake, Bundt Style
(page 233)

Wicked Good Ganache
(page 235)

Cherry Pie *(page 238)* **made with Perfect Flaky & Tender Cream Cheese Pie Crust** *(page 236)*

Hanaa's Moroccan Almond Cookies *(page 242)*

My Dream Chocolate Chip Cookies *(page 240)*

Zach's Chocolate-Studded Truffle Cookies *(page 244)*

Bulgur & Duxelles
(page 247)

Spaghetti Carbonara
(page 248)

Multigrain Bread Loaf
(page 250)

Lemon Poppy Seed Pound Cake

MAKES: One loaf or fluted tube cake
SERVES: 8
OVEN TEMPERATURE: 350°F
BAKING TIME: 55 to 65 minutes for loaf; 35 to 45 minutes for fluted tube pan

Since the first printing of *The Cake Bible*, this variation of my Classic Pound Cake has become my signature cake. My goal had been to have a cake that had the silky smooth dissolving-moist texture of the Sara Lee pound cake, but with the pure buttery flavor of a home-baked cake. It took over 40 tests to arrive at my goal. The addition of lemon and poppy seeds made it my idea of perfection.

PLAN AHEAD: For best flavor and texture, complete the cake 1 day ahead.

SPECIAL EQUIPMENT: One 8 by 4 by 2½ inch (4-cup) loaf pan, bottom coated with shortening, topped with parchment (or a 6-cup fluted tube pan). Either pan coated with baking spray with flour.

BATTER: 710 grams
eggs and butter cut in 1 tablespoon pieces, room temperature (65° to 75°F)

INGREDIENTS	GRAMS	VOLUME
3 large eggs	150	½ cup plus 2 tablespoons
whole milk	45	3 tablespoons
pure vanilla extract	7	1½ teaspoons
bleached cake flour	150	1½ cups (sifted into the cup and leveled off)
sugar, preferably superfine	150	¾ cup
baking powder	3.4	¾ teaspoon
fine sea salt		¼ teaspoon
lemon zest, finely grated	6	1 tablespoon, loosely packed
poppy seeds	27	3 tablespoons
unsalted butter	184	13 tablespoons (1½ sticks plus 1 tablespoon)
Lemon Syrup, for brushing		see chart and recipe on page 225

PREHEAT THE OVEN Set the oven at 350°F with the oven rack in the lower third.

MIX THE LIQUID INGREDIENTS In a 2-cup glass measure, lightly whisk the measured egg yolks and egg whites. Whisk in the milk and vanilla.

MAKE THE BATTER In the bowl of a stand mixer fitted with the flat beater, mix the flour, sugar, baking powder, salt, lemon zest, and poppy seeds on low speed for 30 seconds. Add the butter and one-half of the egg mixture. Mix on low speed until the dry ingredients are moistened. Raise the speed to medium and beat for 1 minute.

Gradually add the remaining egg mixture in two parts, beating on medium speed for 20 seconds after each addition to incorporate the ingredients and strengthen the structure.

Scrape the batter into the prepared pan and smooth the surface evenly with a small offset spatula. The batter will fill the loaf pan about ½ inch from the top.

Make the Lemon Syrup shortly before the cake is done.

BAKE THE CAKE Bake for 30 minutes.* Cover the pan loosely with foil, that is lightly coated with nonstick cooking spray, to prevent overbrowning. Continue baking for 25 to 35 minutes (5 to 15 minutes for the fluted tube pan), or until a wooden skewer inserted near the center comes out clean. The cake should start to shrink from the sides of the pan only after removal from the oven.

* **Loaf pan:** At around 20 minutes, the cake will begin to develop a natural split. For an attractive split, use a lightly oiled sharp knife or single-edged razor blade to make a shallow 6 inch long mark down the middle of the cake. This needs to be done quickly to prevent the cake from falling.

Lemon Syrup

MAKES: 133 grams | ¼ cup plus 3 tablespoons

INGREDIENTS	GRAMS	VOLUME
lemon juice, freshly squeezed and strained (about 2 lemons)	63	¼ cup
sugar	75	¼ cup plus 2 tablespoons

MAKE THE LEMON SYRUP In a small saucepan, over medium heat, stir the lemon juice and sugar until dissolved. Cover and set it aside.

APPLY THE SYRUP, COOL, AND UNMOLD THE CAKE As soon as the cake comes out of the oven, place the pan on a rack, poke the cake all over with a wire cake tester, and brush it with about one-half (66 grams) of the hot syrup. Cool the cake in the pan for 10 minutes. Have ready two wire racks, lightly coated with nonstick cooking spray.

For a loaf pan: Run a small metal spatula between the sides of the pan and the cake, pressing firmly against the pan. Invert the cake onto a prepared wire rack and peel off the parchment. Poke the bottom of the cake and brush the bottom and sides with the remaining syrup. Then reinvert the cake onto a prepared wire rack or serving plate.

(Recipe continued on next page)

(Recipe continued from previous page)

For a fluted tube pan: Use a wooden skewer to loosen the cake from around the center tube and the edge of the sides. Invert the cake onto a prepared wire rack or serving plate and brush with the remaining syrup.

For both pans: Cool completely and cover with plastic wrap.

FINISHED HEIGHT:
Loaf pan: 3½ inches in the middle and 2¼ inches at the sides.
Fluted pan: 2¼ inches in the middle.

STORE: Airtight: with or without syrup, room temperature, 3 days; refrigerated, 1 week; frozen, 3 months.

VARIATIONS:
MY CLASSIC POUND CAKE
Make the cake the same as above without the lemon zest and poppy seeds, and without the syrup.

MY CLASSIC DOUBLE-VANILLA POUND CAKE
Tiny black grains of aromatic vanilla bean offer a round, full flavor and a barely perceptible but delightful crunch. The seeds from the vanilla bean provide a deeper more aromatic flavor because it does not dissipate on baking.

Make My Classic Pound Cake with the following addition: Split 1 Madagascar vanilla bean in half lengthwise. Set the bean into the bowl with the sugar and scrape the vanilla grains into the sugar. Use your fingers to rub the grains into the sugar to distribute them evenly. Remove the bean and save it for another use.

BOOKS: *The Cake Bible; Rose's Melting Pot; The Cake Bible, 35th Anniversary Edition*

Lemon Curd

MAKES: about 1¼ cups | 375 grams
ONE CUP: 300 grams

This easy, new technique offers the purist flavor, silkiest texture, and maximum yield. It does not require straining. The absence of the usual slightly metallic taste comes from avoiding any contact with metal.

egg yolks and butter at room temperature (65° to 75°F)

INGREDIENTS	GRAMS	VOLUME
lemon juice, freshly squeezed and strained (from 2 to 3 lemons)	95	¼ cup plus 2 tablespoons
5 (to 8) large egg yolks*	100	⅓ cup plus 1⅓ tablespoons
unsalted butter, softened*	57	4 tablespoons (½ stick)
sugar, preferably superfine	150	¾ cup
fine sea salt		1⁄16 teaspoon (a pinch)

*When separating the eggs, use your fingers to pinch off any chalazae (the little white substance clinging to the egg yolks).
* Butter must be very soft to coat yolks and prevent curdling.

MAKE THE LEMON CURD With dishwashing liquid, wash, rinse, and dry the lemons and zest them. Freeze it for a future use.

- Into a 1-cup glass measure, weigh or measure the lemon juice.
- Into a 2-cup glass measure, weigh or measure the egg yolks. Be sure to remove the chalazae.

With a small silicone spatula, stir in the butter until the yolks are mixed in and the butter is in small pieces. Then, stir in the sugar until well blended. Gradually stir in the lemon juice and salt. Leave the spatula in the cup.

MICROWAVE THE LEMON CURD In the microwave, on high power, stir every 20 seconds until the curd begins to pool when a little is dropped on the surface. Then, check after 10 seconds until it pools more thickly. An instant-read thermometer will read 180°to 185°F, but the visual cue is most reliable. If the lemon curd comes out grainy, strain it through a plastic, non-metal strainer.

COOL THE LEMON CURD Transfer to a glass bowl. Cool completely. Cover tightly with plastic wrap and refrigerate. The curd will continue to thicken during cooling and chilling.

STORE: Airtight: refrigerated, 3 weeks. Longer will dull the citrus flavor.

BOOKS: *The Cake Bible; Rose's Heavenly Cakes; The Baking Bible; Rose's Baking Basics; The Cake Bible, 35th Anniversary Edition* (with stovetop method)

All-Occasion Downy Yellow Cake

MAKES: Two 9 inch layers
SERVES: 16 to 20
OVEN TEMPERATURE: 350°F
BAKING TIME: 30 to 40 minutes

The Cake Bible had many of my original techniques. The reverse-creaming method, for one, is said to have changed the way people bake cakes, producing a finer crumb and better texture. The method of first mixing the dry ingredients, followed by the butter and some of the liquid to coat the flour, and then the egg and remaining liquid, for softened butter recipes, was a daring counter method to the established creaming the butter and sugar first for bake-from-scratch cakes for home bakers. It should not have seemed too odd, considering box cake mixes have one mixing the eggs and liquids into the dry mix.

SPECIAL EQUIPMENT: Two 9 by 2 inch round pans, encircled with cake strips, bottoms coated with shortening, topped with parchment rounds, coated with baking spray with flour

BATTER: 1,530 grams
egg yolks and butter cut in 1 tablespoon pieces, at room temperature (65° to 75°F)

INGREDIENTS	GRAMS	VOLUME
8 (to 12) large egg yolks	160	⅔ cup
whole milk	323	1⅓ cups, divided
pure vanilla extract	15	1 tablespoon
bleached cake flour	400	4 cups (sifted into the cup and leveled off)
sugar, preferably superfine	400	2 cups
baking powder	24	1 tablespoon plus 2⅓ teaspoons
fine sea salt	6	1 teaspoon
unsalted butter	227	16 tablespoons (2 sticks)

PREHEAT THE OVEN Set the oven at 350°F with the oven rack in the lower third.

MIX THE LIQUID INGREDIENTS Into a 2-cup glass measure, whisk the egg yolks, 83 grams/⅓ cup of the milk, and the vanilla.

MAKE THE BATTER In the bowl of a stand mixer fitted with the flat beater, mix the flour, sugar, baking powder, and salt on low speed for 30 seconds.

Add the butter and the remaining milk. Mix on low speed until the dry ingredients are moistened. Raise the speed to medium and beat for 1½ minutes.

Gradually add the egg mixture in 3 parts, beating on medium speed for 20 seconds each. Divide the batter between the pans. Each pan will be half full (765 grams each).

BAKE THE CAKES Bake for 30 to 40 minutes, or until golden brown, a wire cake tester inserted in the centers comes out clean, and the cakes spring back when pressed lightly in the centers.

COOL AND UNMOLD THE CAKES Set the pans on wire racks for 10 minutes.

Run a small metal spatula between the sides of the pans and the cakes, and invert the cakes onto wire racks that have been lightly coated with nonstick cooking spray.

Peel off the parchments and reinvert the cakes so that the tops are up. If the cakes domed during baking, cool them bottom side up. Cool completely.

FINISHED HEIGHT: Each layer is 2 inches.

STORE: Airtight: room temperature, 3 days; refrigerated, 1 week; frozen, 3 months.

COMPLEMENTARY ADORNMENT: NEOCLASSIC BUTTERCREAM (Recipe on page 230)

BOOKS: *The Cake Bible; Rose's Heavenly Cakes; The Baking Bible; The Cake Bible, 35th Anniversary Edition*

Neoclassic Buttercream

MAKES: 4 cups | 840 grams (without additions)
ONE CUP: 210 grams

I was thrilled to discover that substituting a mixture of corn syrup and sugar for the traditional sugar and water syrup guaranteed that the critical temperature would be reached. Rather than relying on a thermometer, when the corn/sugar syrup comes to a full boil, your syrup is ready to use.

If making a half recipe or smaller, a handheld mixer works best.

egg yolks and butter in 1 tablespoon pieces, at room temperature (65° to 75°F)

INGREDIENTS	GRAMS	VOLUME
6 (to 9) large egg yolks	120	½ cup
superfine sugar	150	¾ cup
corn syrup	164	½ cup
unsalted butter	454	4 sticks
liqueur of your choice OR pure vanilla extract (optional)	30 OR 10	2 tablespoons OR 2 teaspoons

** Have ready a 1-cup glass measure, lightly coated with nonstick cooking spray.*

MEASURE AND BEAT THE EGG YOLKS In the bowl of a stand mixer fitted with the whisk beater, beat the measured egg yolks on medium speed until light in color.

MAKE THE SYRUP In a small saucepan, preferably with a nonstick lining, stir together the sugar and corn syrup until all the sugar is moistened. Cook on medium heat, stirring constantly, until the sugar dissolves and the syrup comes to a rolling boil and is bubbling all over the surface. Immediately transfer the syrup to the prepared glass measure to stop the cooking.

MAKE THE BUTTERCREAM Add the syrup to the yolks with the mixer off to keep it from spinning onto the sides of the bowl. Begin by pouring in a small amount of syrup. Immediately beat on high speed for 5 seconds. Stop the mixer and add a larger amount of syrup. Beat on high speed for 5 seconds. Continue with the remaining syrup. Remove the syrup clinging to the glass measure and scrape it against the beater. (If using a handheld mixer, it's fine to add the syrup gradually, keeping it well away from the beaters.) Continue beating on high speed for 5 minutes. Then allow the mixture to cool completely to cool room temperature.

When the outside of the bowl feels cool to the touch, beat in the butter by the tablespoon on medium speed. The buttercream will not thicken completely until almost all of the butter has been added. If desired, beat in the optional liqueur or vanilla on low speed until it is incorporated, and/or any additional flavorings.

Place the buttercream in an airtight bowl. Use it at once or up to 4 hours. If keeping it longer, refrigerate the buttercream and bring it to room temperature before beating to restore the texture. To avoid curdling, do not beat when it is still cold.

STORE: Airtight: room temperature, 6 hours; refrigerated, 1 week; frozen, 6 months.

BOOKS: *The Cake Bible; Rose's Heavenly Cakes; The Baking Bible; Rose's Baking Basics; The Cake Bible, 35th Anniversary Edition*

Chocolate Domingo Cake

MAKES: One 9 inch layer
SERVES: 8 to 10
OVEN TEMPERATURE: 350°F
BAKING TIME: 35 to 45 minutes

This is my favorite chocolate cake for its deep chocolate flavor, moist tender texture, and versatility for sheet cakes, layer cakes, Bundts, and muffins. It can serve as a base for suspending bits of brownies or chocolate chip cookies. It was my first cake to be dedicated to an opera singer—Plácido Domingo.

SPECIAL EQUIPMENT: One 9 by 2 inch round pan, encircled with a cake strip, bottom coated with shortening, topped with a parchment round, coated with baking spray with flour

BATTER: 860 grams
eggs and butter cut in 1 tablespoon pieces, at room temperature (65° to 75°F)

INGREDIENTS	GRAMS	VOLUME
2 large eggs	100	⅓ cup plus 1 tablespoon
pure vanilla extract	7	1½ teaspoons
unsweetened alkalized cocoa powder	42	½ cup plus 1 tablespoon (sifted before measuring)
boiling water	45	3 tablespoons
full-fat sour cream	121	½ cup
bleached cake flour (or bleached all-purpose flour)	156	1½ cups plus 1 tablespoon OR 1¼ cups plus 2 tablespoons (sifted into the cup and leveled)
sugar, preferably superfine	200	1 cup
baking powder	3.4	¾ teaspoon
baking soda		¼ teaspoon
fine sea salt	3	½ teaspoon
unsalted butter	200	14 tablespoons (1¾ sticks)

PREHEAT THE OVEN Set the oven at 350°F with the oven rack in the lower third.

EGGS AND VANILLA MIXTURE Into a 1-cup glass measure, whisk the eggs and vanilla.

MIX THE LIQUID INGREDIENTS Into a 4-cup glass measure, stir together the cocoa and boiling water until all the cocoa is moistened. Immediately, to prevent evaporation, stir in the egg mixture until well mixed. Add the sour cream and whisk until incorporated. It will be a slightly lumpy batter.

MAKE THE BATTER In the bowl of a stand mixer fitted with the flat beater, mix the flour, sugar, baking powder, baking soda, and salt on low speed for 30 seconds.

Add the butter and half the cocoa mixture. Mix on low speed until the dry ingredients are moistened. Raise the speed to medium and beat for 1½ minutes.

Starting on medium-low speed, gradually add the remaining cocoa mixture in two parts, beating on medium speed for 30 seconds after each addition to incorporate the ingredients smoothly. Scrape the batter into the prepared pan. The pan will be half full.

BAKE THE CAKE Bake for 35 to 45 minutes, or until a wire cake tester inserted in the center comes out clean and the cake springs back when pressed lightly in the center. The cake domes but cools totally flat.

COOL AND UNMOLD THE CAKE Set the pan on a wire rack for 10 minutes.

Run a small metal spatula between the side of the pan and the cake, and invert the cake onto wire rack that has been lightly coated with nonstick cooking spray.

Peel off the parchment and reinvert the cake so that the top is up. Cool completely.

FINISHED HEIGHT: 1½ inches.

COMPLEMENTARY ADORNMENT: WICKED GOOD GANACHE (Recipe on page 235)

STORE: Airtight: room temperature, 3 days; refrigerated, 1 week; frozen, 3 months.

BOOKS: *The Cake Bible; Rose's Heavenly Cakes; Rose's Baking Basics; The Cake Bible, 35th Anniversary Edition*

Bundt-Style Domingo Cake (VARIATION)

MAKES: One 10 cup Bundt Cake
SERVES: 16 to 20
OVEN TEMPERATURE: 350°F
BAKING TIME: 45 to 55 minutes

This cake differs in texture from the layer cake in that it magically will have swirls of slightly fudgier cake, especially at its top.

SPECIAL EQUIPMENT: One 10 cup metal fluted tube pan, coated with baking spray with flour

BATTER: 1,045 grams
eggs and butter cut in 1 tablespoon pieces, at room temperature (65° to 75°F)

(Recipe continued on next page)

(Recipe continued from previous page)

INGREDIENTS	GRAMS	VOLUME
3 large eggs *(separated for amounts below)* 3 (to 4) yolks 2 whites	 60 60	 ¼ cup ¼ cup
pure vanilla extract	9	2 teaspoons
unsweetened alkalized cocoa powder	50	⅔ cup (sifted before measuring)
boiling water	54	3 tablespoons plus 2 teaspoons
full-fat sour cream	174	¾ cup
bleached cake flour (or bleached all-purpose flour)	187	1¾ cups plus 2 tablespoons OR 1⅔ cups (sifted into the cup and leveled off)
sugar, preferably superfine	240	1 cup plus 3 tablespoons
baking powder	5.6	1¼ teaspoons
baking soda	1.4	¼ teaspoon
fine sea salt	4	⅔ teaspoon
unsalted butter	226	16 tablespoons (2 sticks)

Separate the eggs and re-combine the specified amounts for yolks and whites.

Make the batter the same as for the layer cake; be sure to scrape the batter from the bottom off the bowl to ensure it is uniform throughout.

Spoon enough batter to fill the pan about one-third full and thump the pan a few times on the counter to ensure it has filled the pan's design. Continue filling the pan. Use an offset metal spatula to slope the batter to be higher towards the rim. This will minimize the center from doming.

Bake for 40 to 50 minutes, or until a wire cake tester inserted between the tube and the sides comes out clean and the cake springs back when pressed lightly near the center. An instant-read thermometer should read 207° to 210°F.

Cool on a wire rack for 10 minutes. Run a small metal spatula between the sides of the pan and the cake, pressing firmly against the pan, and invert the cake onto a wire rack that has been lightly coated with nonstick cooking spray. Cool completely.

GLAZE THE CAKE The ganache should be applied as a glaze once it has been pressed through the stainer while it is warm and fluid (80° to 85°F). Serve remaining ganache with the cake.

FINISHED HEIGHT: 3 inches.

NOTE: *For this larger batter, the specified amounts of yolks is needed for the proper texture of the cake. Virtually all of the ingredients, except the leavenings, are increased by 20 percent from the layer cake batter. However, the butter was slightly decreased and the sour cream increased to be logical measurements.*

Wicked Good Ganache

MAKES: 3⅔ cups | 915 grams
ONE CUP: 250 grams

I invented this easier method for making ganache using a food processor, when conventional wisdom said it could never be done. Adding the scalded cream to the finely ground chocolate ensured perfect blending without the risk of curdling. Adding cayenne pepper gives the ganache a wine-like finish.

INGREDIENTS	GRAMS	VOLUME
unsweetened chocolate or 99% cacao	48	coarsely chopped (1.7 ounces)
dark chocolate, 60% to 62% cacao	340	coarsely chopped (12 ounces)
heavy cream	464	2 cups
corn syrup	123	¼ cup plus 2 tablespoons
cayenne pepper (optional)		½ to 1 teaspoon

** Have ready a fine-mesh strainer suspended over a medium glass bowl.*

GRATE THE CHOCOLATE In a food processor, process the chocolates until very fine.

MAKE THE GANACHE In a 2-cup glass measure in a microwave (or small saucepan over medium heat, stirring often), heat the cream just to a boil. With the food processor running, pour the cream through the feed tube in a steady stream. Process for a few seconds until smooth, scraping the sides of the bowl as needed. Add the corn syrup and optional cayenne pepper and pulse briefly to incorporate.

Press the ganache through the prepared fine-mesh strainer and scrape any mixture clinging to the underside into the bowl. Let it sit for 1 hour.

COOL THE GANACHE Cover the ganache with plastic wrap and let it sit for several hours, until the mixture reaches a soft frosting consistency (75° to 80°F).

TO REHEAT: Use a double boiler, stirring gently, or a microwave oven on high power, stirring and folding every 5 seconds, using a silicone spatula.

STORE: Airtight: cool room temperature, 3 days; refrigerated, 2 weeks; frozen, 3 months

BOOKS: *The Baking Bible; The Cake Bible, 35th Anniversary Edition*

GANACHE WITHOUT THE CAYENNE PEPPER AND CORN SYRUP: in virtually all of my books.

SPECIAL ENHANCEMENT FOR OTHER GANACHE: In a microwave or on a cooktop, bring the corn syrup just to a boil. Remove it from the heat and stir in the chopped unsweetened chocolate until melted and smooth. Keep a batch of this enrichment in your fridge to stir into ganache, to taste. It will keep for months.

Perfect Flaky & Tender Cream Cheese Pie Crust

This is my favorite pie crust because it is the most flavorful as well as having the ideal texture for pies and tarts—tender, flaky, and sturdy enough even for lattices. Sugar is added only when using unbleached flour to ensure tenderness. It can be made by hand, but the food processor is much faster and easier.

DOUGH FOR A 9 INCH, OPEN-FACE PIE OR TART SHELL | MAKES: 312 grams

INGREDIENTS	GRAMS	VOLUME
unsalted butter, cold	85	6 tablespoons (¾ stick)
pastry flour OR bleached all-purpose flour	145	1¼ cups (or 1 cup plus 3 tablespoons), lightly spooned and leveled off
fine sea salt	1.5	¼ teaspoon
baking powder, aluminum free	0.6	⅛ teaspoon
sugar, if using unbleached all-purpose flour	13	1 tablespoon
full-fat cream cheese, cold, cut into 4 pieces	64	¼ cup
heavy cream	29	2 tablespoons
cider vinegar		1½ teaspoons

DOUGH FOR A 9 INCH, WITH A 10 STRIP LATTICE PIE | MAKES: 480 grams

INGREDIENTS	GRAMS	VOLUME
unsalted butter, cold	128	9 tablespoons (1 stick plus 1 tablespoon)
pastry flour OR bleached all-purpose flour	213	1¾ cups plus 2 tablespoons (or 1¾ cups), lightly spooned and leveled off
fine sea salt	2.2	¼ plus ⅛ teaspoon
baking powder, aluminum free	0.8	⅛ plus 1/16 teaspoon
sugar, if using unbleached all-purpose flour	21	1 tablespoon plus 2 teaspoons
full-fat cream cheese, cold, cut into 4 pieces	100	⅓ cup plus 1 tablespoon
heavy cream	50	3 tablespoons plus 1 teaspoon
cider vinegar		2½ teaspoons

MAKE THE DOUGH Cut the butter into ½ inch cubes. Wrap it in plastic wrap and freeze for at least 30 minutes, until firm.

In a medium bowl, whisk together the flour, salt, and baking powder—sugar, if using unbleached flour. Set in the freezer until the butter is well chilled.

FOOD PROCESSOR METHOD Empty the flour mixture into a food processor. Cut the cream cheese into 3 or 4 pieces and add it to the flour. Process for about 20 seconds or until the mixture resembles coarse meal.

Add the frozen butter and pulse until none of the butter is larger than peanut size. Toss with a fork to see better.

Remove the cover and evenly pour in the cream and vinegar. Pulse until most of the butter is the size of small peas. The mixture will be in particles and will not hold together unless pinched. If there are dry particles, sprinkle in a little extra cream.

Spoon the dough mixture into a gallon-size freezer bag (or two freezer bags if making a lattice crust—312 grams for the shell, remainder for the lattice OR for a double crust—divide evenly).

FORM THE DOUGH INTO DISC(S) Hold either side of the bag opening and use the heel of your hand and your knuckles to knead and press the mixture from the outside of the bag, alternating sides, until most of it holds together in one piece. Use a rolling pin to flatten any larger pieces of butter into flakes.

Cut open the bag and empty the dough onto a large sheet of plastic wrap. Use the plastic wrap to finish kneading the dough just until it feels slightly stretchy when pulled. Use your hands and the plastic wrap to shape the dough into a rough disc or discs.

Use a rolling pin to flatten it and your hands to press in the edges, which tend to crack, to make them smooth. There should be thin flakes of butter throughout the dough. If there are any large pieces of butter, spread them using the heel of your hand.

If desired, for extra flakiness, give it 1 or 2 three-fold turns, and then press in the corners to shape into a disc. (Repeat with the second dough mixture bag.)

FOR A SINGLE CRUST PIE OR TART, flatten the dough into one 6 to 7 inch disc.

FOR A PIE SHELL AND 10 STRIP LATTICE PIE, shape the 316 grams of dough for the shell into a disc, and the lattice/smaller part into a rectangle.

Wrap the dough with plastic wrap and refrigerate for 40 minutes up to 2 days before rolling. If longer than 40 minutes, the dough needs to soften for a few minutes at room temperature. I like to roll the dough slightly under ⅛ inch thick.

ROLLING AND CUTTING THE DOUGH

For a single crust pie: First roll into a round, large enough to cut 12½ inches or large enough to line the pie plate and extend enough to turn about halfway under the border, just past the edge. Ease the dough into the pie plate with stretching. If necessary, trim the edge and then turn it under so that it is even with the pie plate. Crimp, if desired. Cover the plate with plastic wrap and refrigerate.

For the lattice: Add any scraps and roll into a 12 to 11 inch wide oval. Cut 10 long ¾-inch-wide strips, using a ruler and pastry jagger, pizza wheel, or sharp knife.

For a double crust pie: Make a double recipe of the single crust: Cut 12½ inches for the bottom crust, then 12 inches for top crust or larger if the filling is mounded.

Cherry Pie

SERVES: 6 to 8
OVEN TEMPERATURE: 425°F
BAKING TIME: 35 to 45 minutes

Tart sour cherries have a color and vibrancy unlike any other fruit. They can be frozen for many months so that you can enjoy this pie any time of the year. (To keep their color and texture, freeze them in batches adding ¼ cup/50 grams of sugar. When making the pie, subtract that amount of sugar from the filling.) A woven lattice crust is the most spectacular but alternatively five strips can be placed evenly on top of the filling and then the remaining five placed perpendicularly on top.

SPECIAL EQUIPMENT: One 9 inch standard pie plate; A baking stone or baking sheet; a foil ring to protect the edges of the crust

PERFECT FLAKY AND TENDER CREAM CHEESE PIE CRUST FOR A LATTICE PIE, 480 grams (recipe on page 236)

CHERRY FILLING: Makes 2 cups | 720 grams

INGREDIENTS	GRAMS	VOLUME
sour cherries (1½ pounds/680 grams)	567	about 3¾ cups (3½ cups pitted)
granulated sugar	175	¾ cup plus 2 tablespoons
cornstarch	23	2½ tablespoons
fine sea salt		a pinch
pure almond extract		¼ teaspoon

ROLL OUT THE BOTTOM CRUST Follow the instructions on page 237 for rolling the crust and lining the pie plate. Roll and cut the crust 12½ inches in diameter, or large enough to line the pie plate and extend enough to turn about halfway under the border. If necessary, trim the edge and then turn it under so that it is even with the pie plate. Cover the pie crust-lined pie plate with plastic wrap and refrigerate.

MAKE THE CHERRY FILLING Pit the cherries, placing them in a medium bowl along with any juices that form. There should be 567 grams/3½ cups.

In a medium saucepan, stir together the sugar, cornstarch, and salt. Gently stir in the cherries along with any juices. Allow the mixture to sit for at least 10 minutes to liquefy the sugar mixture.

Over medium heat, stirring constantly, bring the cherry mixture to a boil and simmer for about 1 minute until thickened. Scrape the mixture into a wide bowl. Cool completely. Stir in the almond extract.

Transfer the cherry filling into the dough-lined pie plate. Leave the pie unrefrigerated so that the crust border softens in order to be able to attach the strips.

ROLL THE DOUGH FOR THE LATTICE AND CUT STRIPS Roll the second piece of dough into a 12 by 11 inch wide oval (the same thickness as the bottom crust—under ⅛ inch) and cut 10 long, ¾-inch-wide strips, using a ruler and pastry jagger, pizza wheel, or sharp knife. (If you are right-handed, start from the left side.) Set aside any remaining dough, if desired, to make the optional cherry cutout.

WEAVE THE LATTICE Arrange 5 of the strips spaced evenly over the filling, starting at the center. Carefully curve back every other strip, a little past the center, so that the next strip can be placed perpendicular to the first strips, at the center of the pie. Uncurve the strips so that they lie flat on top of the perpendicular strip. Working in the same direction, curve back the strips that were not curved back the first time. Lay a second perpendicular strip on top and uncurve the strips. Repeat with the third strip.

Apply the remaining 2 strips to the other side of the pie. Start toward the center and work in the opposite direction toward the edge. Always alternate the strips that are curved back so that the strips weave in and out.

FORM THE BORDER Use sharp scissors to trim the strips to ½ inch longer than the edge of the pie plate. Use water to moisten under the ends of each strip, and tuck the overhang under the bottom crust border, pressing down to attach it and to keep the border from becoming too thick.

CHILL THE PIE Cover the pie loosely with plastic wrap and refrigerate it for 1 hour before baking to chill and relax the pastry. This will maintain flakiness and minimize shrinking.

PREHEAT THE OVEN Set the oven at 425°F with the oven rack at the lowest level and place the baking stone or baking sheet on it.

BAKE THE PIE Place the foil ring on top of the pie to protect the edges from overbrowning, and set the pie on the baking stone. Bake for 20 minutes. Rotate the pie halfway around. Continue baking for 15 to 25 minutes, or until the juices bubble thickly near the edges and the center is slightly puffed.

COOL THE PIE Set the pie on a wire rack and cool for at least 3 hours before cutting. Serve warm or room temperature.

STORE: Room temperature, 2 days; refrigerated, 4 days.

BOOKS: *The Pie and Pastry Bible, The Baking Bible, Rose's Baking Basics*

My Dream Chocolate Chip Cookies

MAKES: Twenty-two 2¾ inch round cookies
OVEN TEMPERATURE: 350°F
BAKING TIME: 5 minutes for the walnuts; 8 to 10 minutes for the cookies (for each of two batches)

My dream chocolate chip cookie has crisp edges and a moist and chewy interior. Here's how I accomplish it: I discovered that browning the butter to remove the water promotes crispness and also adds flavor. I add golden or corn syrup to make the inside of the cookies moist and chewy. Golden syrup also adds a delicious butterscotch note.

SPECIAL EQUIPMENT: Two 17 by 14 inch cookie sheets, lined with parchment

DOUGH: 690 grams
butter cut in 1 tablespoon pieces, at room temperature (65° to 75°F)

INGREDIENTS	GRAMS	VOLUME
unsalted butter	113	8 tablespoons (1 stick)
1 large egg	50	3 tablespoons plus ½ teaspoon
pure vanilla extract		1 teaspoon
walnut halves	75	¾ cup
all-purpose flour, preferably unbleached	161	1⅓ cups (lightly spooned and leveled off)
baking soda	2.7	½ teaspoon
fine sea salt		¼ teaspoon
light brown sugar, preferably Muscovado	81	¼ cup plus 2 tablespoons (firmly packed)
granulated sugar	25	2 tablespoons
golden syrup (or corn syrup)	42	2 tablespoons
dark chocolate chips, 52% to 63% cacao	170	(6 ounces)

PREHEAT THE OVEN Set the oven at 350°F with the oven rack in the middle.

CLARIFY AND BROWN THE BUTTER: Have ready by the cooktop a 1-cup glass measure. In a small heavy saucepan, melt the butter over very low heat, stirring often with a light-colored silicone spatula. Raise the heat to low and boil, stirring constantly, until the milk solids on the spatula have become little brown specks. An instant-read thermometer should read 285° to 290°F.

Immediately pour the butter into the glass measure, scraping in the browned solids as well. You should have about 94 grams/½ cup minus 1 tablespoon. Allow the browned butter to cool to 80°F.

MIX THE LIQUID INGREDIENTS Into the bowl of a stand mixer, weigh or measure the egg. Whisk in the vanilla extract. Cover tightly with plastic wrap.

TOAST AND BREAK THE WALNUTS Spread the walnuts evenly on a baking sheet and bake for 5 minutes. Turn the walnuts onto a clean dish towel and rub them to loosen the skins. Discard any loose skins and let the nuts cool completely; then break into coarse pieces.

MAKE THE DOUGH In a small bowl, whisk together the flour, baking soda, and salt.

Into the bowl of the stand mixer, fitted with the flat beater, add the browned butter with the solids, the sugars, and golden syrup and mix on low speed for 1 minute.

Add the flour mixture. Starting on the lowest speed, beat just until the flour is moistened. Continue beating on low speed for 30 seconds, or until well mixed. Add the chocolate chips and walnuts and continue beating, just until evenly incorporated.

Divide the dough in half (about 345 grams each). Wrap each piece in plastic wrap. If the dough is very sticky, refrigerate for about 30 minutes.

SHAPE THE DOUGH Divide one piece of dough into 11 walnut-size pieces (31 grams each). Roll each piece of dough in the palms of your hands to form a 1½-inch ball.

Place the balls 2 inches apart on a cookie sheet. Flatten the cookies to about 2 inches wide by ½ inch high.

BAKE THE COOKIES Bake for 4 minutes. Rotate the cookie sheet halfway around. Continue baking for 4 to 6 minutes, or until the cookies are just beginning to brown on the tops. When gently pressed with a fingertip, they should still feel soft in the middle. To create perfectly round cookies, immediately after removing the cookies from the oven, use a round cookie cutter to swirl around the cookie to give them a uniform appearance.

COOL THE COOKIES Set the cookie sheet on a wire rack and let the cookies cool for 1 minute, or until firm enough to lift from the sheet. Use a thin pancake turner to transfer the cookies to another wire rack. Cool completely. Repeat with the second batch.

STORE: Airtight: room temperature, 2 weeks; refrigerated, 1 month; frozen, 3 months.

BOOKS: *The Baking Bible, Rose's Baking Basics, The Cookie Bible*

Hanaa's Moroccan Almond Cookies
(called "Mlouza" in Northern Morocco)

MAKES: Eighteen to twenty 2½ inch round cookies
OVEN TEMPERATURE: 350°F
BAKING TIME: 15 to 17 minutes

How wonderful to have an amazingly delicious gluten-free cookie that is crispy, chewy inside, and flavored with a hint of orange blossom water.

SPECIAL EQUIPMENT: One 17 by 14 inch cookie sheet, lined with parchment;
A #40 (1½-tablespoon) cookie scoop

DOUGH: 690 grams
butter at room temperature (65° to 75°F)

INGREDIENTS	GRAMS	VOLUME
blanched almond flour (no skin)	250	2½ cups
granulated sugar	125	½ cup plus 2 tablespoons
fine sea salt		⅛ teaspoon
lemon zest, finely grated	3	1½ teaspoons, loosely packed
orange blossom water (or orange juice)	6	1⅓ teaspoons
butter	10	2 teaspoons
corn syrup	14	2 teaspoons
2 large eggs	100	¼ cup plus 2⅔ tablespoons
baking powder	3.4	¾ teaspoon
powdered sugar, for coating*	57	½ cup
whole almonds (optional decoration)		one per cookie for topping

**Have ready the powdered sugar placed in a shallow bowl.*

PREHEAT THE OVEN Set the oven at 350°F with the oven rack in the middle.

MIX THE DOUGH In a large bowl, combine all of the ingredients. Knead them together for a few minutes. The dough should be very soft and sticky.

Using the cookie scoop, fill it with the cookie dough and scrape off the excess against the side of the bowl, around 36 grams each. Place the dough ball in the powdered sugar bowl. Roll it in powdered sugar
until it is covered on all sides and press your index finger into the middle of each cookie to create a small indentation.

Place it on the cookie sheet. Continue with placing the balls 2 inches apart. (If using, lightly press in a whole almond on top of each cookie.)

BAKE THE COOKIES Bake for 15 to 17 minutes. The cookies will be too soft at this stage to move without breaking or denting them.

COOL THE COOKIES Set the cookie sheet on a wire rack and let the cookies cool for 5 minutes. Use a thin pancake turner to move the cookies directly onto another wire rack. Cool completely.

The cookies will remain pale in color, the bottom will be light golden brown, and the top will be beautifully cracked.

STORE: Airtight: room temperature, 1 week; frozen, 2 to 3 months.

Zach's Chocolate-Studded Truffle Cookies

MAKES: Twelve to fourteen 3 inch round cookies
OVEN TEMPERATURE: 350°F
BAKING TIME: 14 to 15 minutes for each of two batches

Several years ago, I created a chocolate lava cake for my book *Rose's Heavenly Cakes* with a ganache truffle for the center to ensure that it would have a flow even if overbaked. But it was my kindred spirit, chocolatier Zach Townsend, who recently crafted these stellar chocolate cookies using the same concept. The cookies have a chewy, brownie-like texture, with a pleasing crunch from the undissolved turbinado sugar and the addition of tiny bits of chocolate—but oh, the centers! They are chocolate at its finest moment: lusciously, enticingly creamy.

SPECIAL EQUIPMENT: Six or twelve 3 to 3¼ by ¾ inch high or higher pastry rings (measured from the inside)*; Two 17 by 14 inch cookie sheets, lined with silicone baking mats or parchment

CHOCOLATE GANACHE TRUFFLE CENTERS (can be made several weeks ahead and frozen)
MAKES: 172 grams
butter at room temperature (65° to 75°F)

INGREDIENTS	GRAMS	VOLUME
dark chocolate, 61% to 66% cacao	88	coarsely chopped (3 ounces)
heavy cream	77	⅓ cup
unsalted butter	14	1 tablespoon

MAKE THE GANACHE In a food processor, pulse the chocolate until finely chopped. (Alternatively, use a chef's knife to chop it.) Empty it into a medium bowl. In the microwave, scald the cream (heat it to the boiling point; small bubbles will form around the periphery).

Pour the hot cream on top of the chocolate. Cover with plastic wrap and let sit for 1 minute.

With a silicone spatula, start stirring vigorously in the center of the bowl until the mixture turns dark and smooth. Then continue stirring in larger concentric circles until all of the cream is incorporated and the mixture is completely smooth. Stir in the butter until fully melted and incorporated. The mixture should be glossy and smooth.

Let the ganache stand for a few minutes, or until cooled, then cover the bowl with plastic wrap and refrigerate until firm, 30 minutes or longer.

SHAPE THE GANACHE CENTERS At least 1 hour before making the cookies, remove the ganache from the refrigerator. Have ready a small plate or tray lined with plastic wrap.

Using a spoon, scrape up 12 to 14 medium balls (12 grams each) from the ganache for the truffle centers. It works well to set each ball of chocolate onto a piece of plastic wrap as you scoop it and then use the plastic wrap to help shape the truffle. The centers do not need to be perfectly round.

Place the ganache balls on the prepared plate, cover with plastic wrap, and place in the freezer until the balls are completely frozen, 30 minutes to 1 hour.

CHOCOLATE-STUDDED COOKIE DOUGH

DOUGH: 690 grams

butter cut in 1 tablespoon pieces, at room temperature (65° to 75°F)

INGREDIENTS	GRAMS	VOLUME
all-purpose flour, bleached	201	1⅔ cups (lightly spooned into the cup and leveled off)
unsweetened alkalized cocoa powder	19	¼ cup (sifted before measuring)
baking soda	2.7	½ teaspoon
fine sea salt		⅛ teaspoon
unsalted butter	126	9 tablespoons (1 stick plus 1 tablespoon)
instant espresso powder		¼ teaspoon
pure vanilla extract		½ teaspoon
turbinado sugar, preferably Sugar in the Raw	150	¾ cup plus 1 teaspoon
1 large egg	50	3 tablespoons plus ½ teaspoon
dark mini chocolate chips or finely chopped chocolate, 55% to 62% cacao	150	(5.3 ounces)

MAKE THE DOUGH In a medium bowl, whisk together the flour, cocoa, baking soda, and salt. Then sift into another bowl.

In a 2-cup or larger microwavable measure with a spout, in a microwave (or in a small saucepan over medium-low heat, stirring often) melt the butter. Allow the butter to cool slightly so that it is not hot when added to the sugar, or it could dissolve some of it.

In a custard cup, dissolve the coffee granules in the vanilla. Add to the melted butter and stir to combine.

Into the bowl of the stand mixer, add the sugar. Scrape the melted butter mixture into the sugar. Whisk by hand until smooth (the sugar will not dissolve). Whisk in the egg until thoroughly combined.

Attach the flat beater. Add the flour mixture to the bowl in three parts, mixing on low speed and incorporating each addition before adding the next. Scrape down the sides of the bowl as needed and mix just until a smooth dough is formed. Add the chocolate and continue beating just until evenly incorporated.

(Recipe continued on next page)

(Recipe continued from previous page)

SHAPE THE DOUGH LOG AND CUT THE COOKIES Scrape the dough onto a large piece of plastic wrap and shape it into a 14-inch-long log, 1¾ inches in diameter, with flat or slightly rounded ends. Wrap the log in the plastic wrap and place it in the refrigerator until firm, a minimum of 1 hour, up to 24 hours.

Using a sharp knife, cut off 1 inch from each end of the dough log to form a 12 inch long log. (Wrap and refrigerate the cut-off pieces to make 2 more cookies.) Slice the dough into twelve 1-inch-thick cookies, around 53 grams each.

SHAPE THE COOKIES If necessary, let the cookies sit at room temperature for about 10 minutes to soften slightly. Lightly sprinkle a dough mat or the counter with flour. Using a rolling pin (preferably a small one), roll the cookies into discs measuring about 3¼ inches in diameter. They do not have to be perfectly round.

Remove the frozen ganache balls from the freezer (for one batch at a time). Place a frozen ganache ball in the center of each cookie and wrap the dough around the ganache ball to encase it completely. Pinch the dough together at the top and press all around the cookie in places where it may have cracked to ensure that the ganache ball is well sealed inside.

Using the palm of your hand, press down gently on the cookie to flatten it to about 2¼ inches in diameter. Place the cookies on a tray, cover with plastic wrap,* and set in the freezer or refrigerator while the oven preheats.

**You can also wrap the cookies individually with plastic wrap and freeze for up to 1 month.*

PREHEAT THE OVEN Set the oven at 350 ° F with the oven rack in the middle.

BAKE THE COOKIES Working with one batch at a time, place six of the pastry rings evenly spaced on a prepared cookie sheet. Set a chilled or frozen cookie in the center of each ring.

Bake for 14 to 15 minutes, or until the edges of the cookies are firm when pressed gently with your fingertip but the centers still feel soft. (The centers will dip slightly on removal from the oven.)

*Alternatively, place six cookies on a prepared cookie sheet, bake for 14 to 15 minutes, and when removed from oven and still hot, use a 3-inch to 4-inch round cookie cutter to swirl the cookies in a circular pattern to bring in the edges and create a perfectly round shape.

COOL THE COOKIES Set the cookie sheet on a wire rack and let the cookies cool for 10 minutes. Slowly lift off the rings from the cookies; if necessary, gently press down on one edge of each cookie to release it. With a thin pancake turner, carefully transfer the fragile cookies to another wire rack.

Allow the cookies to cool for at least 5 minutes before eating. A warm cookie will be more liquid in the center, but for the best flavor, allow them to cool completely. They keep moist and chewy if stored airtight.

Repeat with the second batch (and the extra 2 cookies).

STORE: Airtight: room temperature, 5 days; refrigerated, 1 week; frozen, 2 months.

BOOK: *The Cookie Bible*

Bulgur & Duxelles
(Mushroom Pilaf)

MAKES: 2 to 3 servings

I learned how to make this delicious mushroom recipe from James Beard over a half-century ago! The earthiness of the mushrooms blends beautifully with the bulgur wheat.

butter at room temperature (65° to 75°F)

INGREDIENTS	GRAMS	VOLUME
fresh mushrooms 1 pound, preferably portobello	454	(will reduce to 100 grams duxelles)
unsalted butter	71	5 tablespoons
2 medium cloves garlic	5	lightly smashed
medium bulgur	100	⅔ cup
fine sea salt	6	1 teaspoon
black pepper, freshly ground		¼ teaspoon
boiling water	232	1 cup
parsley, preferably flat-leafed, minced		1 tablespoon

PREPARE THE MUSHROOMS Clean the mushrooms by brushing off any dirt with a damp paper towel and cutting off the tough stem ends. If you are using a food processor, cut any large mushrooms in quarters first and then process the mushrooms until finely minced.

COOK THE MUSHROOMS In a large skillet, over medium heat, melt the butter. Add the mushrooms and garlic and simmer covered over low heat for 5 minutes. The mushrooms will release a lot of water. Uncover and continue cooking about 30 minutes, stirring occasionally, until the mushrooms turn dark brown and all the water has evaporated.

COMPLETE THE DUXELLES Add the bulgur to the skillet and fry, stirring often, for two to three minutes. Reduce the heat to low. Sprinkle with the salt and pepper

Add boiling water and simmer tightly covered for 15 minutes. Fluff the mixture with a fork and allow it to stand covered for at least 5 minutes. Sprinkle with parsley before serving.

NOTE: *The processor releases a good deal of water from the mushrooms. Some people drain it off to speed up cooking time, but I like to use it all for intensity of flavor.*

Spaghetti Carbonara

MAKES: 2 servings

This was the recipe that got me my first magazine job with *Ladies' Home Journal* over 50 years ago! It's still one of my top favorite dinners. If you're lucky enough to get duck eggs, their yolks have an even more delicious flavor and creamy texture.

eggs and butter cut in 1 tablespoon pieces, at room temperature (65° to 75°F)

INGREDIENTS	GRAMS	VOLUME
bacon, preferably corn cob smoked	170	cut into ¼ inch strips (6 ounces)
unsalted butter	14	1 tablespoon
4 large cloves garlic, thinly sliced	14	about 2 tablespoons
about 3 large egg yolks	50	3 tablespoons
heavy cream	29	¼ cup
Parmesan cheese (can use half Romano)	16	a rounded ⅓ cup + extra
fine sea salt		¼ teaspoon
black pepper, freshly ground		¼ teaspoon
cayenne pepper		a sprinkling
coarse salt (Diamond Crystal)	24	a rounded tablespoon
spaghetti	227	(8 ounces)
water from the boiling pasta		¼ cup (divided)
parsley, minced (optional)	14	¼ cup

HEAT THE PASTA WATER Fill a large saucepot with at least 4 quarts of cold water; cover it and bring the water to a near boil.

MAKE THE CARBONARA MIXTURE Meanwhile, in a large wok or fry pan, fry the bacon until medium crisp. Remove all but 2 tablespoons of the bacon fat and add the butter. Add the garlic and sauté for about a minute or until softened, stirring constantly. Do not allow the garlic to brown or it will be bitter. Turn off the heat and set aside.

MAKE THE EGG MIXTURE In a small bowl, whisk the egg yolks lightly. Whisk in the heavy cream.

MAKE THE PARMESAN MIXTURE In another small bowl, stir together the Parmesan cheese, the sea salt, and the black and cayenne peppers.

COOK THE PASTA Bring the water for the pasta to a boil. Add a rounded tablespoon (13 grams) of coarse salt, and then the pasta. Cook until al dente, until no white appears in the center when a strand is cut.

Shortly before the end of cooking, remove ¼ cup of the boiling water with a ladle and whisk 2 tablespoons of it into the egg mixture. Reserve the rest.

COMPLETE THE SPAGHETTI CARBONARA Drain the cooked pasta and add it to wok. Sauté, stirring with a large spatula until evenly coated with the bacon mixture. Remove the pan from the heat. Insert an instant-read thermometer into the center of the pasta. If it is higher than 155°F, add an ice cube and stir it in until the temperature lowers.

Add the egg yolk mixture and toss quickly to blend it in without scrambling the yolks. Add the Parmesan mixture. If too thick add a little of the reserved pasta water.

SERVE Transfer the carbonara at once to the serving bowls. Sprinkle with the parsley. Have extra grated cheese, salt, and a pepper mill at the table.

Multigrain Bread Loaf

MAKES: One 8 by 4¾ inch high loaf (5 inches if using a baking steel)
OVEN TEMPERATURE: 425°F
BAKING TIME: 35 to 45 minutes

I make this favorite bread on a regular basis for grilled cheese sandwiches. Jennifer Garner made it famous when she put it on her "Pretend Cooking Show." The starter extends the shelf-life of the bread as well as giving it extra flavor.

PLAN AHEAD: Soak the grain mixture for a minimum of 8 up to 24 hours before mixing the bread. Defrost the starter overnight or prepare the Biga (recipe on page 253).

SPECIAL EQUIPMENT: One 8½ by 4½ inch (6 cup) loaf pan, coated with nonstick cooking spray; A baking steel or stone

DOUGH: 850 to 870 grams, depending on combination of grains and water

INGREDIENTS	GRAMS	VOLUME
10-grains mixture*	100 to 113	about ½ cup plus 2 tablespoons
water, for the grains mixture	100 to 113	½ cup minus 1 to ½ tablespoon
firm sourdough starter OR Biga (recipe on page 253)	75	⅓ cup
water	177	¾ cup
non-diastatic malt powder OR barley malt syrup	9.3 OR 21	1 tablespoon
bread flour, preferably King Arthur 12.7% protein (see Note)	312	2⅓ cups (lightly spooned and leveled off), divided (300/12 grams for shaping)
instant yeast	3.2	1 teaspoon
sunflower or safflower oil	54	¼ cup, divided
fine sea salt	9	1½ teaspoons
wheat bran	5	about 1 tablespoon

NOTE: *If using a lower percentage of bread flour, add up to 4 teaspoons/12 grams of vital wheat gluten when adding the bread flour to the starter mixture.*

**Soak the Grains: 8 hours up to 24 hours. (Refrigerate if longer than 8 hours.)*

MAKE THE 10-GRAINS MIXTURE In a 1-quart container with a lid, place 1 tablespoon of each of these grains and seeds: coarse buckwheat, sunflower seeds, pumpkin seeds, millet, polenta, poppy seeds, barley flakes, flax seeds, steel cut oats, and cracked wheat or bulgur. You can also use different combinations or grains and seeds to your taste.

Weigh the water to match the weight of the grains mixture. Heat it until hot. Add it to the mixture. Cover, cool to room temperature, and refrigerate for 8 hours to 2 days.

MAKE THE DOUGH 30 minutes to 1 hour before mixing the dough, into the bowl of a stand mixer, with small sharp scissors, cut the starter into small pieces.

Add ¾ cup water and malt to the starter and allow it to sit to soften, 30 minutes to 1 hour.

Add 300 grams of the bread flour to the starter mixture (and the vital wheat gluten if using). Sprinkle the yeast on top.

Attach the dough hook and mix on low speed for 1 minute or until the flour is moistened and the dough is in shaggy pieces. Cover the bowl and allow it to rest for 20 minutes.

On medium-low speed, add half of the oil, and knead for 7 minutes. (Pour the other half of the oil into the grain mixture.) The dough will be soft and smooth and form a firm ball around the dough hook.

With the mixer off, add the grain mixture. Knead for another 3 minutes or until evenly incorporated. Check to be sure! The dough will be very sticky.

With the mixer on, evenly sprinkle in the salt and bran and knead for another 2 minutes.

Remove the mixer from the stand. Use your hand to knead the very sticky dough, adding the rest of the rest of the reserved flour as needed, until the dough is only slightly sticky.

LET THE DOUGH RISE Into a 2-quart dough rising container, lightly coated with nonstick cooking spray, place the dough. Press it down and lightly spray the top of the dough. (It will weigh 824 to 828 grams or 857 if adding 113 grams of grains and 113 grams of water.) Adding the bran means not adding too much extra flour!

Cover the container with a lid or plastic wrap. With a piece of tape, mark on the side of the container approximately where double the height would be (up to the indentation on the bowl). Let the dough rise at 80°F for 1 to 1½ hours.

Remove the dough to a floured counter. Lightly flour the dough and press down on it gently to form a rectangle. Give it 2 stretches, folding it in thirds after each one. Round the corners by folding them under and set it back in the container.

Again, spray the top of the dough, cover and let it continue rising until doubled to the 2-quart mark. At 80°F, it will take 50 minutes to 1 hour.

SHAPE THE DOUGH AND LET IT RISE Turn the dough onto a lightly floured counter and sprinkle a little flour on top.

Dimple the dough with your fingertips, stretching it gently to a 10 to 11 inches long by 7 inches wide rectangle. It widens to 8 inches when rolling. (By not rolling, it will rise ½ inch higher and have a more open structure.) Shape it by rolling it tightly into a loaf, and set it, seam-side-down, in the prepared loaf pan. When pressed down it will be ½ inch from the top of the pan.

Cover the pan, and a vessel of hot water set by its side, within a large container. Let the dough rise for 45 minutes to 1 hour, until when pressed gently with a fingertip the depression very slowly fills in. It should be around 1⅝ inches above the sides of the pan at the highest center point.

(Recipe continued on next page)

(Recipe continued from previous page)

PREHEAT THE OVEN 45 minutes before baking, set an oven rack in the lower third and set the baking steel or stone on it.

Place a cast-iron skillet, lined with aluminum foil, on the floor of the oven to serve as a steaming pan. Set the oven at 425°F.

BAKE THE BREAD Spritz the top of the bread with water. Quickly but gently set the loaf pan on the hot steel or stone and toss ½ cup of ice cubes into the pan beneath. Immediately shut the door.

Bake the bread for 15 minutes. Rotate the pan halfway around and continue baking 20 to 30 minutes, or until the bread is deep golden brown. A skewer inserted into the center will come out clean and an instant-read thermometer should read 205° to 208°F.

COOL THE BREAD Remove the bread from the oven, unmold it from the pan, and transfer it to a wire rack to cool completely, top-side up.

STORE: Airtight: room temperature, 3 days; frozen, 3 months.

BOOKS: *The Bread Bible as a torpedo shape*

Bread Dough Enhancer
(Biga)

MAKES: 80 grams | almost ⅓ cup

PLAN AHEAD: Make the Biga a minimum of 6 hours, preferably 3 days before adding it to the dough on the fourth day.

SPECIAL EQUIPMENT: One small mixing bowl

BIGA (DOUGH ENHANCER)

INGREDIENTS	GRAMS	VOLUME
water	30	2 tablespoons
bread flour, preferably King Arthur	50	¼ cup (lightly spooned and leveled off) plus 2 tablespoons
instant yeast	0.2	1/16 teaspoon

ROOM TEMPERATURE WATER Into a custard cup, add the water, cover, and let it come to room temperature.

MAKE THE BIGA In a small bowl, whisk together the flour and yeast. With a silicone spatula or wooden spoon, stir in the water. Continue stirring or kneading with your fingers for 3 to 5 minutes, or until very smooth and just barely tacky. If toward the end of mixing there are a few dry particles, add water by the droplet.

LET THE BIGA RISE Cover the bowl tightly with plastic wrap that has been lightly coated with nonstick cooking spray (or place it in a sprayed 1 cup food storage container and cover it with a lid). Set it aside in a warm place (80°F), until doubled in volume (almost ⅔ cup). If stored in a clear container, you will see large bubbles on the sides. It will take about 4 to 6 hours.

With the back of your fingers, press down the Biga to deflate it to its original size. Refrigerate the Biga, preferably for 3 days, before making the dough.

BOOKS: *The Bread Bible, Rose's Baking Basics*

Acknowledgments

Thanks first and foremost to Woody Wolston, my husband, who was an equal partner in every way in writing this book. Over the years, he actually kept notes when I told him my many stories. He never lost patience when I repeated some of them either! Woody's talents and exceptional skills for taking photos and improving the photography of many of the photos and assisting in the book's design were vital contributions. He also was responsible for writing and editing the featured recipes, and he had the stellar idea to add "time capsules" of significant events in the food world, interspersed with my stories and events.

To my publisher and dear friend Brian Hart Hoffman of 83 Press and *Bake from Scratch* magazine at Hoffman Media, your enthusiasm and respect for my work and stories were inspirational. I was also so fortunate to have Amber Wilson as editor. I've adored working with her on my column as contributing editor to the magazine. She has become a most treasured friend.

I am also so grateful for the extraordinary team at 83 Press who produced this beautiful beyond-my-dreams book. I entrusted them to put my life in their hands, and they made the most of it.

Rachel Q. West, *Editorial Director*
Kristy Harrison, *Chief Strategy Officer of 83 Press*
Adrienne Davis, *Copy Editor*
Karissa Brown, *Art Director*
Ellen Gillespie, *Contributing Assistant Art Director*
Stephanie Welbourne Steele, *Director of Photography*
Laura Crandall, *Test Kitchen Director*
Katie Moon, *Food Stylist*
Madison Harvel, *Assistant Food Stylist*
Giovanna Vazquez, *Recipe Tester*
Haley Bowen, *Prop Stylist*
Delisa McDaniel, *Senior Digital Imaging Specialist*
Amanda Golz, *Director of Business Development*
Kari Parker, *Director of Marketing*

Thank you, everyone, for being such an invaluable part of my life's story:

David Shamah was the ideal person to write the foreword. I've known him for decades—longer than just about anyone I mention in this book. His contribution to my life and work is immeasurable.

Much appreciation to Cassie Jones, my editor for *The Cake Bible, 35th Anniversary Edition*, for advising me to add a common thread to the memoir, which became Woody's time capsules.

Lisa Lucas, our literary lawyer and close friend, has navigated us through the contractual complexities of this new publishing venture. She brought her razor-sharp mind, intellect, and also her good heart.

My dearest cousin Richard G. Morris, who has always been there for me, contributed some heartwarming stories, especially about the 60-year reunion of our grandmother and her brother. As a biochemist, he also made an important contribution to the food world by creating a microchip insertion, ensuring its true production date.

My dearest cousin Daniel Howe, who gave me a head start writing this memoir by asking for family history.

My dearest cousin Joan Wager, who found the perfect blouse for my cover portrait.

Tai Blanche is the brilliant artist who designed several of my cookbooks. We were close friends from the start, bonding over our shared experience of attending the High School of Music & Art in New York City. Over the years, I bought several of her paintings, which inspired me to commission the portrait for the cover of this book.

Tai Blanche and Rose in Oil

My feeling about this memoir is that it is so personal the audio version had to be in my own voice. I'm so happy to have found the talented audio engineer and producer Andrew Santiago of ANJ Media.

Team *Ma Vie en Rose*

I gave Amber Wilson, editor for *Bake from Scratch*, some chapters of my memoir in the summer of 2025, and she really enjoyed them. Just a few months later, Brian Hart Hoffman said, "I want you," and Amber became the editor for *Ma Vie en Rose*. I finished the manuscript with Woody contributing his time capsules. Rachel West assembled a dream team of 13 that was beyond anything that I expected. For our previous books, once we submitted the manuscript and participated in the recipes' photography sessions, we mainly just made choices for design and layout. From starting to submitting the book for printing in early April 2026, Team *Ma Vie en Rose* was going to complete the memoir in just three months!

In early January, Woody was able to format my manuscript to the same font and layout as Brian's book, *The Ribbon in Her Journal*, which allowed him to work hand in hand with Karissa Brown, our art director, in charge of laying out the manuscript, as well as including over 40 time capsules and 100 photos. Woody expressed that the time capsules be in shaded boxes, sometimes into the margin's white space similar to highlighted boxes used in a few of my books. "It will be different from any other memoir," Woody promised. Karissa had a great talent for incorporating our supposedly "this is the last addition" edits. For impact, she chose having a photo of my 14 stacked cookbooks as the memoir's back cover.

Our copy editor, Adrienne Davis, brilliantly transformed my speaking voice text into a more readable memoir text, but with agreeing to my including some made-up words for context. As Woody and I read, I would comment: "You two are 'the comma queens.'"

For the styling and photography phase, Woody and I joined the kitchen and photography team in early March at *Bake from Scratch*'s home office. Katie Moon and the kitchen staff did brilliantly in making each recipe as we would have done. We were in awe at how Katie, photographer Stephanie Welbourne Steele, and prop stylist Haley Bowen seamlessly worked in unison to create incredible "beauty shots" of the recipes. When possible, they incorporated Woody's styling ideas for my innovative techniques. We also met with Rachel and Karissa to go over the layout and design for the entire book. The highlight was Amber presenting me the printed-out pages for us to bring home.

Tai Blanche is a fantastic artist, and we have four of her paintings. I was so impressed with her oil portrait of Ruth Bader Ginsburg, that I asked her to paint my portrait in oil. How wonderful it is that it will now grace my memoir's front cover.